Londo

Ben West has written for many
newspapers and magazines including
the *Guardian*, the *Independent*, the *Daily
Telegraph*, the *Sunday Telegraph*, the
Daily Mail, *Today*, the *Evening Standard*,
Time Out and the *Sunday Times
Magazine*. He specialises in writing
articles about lightweight subjects of
little consequence to anyone.

London for Free

How to get the most out of the capital without having to pay for it

Ben West

PAN BOOKS

First published 1996 by Pan Books
an imprint of Macmillan Publishers Ltd
25 Eccleston Place, London SW1W 9NF
and Basingstoke

Associated companies throughout the world

ISBN 0 330 34438 2

9 8 7 6 5 4 3 2

A CIP catalogue record for this book is available from
the British Library.

Typeset by CentraCet Limited, Cambridge
Printed and bound in Great Britain by
Mackays of Chatham PLC, Chatham, Kent

Contents

1   *Introduction*
6   *A few points about this book*

9   Accommodation
9   Adventure playgrounds
14   Advertising
14   Advice and counselling
24   American football
24   Animal and bird enclosures in parks
27   Annual events: festivals and festivities
52   Art galleries and exhibitions
74   Buddhism
74   Business information
75   Careers information
76   Charity sponsorship
76   Christmas
79   Churches
84   City Farms
89   Cloakrooms
91   Comics

91	Consumer information
92	Contraception and abortion
93	Cosmetics and perfumes
94	Cycling
95	Dental treatment
96	Disabled information
97	Drink
101	English Heritage
102	Fashion
103	Film and video
104	Food from street markets
105	Food information
106	Food plants
110	Food shops
113	Football
113	Frequent events
114	Fun-fairs
115	Gardening
116	Gymnasium equipment
117	Haircuts
118	Hitch-hiking
119	Lectures, talks and discussions
125	Libraries
135	The life of a ligger: there is such a thing as a free lunch
139	Magazines and newspapers
141	Make-overs and beauty care
143	Markets
148	Medical treatment

152	Museums and collections
182	Music
194	National Trust
197	Nature reserves and open spaces of particular wildlife interest
208	Opera
209	Paper
209	Parks and open spaces
222	Playgrounds
223	Postcards
223	Publicity
224	Sightseeing and places of interest
250	Sightseeing after dark
253	Softball
253	Sun-tanning
255	Swimming
256	Telephone directory enquiries
256	Television and radio shows
258	Theatre
259	Tourist Information Centres
263	Valuations
263	Volunteering
264	Walking in London
282	Working London
290	Workshops and demonstrations

Introduction

Whoever said that the best things in life are free has clearly never driven a factory-fresh Ferrari. But that doesn't mean to say that obtaining something without paying for it isn't gratifying. Especially when the basic art of existing can be prohibitive at the best of times.

Whatever your age and interests, whether you are a Londoner wishing to discover more of this great city, a parent with children to entertain, or a visitor to the capital who after shelling out on transport, board and lodgings doesn't wish to also have to travel the expensive tourist trails so many end up on, this book is for you.

The many suggestions in this publication counteract the frequent charge made about London – that it is exceptionally expensive. Everything included here is genuinely free; there are no free offers which require a prior purchase.

Many people know *vaguely* of a few things that are free in London. This guide clearly and concisely explains when, where and how they can obtain a wealth of them. Do you have to turn up early to get an acceptable view? Is something free only at a certain time? Do you have to apply first for tickets?

Most people are aware that some museums are free or that others are free for only some of the week – but who knows exactly? Most of us just turn up and hope, expecting to pay £5 or so for adult entry. How many people must turn up at the National History Museum at 4.15 pm and pay an admission charge, unaware that fifteen minutes later they can enter for free?

This book includes so many worthwhile activities which do not entail spending money that a reader could follow a couple of suggestions every weekend for a couple of years and still be left with plenty of ideas.

In the same way that it makes sense to discover your own country before jet-setting around the world (but how many people in southern England see the Yorkshire Dales, Durham or the islands of Scotland before booking their first flight to Spain?), equally does it not make sense to experience the abundance of things on offer for free in the capital before spending a small fortune on London leisure?

And it is a small fortune. A couple of adults visiting, say, the London Dungeon, the Guinness World of Records, the London Planetarium, Rock Circus, Madame Tussaud's and the Tower of London would presently receive little change from £80.

Splashing out for admission tickets to a well-known tourist attraction is no guarantee of satisfaction. When I last paid a visit to a couple of London's most popular tourist attractions, at considerable expense, there seemed to be no restriction on numbers admitted and I was herded around in a flash, pushed onwards by the crowd if I dared pause at any exhibits.

It is surprising how badly designed many attractions are. The most common problems are sharp edges at toddler level around display cases (just waiting to cause an accident), bad signposting and inadequate facilities for those in wheelchairs, those otherwise disabled and those with push-chairs. Paying a big admission charge on top of such trials hardly pacifies the harassed visitor.

You can experience many of London's wonders most adequately without paying for the privilege. For instance, a better sense of the excellence of Tower Bridge is obtained by walking over the bridge at car level for free rather than by paying £5 adult admission for the tour of the bridge, which lasts over an hour, and includes a walk across the upper walkways. These are so enclosed by glass and metal, you might as well be looking out from any old office building.

This fairly strenuous tour, with an over-the-top and often irrelevant audio-visual trip back 100 years, is much populated by international tourists sporting ludicrous 'Acoustiguide' translating handsets. The tour offers no flexibility to look around at your own pace. And after paying an admission fee, to see modern drink- and food-vending machines mingling with the Victorian exhibits is a trifle irritating. I'm sure others share these views: when I demanded to be freed from the tour midway, the whole party followed.

Theme parks are especially expensive to visit. Their phenomenal success is difficult to understand when you consider what they offer. If you've been to one you'll be aware of the yells and screams, becoming louder the nearer you get to the entrance gates. These are not due to the thrills of the roller-coasters and other terrifying rides, but are the reactions of visitors on discovering the admission charges.

For example, Chessington World of Adventures currently charges around £15 for an adult and £12 for a child, so a family of four would pay out over £50 before buying any drinks or food. Incredibly, some of the attractions require further expenditure. And there's no prior warning that because so many people are admitted, half an hour or an hour's wait for the more popular rides is not unusual. Many visitors therefore only experience the less exceptional attractions, such as fairground rides, the playground and zoo – at an exceptionally high cost.

Many of the free events and venues on offer in London explain the capital, its rich history and people far more effectively than the obvious, expensive tourist spots. A number of these famous but pricey stops on the well-worn tourist trail could have been located in any city in the world, having no particular relevance to London.

As an example, an hour in the public gallery of the

Old Bailey can effortlessly reveal aspects of the British character and past and present in a way that Rock Circus and the like never could.

People used to believe that the more you paid, the better something was. The recession swiftly put an end to that idea. In our new haggling society, obtaining something free of charge has to be the ultimate in good value.

When covering an area as big as the capital it can be difficult to know where London ends. Some people define the place as anywhere with an 0171 or 0181 telephone code; others would say that a north, south, east and west postcode plus their variants would suffice. Then there's the 32 boroughs that make up Greater London to consider, and the area within the M25 or the A–Z street map. Whatever definition you subscribe to, I trust that on the whole the entries in this book represent your idea of London.

A Few Points About This Book

Every endeavour has been made to ensure details were correct when going to press, and that any organisation offering something for free in this book has no plans to stop the facility. Nevertheless, policies do change so check details before setting out.

Several institutions that previously allowed free admission to individual members of the public have either stopped, such as Lloyds of London, the London Metal Exchange and the Stock Exchange, or now charge admission fees, such as The Jewish Museum, Highgate Cemetery and the Commonwealth Institute. Yet for those places lost to the world of commerce or hidden from the public gaze, other attractions appear to replace them, including newcomers like Morden's Dene City Farm and Croydon's Clocktower complex.

Although opening times are included where possible, these are of course subject to change so it's a good idea to call ahead to check such details. Many places may be closed or alter opening times on particular days, especially around Christmas and on bank holidays.

Some places listed are administered by trusts, charities and associations that do no charge admission fees, but would welcome a voluntary donation to help keep the establishment open to the public. As far as possible this is indicated when relevant, although very few entries in this book would turn down voluntary donations whether they have a donation box or not.

Any books mentioned in the text are not necessarily currently in print, but should be easily available from your local library.

When visiting open spaces and nature reserves, visitors should keep to any marked paths to avoid causing any damage or disturbance.

Opening times shown are solely for when the facility is free: it may be open at other times too.

The nearest British Rail station and/or underground station is included for many entries, although for some of them a further walk or bus ride may be necessary.

Once you have this book, you will need two more things: a street atlas with a street index, either the LONDON A–Z (Geographers' A–Z Map Co Ltd) or the NICHOLSON LONDON STREETFINDER, both around £4 from bookshops and many newsagents, and a TRAVELCARD, allowing you to travel within certain zones in London on the underground system, London Regional Transport buses and most London British Rail trains.

Please always bear in mind that it is only because of the generosity of the many relevant organisations whose

offerings are listed here that we are so fortunate in
having such a rich choice of activities available in
London that cost us nothing. Please don't abuse such
privileges, which could spoil things for everyone else.

Any comments or suggestions of things for inclusion in
future editions of this book would be welcomed. Write
to: *London for Free, P.O. Box 8672, London, SE3 7ZB.*

ACCOMODATION

ADVISORY SERVICE FOR SQUATTERS, 2 *St Paul's Road, N1 (0171 359 8814). Open Mon–Fri 2–6 pm. Highbury and Islington BR/underground*. Has details of empty properties and can inform you of squatters' rights.

SHAC General housing advice and help for families is available from the *0171 404 6929* advice line *(Mon–Fri 10 am–1 pm)*. There is also a single persons' advice line, *0171 404 2614 (Mon–Fri 10 am–1 pm, 2–5.30 pm)*. SHAC can help with temporary hostel accommodation and possibly also long-term housing.

There's also the SHELTER NIGHTLINE *(Mon–Fri 6 pm–9 am; Sat, Sun 24-hour) 0800 446441*; PICCADILLY ADVICE CENTRE on *0171 434 3773 (after 2 pm)*; and for homeless under-21s, ALONE IN LONDON *(0171 278 4224)*.

ADVENTURE PLAYGROUNDS

The age range for these is usually 5–16. Telephone before turning up for the first time, as sometimes children have to be registered.

ACKLAM ROAD, 6 *Acklam Road, W10 (0181 969 5058)*.

Open term-times Tues–Sat 3.30–7.30 pm; school holidays Mon–Fri 10.30 am–5.30 pm. Westbourne Park BR/underground. Lots of activities including swings, a pool table, art, swings, a pool table, art, sport and games.

ANGELL TOWN, *Gordon Grove, SE5 (0171 737 0956). Open term–times Mon–Fri 3.30–7 pm; school holidays (registration fee in Summer) Mon–Fri 11 am–6 pm. Loughborough Junction BR.* Climbing frames, swings and lots of other activities.

ATTLEE, *28 Commercial Street, E1 (0171 247 1281). Open term-times: Tues, Wed 3.30–7.45 pm; Thur, Fri 3.30–5 pm; school holidays: Tues. Wed 9.45 am–5 pm; Thurs, Fri 12.45–7.45 pm; Sat 9.45 am–4.45 pm. Aldgate East underground.* Various play structures, inflatables, etc.

CHARLIE CHAPLIN, *Bolton Crescent, SE5 (0171 735 1819). Oval underground.* A playground for disabled children only. To visit, telephone for details.

CRUMBLES CASTLE, *Bingfield Street, N1 (0171 278 8640). Open term-times: Mon–Wed 3.30–7.15 pm; Thurs 4–6 pm; Sun noon–6 pm; school holidays: Mon–Fri 10 am–1.30 pm, 2.30–6 pm. King's Cross BR/underground.* Facilities include table tennis, art and craft activities and outdoor play structures.

THE DUMBS, *14 Oakview Road, SE6 (0181 698 2991) Open term-times: Mon–Fri 3.30–7 pm; Sat, Sun noon–6 pm; school holidays: daily 11 am–7 pm. Beckenham Hill BR*. Quite a big set-up with art and craft activities, trips, games and sports including basketball, table tennis, and a football field.

EAST DULWICH, *Dog Kennel Hill, SE5 (0171 274 6197). Open term-times: Tues–Thur 3.30–7.30 pm; Sat 10.30 am–4.30 pm; school holidays: Mon–Fri 10.30 am–6 pm. East Dulwich BR*. Swings, cricket, football, table tennis and other games as well as arts and crafts.

ELHAP, *119 Roding Lane North, Woodford Bridge, Essex (0181 550 2636). Open Mon–Fri 9 am–5 pm but telephone first. Woodford underground*. A special-needs playground with a fortnightly Saturday club that integrates mainstream children with those with special needs. Also adult day care and holiday play schemes. Facilities include play structures, play areas, a giant see-saw, water play, sand play, music, a soft room and play room.

EVERGREEN PLAY ASSOCIATION, *Richmond Road, E8 (0171 275 9004). Open term-times: Tues–Fri 3.30–6.45 pm; Sat, Sun 10.30 am–5.30 pm; school holidays: Mon–Fri 10.30 am–5.30 pm. Dalston Kingsland BR*. Arts and crafts such as pottery, hockey, table tennis, swings, inflatables, a wildlife garden and bees.

HIGHGATE WOOD, *Muswell Hill Road, N6 (0181 444 6129). Open during daylight hours. Highgate underground.* Includes a good children's playground.

HOLLAND PARK, *Illchester Place, Kensington, W8 (0171 602 9483). Open during daylight hours. Holland Park underground.* Contains an excellent adventure playground.

LOG CABIN, *259 Northfield Avenue, W5 (0181 840 3400). Open Mon, Wed–Fri 9.30 am–6.30 pm. Northfields underground.* A playground offering extensive activities that also has facilities for the disabled. There's a variety of structures including swings and climbing frames, toys, games, a dark-room, inflatables, arts and crafts and a nature area.

MINT STREET, *56 Southwark Bridge Road, SE1 (0171 403 3747). Open term-times: Mon–Fri 3.30–7 pm; school holidays: Mon–Fri 10 am–5 pm. Borough underground.* Has the usual play structures and arts and crafts facilities as well as tennis, table tennis, pool table, hockey and football.

NOTTING HILL, *The Venture Centre, Wornington Road, W10 (0181 969 7919). Open term-times: Tues–Sat 3.30–6.45 pm; school holidays Mon–Fri 11 am–5.45 pm. Ladbroke Grove underground.* A football pitch, tennis, basketball, lots of structures, slides and swings as well as crafts such as jewellery making and gardening.

PALACE, *Bishops Avenue, SW6 (0171 731 2753). Open Mon–Fri 10 am–5 pm but by arrangement. Putney Bridge underground.* A special-needs playground in the grounds of Fulham Palace that has some sessions integrated with mainstream children.

PECKHAM, *Pentridge Street, SE15 (0171 701 7974). Open term-times: Tues–Fri 3.30–6.30 pm, Sat 10 am–6 pm; school holidays: Mon–Fri 10 am–6 pm. Peckham Rye BR.* Facilities include table tennis, a computer and a pool table.

SLADE GARDENS, *Lorn Road, SW9 (0171 737 3829). Open term-times: Mon–Fri noon–1.30 pm, 3.30–7.30 pm; school holidays: Mon–Fri 10 am–7.30 pm. Stockwell underground.* Outdoor facilities include football, towers, ropes and swings, and indoors there are various arts and crafts activities such as model making and painting.

SURREY DOCKS, *Trident Street, SE16 (0171 232 0846). Open term-times: Tues–Fri 3.30–8 pm; Sat 10 am–6 pm; school holidays: Mon–Fri 10 am–6 pm. Surrey Quays underground.* Activities include netball basketball, football, climbing and play structures, pool table, table tennis, arts and crafts, workshops.

TOFFEE PARK, *Ironmonger Row, EC1 (0171 251 0190). Open term-time: Mon–Fri 3.30–8 pm; school holidays: Mon–Fri 10.30 am–6 pm. Old Street underground.* 'The children say what they want to do and we organise it,' said one of the staff. There are swings, arts and crafts, a pool table and other games.

ADVERTISING

It was such a good idea that of course the founder of LOOT, the free ads newspaper available at newsagents, had great difficulty obtaining help from the banks when starting the business up. The London edition is published five times a week and allows private advertisers to advertise anything legal at no charge.

Three advertisements may be placed in any one issue. You can place ads (giving your name, telephone number, classification number – see page 2 of Loot at the newsagents for this – and the wording of your ad) by telephoning *0171 328 1771* 24 hours a day, faxing *0171 328 8249* or bringing/posting the details to *Loot, Lynwood House, 24–32 Kilburn High Road, NW6 5TF*.

ADVICE AND COUNSELLING

The following organisations offer free advice, around the clock if indicated. 0800 calls are free of charge, 0345 calls are at local rates. Some of the organisations offer free information packs and courses.

The CAPITAL HELPLINE *(0171 388 7575)* will try and answer queries about anything, or refer callers to someone who could help. They also have further temporary advice lines during the year, including revision lines before GCSEs, a finance line when there's a budget, and a Christmas line. Details of these are given on *Capital Radio 95.8 FM*, from time to time.

ACCIDENT COMPENSATION National Accident Helpline *(24-hour) 0800 444240*

AIDS/HIV Afro-Caribbean Helpline *0800 567 123*; Body Positive *0171 835 1045*; National Aids Helpline *(24-hour 0800 567123*; Positively Women *0171 734 1794*; Terence Higgins Trust Helpline *0171 242 1010*

ALCOHOL ABUSE Alcoholics Anonymous Helpline *0171 352 3001*; National Alcohol Helpline *0171 332 0202*

ALZHEIMER'S DISEASE Alzheimer's Disease Society *0171 306 0606*

ANIMAL WELFARE Royal Society for the Prevention of Cruelty to Animals *0345 888999*

ARABIC Arabic Helpline *0800 521 361*

ARTHRITIS Arthritis Care *0171 916 1500*

ASIAN Asian Language Helpline *(Wed 6–10 pm)* *0800 282 446*

AUTISM National Autistic Society *0181 451 1114*

ASTHMA National Asthma Campaign Helpline *0345 010203*

BACK PAIN National Back Pain Association *0181 977 5474*

BEREAVEMENT National Child Death Helpline *0800 282986;* Compassionate Friends: for parents *01272 539639;* Cot Death Helpline *(24-hour)* *0171 235 1721;* Cruse Bereavement Line *0181 332 7227;* Stillbirth & Neonatal Death Society *0171 436 5881*

BLIND Guide Dogs for the Blind Association *01734 835555;* Royal National Institute For The Blind *0171 388 1266*

BREAST CANCER Breast Cancer Care *0171 867 1103*

CANCER British Association of Cancer United Patients *0800 181199;* CancerLink *0171 833 2451;* CancerLink Teenagers Helpline *0800 591028;* Cancer Care Society *0117 942 7419*

CANTONESE Cantonese Helpline *(Tues 6–10 pm)* 0800 282447

CARERS Carers National Association CarersLine 0171 490 8898

CEREBRAL PALSY Cerebral Palsy Helpline 0800 626216

CHILDREN Childline *(24-hour)* 0800 1111; Children's Legal Centre Advice Line *(Mon–Fri 2–5 pm)* 0171 359 6251; Kidsline: leisure information *(Mon–Fri 4–6 pm; school holidays Mon–Fri 9 am–4 pm)* 0171 222 8070; National Society for the Prevention of Cruelty to Children Child Protection Helpline *(24-hour)* 0800 800500

CITIZENS ADVICE For nearest Bureau: National Association of Citizens Advice Bureaux 0171 833 2181

CONSUMER Office of Fair Trading Consumer Information Line 0345 224499

CRIME Criminal Injuries Compensation Board 0171 355 6800; National Association of Victims Support 0171 735 9166; Support After Murder and Manslaughter 0171 735 3838; Victims' Helpline 0171 729 1252

CYSTIC FIBROSIS Cystic Fibrosis Trust 0181 464 7211

DEAF National Deaf Children's Society *0113 282 3458*; Royal National Institution for Deaf People *0171 387 8033*; Tinnitus Helpline *0345 090210*

DEPRESSION Arbours Association *0181 340 8125*

DEBT National Debtline *0121 359 8501*

DIABETES British Diabetic Association *0171 323 1531*

DISABLED Benefit Enquiry Line *0800 882200*; DIAL UK Helpline *01302 310123*; Disability Law Service *0171 831 8031*; Disabled Living Foundation *0171 289 6111*; Greater London Association of Disabled People *0171 274 0107*; Royal Association for Disability and Rehabilitation *0171 250 3222*

DIVORCE AND SEPARATION Divorce Conciliation and Advisory Service *0171 730 2422*; National Family Mediation *0171 383 5993*

DOMESTIC VIOLENCE Women's Aid Helpline *01272 633542*

DOWN'S SYNDROME Down's Syndrome Association *0171 682 4001*

DRUGS The Blenheim Project *0181 960 5599*; Narcotics Anonymous Helpline *0171 498 9005*; Release Emergency

Service *(24-hour)* 0171 603 8654; Serious Drugs Misuse *(24-hour)* 0171 278 8671; Turning Point 0171 702 2300

DYSLEXIA British Dyslexia Association 01734 668271

EATING DISORDERS Eating Disorders Association 01603 621414; Overeaters Anonymous 01422 886475

ELDERLY Age Concern 0181 679 8000

EPILEPSY British Epilepsy Association 0345 089599

ECZEMA National Eczema Society 0171 388 4097

FAMILY Parentline 0181 668 4805

GAMBLING Gamblers Anonymous *(24-hour)* 0171 384 3040

GAY AND LESBIAN Acceptance: for parents of lesbians and gay men 01795 661463; Black Lesbian and Gay Centre Project 0171 885 3543; Gay and Lesbian Legal Advice 0171 976 0840; Lesbian and Gay Switchboard *(24-hour)* 0171 837 7324; London Lesbian Line 0171 251 6911

GLAUCOMA International Glaucoma Association 0171 737 3265

HAEMOPHILIA Haemophilia Society *0171 928 2020*

HEAD INJURIES National Head Injuries Association *0115 924 0800*

HEALTH Health Information Service *0800 665544*; Medical Advisory Service: general advice *(Mon–Fri 2–10 pm) 0181 994 9874*

HEART British Heart Foundation *0171 935 0185*

HOMELESSNESS Shelter Nightline *(Mon–Fri 6 pm–9 am; Sat, Sun 24–hour) 0800 446441*; SHAC: general housing advice *(Mon–Fri 10 am–1 pm) 0171 404 6929*; SHAC: single persons' adviceline *(Mon–Fri 10 am–1 pm, 2–5.30 pm) 0171 404 2614*

HYPERACTIVE CHILDREN Hyperactive Children's Support Group *01903 725182*

IMMIGRATION Immigration Advisory Service *0171 357 6917*; Immigration Helpline *0171 587 1997*

LAW Law Centres Federation *(Mon–Fri 10 am–6 pm) 0171 387 8570*

LEUKAEMIA Elimination of Leukaemia Fund *0171 737 4141*

MANIC DEPRESSION Manic Depression Fellowship *0181 974 6550*

MARRIAGE GUIDANCE London Marriage Guidance Council *0171 580 1087*; Relate *0181 680 1944*

MEDICAL ACCIDENTS Action for Victims of Medical Accidents *0181 291 2793*

MENINGITIS National Meningitis Trust *(24-hour)* *01453 755049*

MENTAL HEALTH MIND *0181 519 2122*; Saneline: for carers, sufferers or friends *0171 724 8000*

MENTALLY HANDICAPPED Mencap *0171 454 0454*

MISCARRIAGE The Miscarriage Association *01924 200799*

MISSING PERSONS Missing Persons Bureau Helpline *0181 392 2000*; Salvation Army Family Tracing Service *0171 383 2772*

MOTOR NEURONE DISEASE Motor Neurone Disease Association *0345 626262*

MULTIPLE SCLEROSIS Multiple Sclerosis Counselling Service *0171 222 3123*

MUSCULAR DYSTROPHY Muscular Dystrophy Group *0171 720 8055*

PARKINSON'S DISEASE Parkinson's Disease Society *0171 383 3513*

PHOBIAS Phobic Action *0181 559 2459*

POLICE Liberty: help with complaints against the police *0171 403 3888*

PREGNANCY Abortion Anonymous *0171 350 2229*; Bliss: families with babies in special care units *0171 831 9393*; British Pregnancy Advisory Service *01564 793225*; Brook Advisory Centre *0171 580 2991*; LIFE Hotline: pregnancy counselling *01926 311511*; National Childbirth Trust *0181 992 8637*

PRISON Prisoners Reform Trust *0171 278 9815*

PSORIASIS Psoriasis Association *01604 711129*

RAPE Rape Crisis Centre *0171 837 1600*; Rape and Sexual Abuse Support Centre *0181 688 0332*; Survivors: male rape *(7 pm–10 pm Tues & Thur) 0171 833 3737*

THE SAMARITANS *(24-hour) 0171 734 2800/0181 301 1010/0181 692 5228*

SCHIZOPHRENIA National Schizophrenia Fellowship
0181 974 6814

SEXUAL HARASSMENT Women Against Sexual Harassment *0171 721 7593*

SINGLE PARENTS Gingerbread *0171 240 0953*; National
Council for One Parent Families *0171 267 1361*

SMOKING Smokers Quitline *0171 487 3000*

SOCIAL SECURITY DSS Linkline *0800 666555*

SPEECH IMPEDIMENTS Association for all Speech
Impaired Children *0171 236 3632*

SPINAL BIFIDA Association for Spina Bifida and
Hydrocephalus *01733 555988*

SPINAL INJURIES Spinal Injuries Association *0181 444
2121*

STROKE Stroke Association *0171 490 7999*

TAX TaxAid: advice for those who cannot afford an
accountant *(9 am–11 am Mon–Fri) 0171 624 3768*

WOMEN'S AID London Women's Aid: refuges and advice

0171 251 6537; Refuge Crisis Line (24-hour) 0181 995 4430

YOUNG PEOPLE Teenage Information Network: counselling and information for 13–25 year olds *0181 403 2444*

AMERICAN FOOTBALL

If you like watching American Football, the BRITISH AMERICAN FOOTBALL ASSOCIATION SENIOR LEAGUE *(01205 363522)* can tell you the London fixtures, kick-off times and team telephone numbers for the following weekend. About 80% of games are free.

ANIMAL AND BIRD ENCLOSURES IN PARKS

BATTERSEA PARK, *Queenstown Road, SW8 (0181 871 7530). Sloane Square underground/Battersea Park BR.* Deer enclosure.

BROCKWELL PARK, *Dulwich Road, SE24 (0171 926 0105). Herne Hill BR.* An aviary with birds including finches, canaries, doves and chickens as well as a duck pond.

CLISSOLD PARK, *Green Lanes, N16 (0181 800 1021).*
Finsbury Park BR/underground. Fallow deer, rabbits,
waterfowl and tropical birds such as a peacock and
mina bird.

GOLDERS HILL PARK, *North End Road, NW11 (0181
455 5183). Golders Green underground.* Antelope, fallow
deer, wallabies and pygmy goats; avaries with a good
variety of exotic birds including cranes, magpies, flamingoes and pheasants.

GREENWICH PARK, *Maze Hill, SE10 (0181 858 2608).*
Greenwich/Maze Hill BR. A herd of deer roam a 13-
acre enclosure, and the central pond has a good variety
of wildfowl.

HAINAULT FOREST, *Essex (0181 500 3106). Hainault
underground.* Ponies, pigs, cows, rabbits and wildfowl.

HOLLAND PARK, *Illchester Place, Kensington W8 (0171
602 9483). Holland Park underground.* Peacocks, Muscovy
ducks, bantams and other birds.

HORNIMAN GARDENS, *100 London Road, Forest Hill,
SE23 (0181 699 2339/1872). Forest Hill BR.* A little
children's zoo with small animals.

MARYON WILSON PARK, *Thorntree Road, SE7 (0181 854
0446). Charlton/Woolwich Dockyard BR.* A deer park

and children's zoo with goats, ponies, sheep, rabbits, chickens and donkeys.

PLASHET PARK, *Plashet Grove, E6 (0181 503 5994). Zoo open summer Tues–Sun 10 am–5 pm; winter Tues–Sun 10 am–4 pm. East Ham underground.* A small zoo with ponies, pygmy goats, llamas, wallabies, butterflies and various birds.

ST JAMES'S PARK, *The Mall, SW1 (0171 930 1793). St James's Park underground.* On the island and lake in the centre of the park are over 30 types of bird including pelicans, moorhens and various types of geese and ducks. In addition, many other bird varieties fly in and out – I tell you, it's like Heathrow in July some days.

TRENT COUNTRY PARK, *Cockfosters Road, Barnet, Herts (0181 449 8706). Cockfosters underground.* A variety of animals such as sheep, pigs, rabbits and chickens at Pet Corner.

VICTORIA PARK, *Victoria Park Road, E9 (0181 985 1957). Mile End underground.* Fallow deer and pygmy goats on the eastern side of the park.

ANNUAL EVENTS: FESTIVALS AND FESTIVITIES

LONDON PARADE, *provisionally scheduled to start on Westminster Bridge at noon on 1 Jan. Phone the organisers on 0181 566 8586 for details. Westminster underground.* In recent years this event has been called the Lord Mayor of Westminster's New Year's Day Parade. It has started at noon, 12.30 pm and 1 pm, and has begun from Parliament Square and Piccadilly Circus as well as Westminster Bridge. With an estimated 700,000 to 1 million people attending, there must have been a fair amount of confusion and disappointment. The present route should follow Whitehall, Cockspur Street, Lower Regent Street, Piccadilly Circus, Piccadilly, Berkeley Street and the final marching band reaches Berkeley Square nearly three hours after the start. There are various floats, and horse-drawn carriages carrying the mayors of Westminster and the London boroughs. Also a fair and aerial displays. If you think you'd fit into the procession and could offer some form of street entertainment, you can participate for free. Telephone the organisers for details.

CHARLES I COMMEMORATION, *Whitehall, SW1 (0171 836 3205). Last Sunday in January. Charing Cross BR/ underground.* In 1649 Charles I was removed from the Banqueting House, Whitehall, and executed at the scaffold. To commemorate this, members of the King's Army, in 17th century garb, parade from St James's Palace at *11.30 am*. Going down the Mall, through Horse Guards to the Banqueting House and to King Charles's statue in Trafalgar Square, they lay a wreath at the Banqueting House and then return by the same route.

CHINESE NEW YEAR, *around Gerrard and Lisle Streets and Newport Place, Soho, W1 (0171 439 9805/0171 437 5256). In late January or early February, on the nearest Sunday to the date of the Chinese new year, at approximately 11 am–5 pm. Leicester Square underground.* The high point of the Chinese calendar means Chinatown comes alive with music, colourful dancers, stalls, performers and decorations on windows and balconies. Dragon and lion dancers entertain the crowds.

ACCESSION DAY GUN SALUTES, *Hyde Park, W2 at noon (Hyde Park Corner underground) and the Tower of London, EC3 at 1 pm (Tower Hill underground) on 6 February – or if a Sunday, on the following day.* A striking ceremony; a number of other gun salutes take place during the year.

CLOWN'S SERVICE, *Holy Trinity Church, Beechwood Road, Dalston, E8 (0171 254 5062). First Sunday in February. Dalston Junction BR.* Members of the Clowns International Club attend a special church service here in full costume, laying a wreath on a memorial to Grimaldi, originator of the clown. A clown show follows in the church hall, which is particularly popular with children.

LINCOLN'S INN FIELDS PANCAKE DAY RACES, *Lincoln's Inn, wc2. Shrove Tuesday (last day before Lent), races begin 11 am. Holborn underground*. Also GREAT SPITALFIELDS PANCAKE DAY RACES, *Spitalfields Market, Brushfield Street, E1 (0171 247 6590) Shrove Tuesday, from noon. Oxford Circus underground*. Also COVENT GARDEN PANCAKE DAY RACES, *Covent Garden, wc2 (0171 836 9136) Shrove Tuesday. Covent Garden underground*. Pancake day marks the beginning of Lent when fat and meat were prohibited and therefore used up in savoury pancakes. On this day races are held throughout the country, where the competitors run while tossing pancakes in frying pans. Not as yet an Olympic event, sadly.

INTERNATIONAL WOMEN'S WEEK A week packed with events for women, held all over the London Borough of Greenwich in *early March* has health, fitness and sports events and coaching, talks, poetry, presentations, dance classes, exhibitions and more. Look out for leaflets in the borough earlier in the year.

SPRING EQUINOX DRUID CEREMONY, *Tower Hill Terrace, EC3. Held in March: details from the Druid order on 0181 771 0684. Tower Hill underground.* This is one of the ancient rituals by the Order of Druids, who wear white, hooded gowns to celebrate spring, the season of renewal.

ORANGES AND LEMONS SERVICE, *Church of St Clement Danes, Strand, WC2 (0171 242 8282). Held in March. Aldwych underground.* 'Oranges and lemons, say the bells of St Clements ...' goes the nursery rhyme. After a special service, children from St Clement Danes School are given an orange and lemon to celebrate the day these fruits first appeared in London.

HOLI FESTIVAL, *Roe Green Park, Kingsbury Road, NW9 (0181 900 5659). Kingsbury underground.* A Hindu celebration held in *March*.

HEAD OF THE RIVER RACE, *on the Thames from Mortlake, SW14, to Putney, SW6 (0171 940 2219). Last Saturday in March. Putney Bridge underground.* Although less well known than the Oxford and Cambridge Boat Race, this is probably more fun as over 400 crews of eight-oared boats, starting at 10-second intervals, compete to be fastest.

OXFORD AND CAMBRIDGE BOAT RACE, *on the Thames from Putney, SW6 to Mortlake, SW14 (0171 379 3234/0171 730 3488). March or April. Putney Bridge underground.* This annual clash between the rowing teams of Oxford and Cambridge universities, lasting under 20 minutes, has been held on the Thames since 1849. Along the four-mile, 374-yard course the teams are cheered on by large crowds on the river-banks and bridges even though no-one gets a particularly good view.

CHAUCER FESTIVAL, *Tower of London, Tower Hill, EC3 (0171 229 0635). Early April. Tower Hill underground.* In a celebration of Chaucer's *Canterbury Tales*, a costumed procession goes from Southwark Cathedral to the Tower of London, where there's a medieval fayre.

LONDON MARATHON, *from Greenwich Park, Blackheath, SE3, to Westminster Bridge, SW1, via the Isle of Dogs and Victoria Embankment (0171 620 4117/01925 417744). Early to mid-April.* Crowds line the whole 26-mile route of this, the world's largest road race with over 30,000 participants (many raising money for charity) including celebrities, the disabled and those in fancy dress as well as the international record breakers.

TYBURN WALK, *from the Old Bailey (the Central Criminal Court), Newgate Street, EC4 to Tyburn Convent, 8 Hyde Park Place, W2 (0181 947 2598). Last Sunday in April at 3 pm. St Paul's underground.* A silent procession led by a Catholic bishop takes about two hours to walk the three miles from the site of Newgate Prison (the Old Bailey) to a special service at Tyburn Convent in memory of Catholics martyred at Tyburn Gallows during the 16th and 17th centuries.

QUEEN'S BIRTHDAY GUN SALUTES, *Hyde Park, W2 (Hyde Park Corner underground) or Green Park, SW1 (Green Park underground) at noon (telephone 0171 298 2100 for further details) and the Tower of London, EC3 at 1 pm (Tower Hill underground) on 21 April – or if a Sunday, on the following day.*

EASTER SHOW, *Battersea Park, SW11 (0181 871 7530). Easter Sunday, parade begins around 3 pm. Battersea Park BR.* Large crowds for a carnival of side-shows, a fair, concerts, stalls, children's competitions, a children's threatre, a steel band and various stalls.

KITE FESTIVAL, *Blackheath, SE3 (0181 808 1280). Easter Sunday and Monday. Blackheath BR.* A dazzling collection of stunt kites.

LONDON HARNESS HORSE PARADE, *Battersea Park, Queenstown Road, SW8 (0181 871 7530/01733 234451). Battersea Park BR. On Easter Monday* the parade, first held in 1885, features horse-drawn carriages and side-shows competing for rosettes and brass badges.

MAY DAY INTERNATIONAL WORKERS DAY CELE-BRATION, *Clapham Common, SW4. A Sunday in late April/early May. Clapham Common underground.* Lots of live bands, clowns, jugglers, Morris Dancers and other entertainments.

CANALWAY CAVALCADE, *Little Venice, W2 (0171 874 2787)*. *May Day weekend Sat–Mon. Warwick Avenue underground*. About 30,000 visitors enjoy this pageant of about 150 decorated boats, canoeing displays, boat handling competitions, raft races, folk music, Morris Dancers, jazz and brass bands, a trade and craft show, theatre, children's activities, teddy bears' picnics and other attractions. The Sunday evening sees an illuminated procession of boats.

MAY FAYRE AND PUPPET FESTIVAL, *St Paul's Church Garden, Covent Garden, WC2 (0171 375 0441)*. *Held nearest Sunday to 9 May. Covent Garden underground*. Celebrating the first reported Punch and Judy show (recorded by diarist Samuel Pepys on 9 May 1662), in the doorway of the church. There's a procession and entertainments.

CHESTNUT SUNDAY, *Bushy Park, Hampton Court Road, Middlesex, TW12 (0181 979 1586)*. *Nearest Sunday to May 11 from noon–7p.m. Hampton Wick BR*. An event dating from Victorian times with a parade including veteran bicycles such as Penny Farthings and carriages going along the mile-long Chestnut Avenue with its trees in bloom. Of the 1300 trees only a fifth are chestnuts, curiously. There are also other events including Victorian bands, Victorian re-enactment groups and horse displays.

COVENT GARDEN FESTIVAL OF OPERA AND THE MUSICAL ARTS *(24-hr information line 0181 944 9467/ 0171 240 0560). Held in May. Covent Garden underground.* The two-week festival typically includes a parade, mini-operas, choral and theatrical works, celebrity interviews and an opera troupe performing lunchtimes and evenings in Covent Garden shops and bars.

VICTORIA EMBANKMENT GARDENS SUMMER ENTERTAINMENTS, *Villiers Street, WC2 (0171 375 0441). June/July. Charing Cross BR/underground.* Beginning with weekend festivals celebrating dance and music, mime, poetry and the like, with lunch-time and evening performances of street theatre, mime, music, opera and similar attractions towards the end.

CAMLEY STREET NATURAL PARK FESTIVAL, *Camley Street Natural Park, 12 Camley Street, NW1 (0171 833 2311). A Sunday in late May. King's Cross underground/ Camden Road BR.* A community gathering with music and dancing.

WHITESTONE POND SUMMER OPEN AIR ART EXHIBITION, *Whitestone Pond, Heath Street, NW3. From May to August, Sat, Sun 11 am–6.30 pm. Hampstead underground.* Paintings, prints, pottery and other crafts all on display.

OAK APPLE DAY, *Royal Hospital Chelsea, Royal Hospital Road, SW3 (0171 730 5282). 29 May. Sloane Square underground.* The Chelsea Pensioners honour their founder, Charles II, on the anniversary of his escape after the Battle of Worcester in 1651 where he hid in an oak tree. His statue is decorated with oak leaves. Well, beats watching paint dry, doesn't it?

FAMILY FUN DAYS, *The Albany Centre, Douglas Way, SE8 (0181 692 0231). One day a month from May to August. New Cross BR/underground.* Children's events including music, clowns, and a bouncy castle.

BROADGATE ARENA SUMMER ENTERTAINMENTS, *Broadgate Centre, Eldon Street, EC2 (0171 588 6565). Liverpool Street BR/underground. From May to September, Mon–Fri 12.30–2 pm* this outdoor site is used for a variety of imaginative events including music, dance and theatre. There could be anything from fashion shows, horse displays, Elvis impersonators and tennis coaching to pageantry and jousting, aerobics master-classes, karate, blues, classical, folk, and reggae. There's even giant chess and draughts sets available if you fancy a game. Also events at Halloween, Christmas and on Burns Night.

NOT THE ROYAL ACADEMY, *Llewellyn Alexander Gallery, 124–126 The Cut, SE1 (0171 620 1322). From early June to early September, Mon–Sat 10 am–7.30 pm. Water-*

loo BR/underground. What happens to the 13,000 paintings not hung at the Royal Academy Summer Exhibition? Not the Royal Academy organises a constantly changing exhibition of the best. This event has been held since 1991, echoing the 19th-century 'Salon des Refusés', where Manet and Sargent rebelled against the French Academy and mounted their own Paris exhibition.

BEATING THE RETREAT ON HORSE GUARDS PARADE, *SW1 (0171 298 2100). Early/mid June. Charing Cross BR/underground.* These impressive military displays of marching and drilling bands are held over several days.

UPSTREAM JAZZ, *venues around Richmond Borough (0181 332 0534). Early/mid June.* Five days of jazz with many free events.

JUNE GUN SALUTES, *Hyde Park, W2 (Hyde Park Corner underground) or Green Park, SW1 (Green Park underground) at noon (telephone 0171 298 2100 for further details) and the Tower of London, EC3 at 1 pm (Tower Hill underground) on 2 June (Coronation Day), 10 June (the Duke of Edinburgh's birthday) and 16/17 June (Trooping the Colour) – or if on a Sunday, on the following day.*

TROOPING THE COLOUR, *Buckingham Palace to Horse Guards Parade, SW1 (0171 930 4466/0171 414 2479).*

Second Saturday in June. St James's Park underground. To celebrate her official birthday on 11 June, the Queen leaves Buckingham Palace at *10.40 am* in an open coach, going down the Mall to meet the Brigade of Guards and the Household Cavalry (which amounts to about all we have left of the army after recent defence cuts) at Horse Guards Parade at *11 am*. There is a military display, the national anthem is played, and there is a gun salute (see above). After the Queen returns to the Palace at *1 pm* there is an RAF flypast down the Mall. Attending the event is not free but you can watch the procession down the Mall, and free tickets are available by ballot for the first rehearsal. For tickets write with a stamped addressed envelope to the *Brigade Major (Trooping the Colour), Household Division, Horse Guards, Whitehall, SW1*.

SPITALFIELDS FESTIVAL, *Christchurch, Commercial Street, E1 (0171 377 1362/0171 377 0287). June. Donations requested. Liverpool Street BR/underground, Aldgate East underground*. A lively celebration of music from the 17th to the 20th century with, typically, lunch-time and evening concerts, music, theatre, art exhibitions, educational and visual art events and even live relays of concerts that are not free, to the Old Spitalfields Market.

GREENWICH FESTIVAL, *the London Borough of Greenwich (0181 305 1818). June. Greenwich BR*. Many of this arts festival's events are free including the opening-night celebrations which include a firework display, live music and street theatre at *Cutty Sark Gardens, SE10*. There are often a number of free exhibitions, workshops and classes, children's events, poetry and music. During the festival, nearby is BLACKHEATH VILLAGE FAYRE, *SE3* which has increasingly abandoned its olde worlde feel to become a small modern fair plus jumble sale. It includes displays such as police dogs jumping through hoops of fire, and trapeze artists.

BRENT COUNTRYSIDE DAY, *Fryent Country Park, Fryent Way, Kingsbury, NW9 (0181 900 5659). Wembley Park underground*. Held on a *Sunday in June*, this country festival offers family entertainment in the form of sheep-dog trials, farm animals, nature walks and other events.

CYCLE PROMENADE DAY, *Richmond Park, Holly Lodge, Richmond, Surrey (0181 948 3209). A Sunday in early/mid June. Richmond BR/underground*. Various entertainments, a five-mile easy-to-follow route and free cycle checks to promote cycling.

STOKE NEWINGTON MIDSUMMER FESTIVAL *(0171 254 3735). Mid-June*. A week of events using artists and performers from the locality in various Stoke Newington venues. The very varied attractions include music, dance, carnival, readings, guided walks, art exhibitions and workshops. The grand finale on the Sunday is the Church Street Festival Party with its opening procession, sports displays, dance, circus performance, a fayre and lots of music.

KNOLLYS RED ROSE RENT, *Seething Lane, EC3 to Mansion House, EC2. Around 24 June. Bank underground.* Churchwardens of All Hallows-by-the-Tower present the Lord Mayor and his wife with roses at the Mansion House to commemorate the fining of Sir Robert Knollys for building a foot-bridge in Seething Lane in the 14th century.

NATIONAL MUSIC DAY, *Trafalgar Square, WC1 and elsewhere (0171 491 0044). Last weekend in June. Charing Cross BR/underground.* Founded in 1992 by the Right Hon. Timothy Renton, MP and the right-on Mick Jagger, this is a musical celebration with many events (not all of them free) held around the country. At no other time in the year do so many people gather to celebrate music in so many ways. At the centre of it all are bands and orchestras gathered around Nelson's Column.

LESBIAN AND GAY PRIDE FESTIVAL, *Victoria Park, Victoria Park Road, E9 (0171 737 6903). Third Saturday in June. Bethnal Green underground.* An increasingly huge event with a turn-out of about 150,000, with half of that number taking part in the march. Of the many events, there's live music and cabaret.

CITY OF LONDON FESTIVAL, *in the City (0171 377 0540). Around three weeks from late June.* 20 to 30 events that could range from classical, jazz and pop to operetta, opera and theatre in some of the square mile's most beautiful churches, squares and other venues.

GREENWICH PARK FAMILY DAY, *SE10 (0181 858 2608). A Saturday in late June/early July from noon to 5pm. Greenwich/Maze Hill BR.* Lots of fun events for all the family that could include steam-engine rides, archery displays, farm animals, bands, clowns and gymnastic displays.

DEPTFORD FESTIVAL *(0181 692 4446). Around late June to late July.* A month-long festivity in the area with a greatly varied programme including a carnival procession.

HACKNEY SHOW, *Hackney Downs, Downs Road, E5 (0171 739 7600). A Saturday in late June/early July from noon–8pm. Hackney Downs/Hackney Central BR.* Over 40,000 people attend this fun, family event that allows the Hackney borough to 'get together and let its collective hair down'. The show features music, comedy, variety entertainment, a dog show, a children's play area, stalls and side-shows.

BEXLEY FESTIVAL, *various Bexley venues (01322 351666/0181 308 4836). First two weeks of July.* Includes international street theatre and cycle races in the town centre, the opportunity to try sports and water activities such as water-skiing, wind-surfing and sailing in Danson Park, a regatta, a rugby festival, and live music.

CATFORD ARTS FESTIVAL, *St Dunstan's College, Stanstead Road SE6 (0181 690 1274). Early July. Catford/ Catford Bridge BR.* Although many of the events are not free, there are workshops and demonstrations covering such subjects as silk screen printing, doll making and pottery, and there are several visual art events.

SHELL LSO MUSIC SCHOLARSHIP FINAL, *Barbican Concert Hall, Silk Street, EC2 (0171 638 8891). Barbican/ Moorgate underground.* In *early July* four young musicians play classical music alongside the London Symphony Orchestra to compete in this prestigious event. Apply early for tickets; for more information telephone *0171 588 1116.*

PADDINGTON PERFORMANCE FESTIVAL, *Paddington Recreation Ground, Grantully Road, W9 (0171 375 0441). First Sunday in July, noon–6 pm. Maida Vale underground.* A celebration of performing arts as clowns, jugglers, stilt-walkers, acrobats, trapeze artists, unicyclists and other circus acts merge with lots of music, workshops and games.

RICHMOND FESTIVAL, *the London Borough of Richmond*

(0181 332 0534). Early/mid July. A number of events are free, which usually include music, dance, theatre and various art exhibitions.

COIN STREET FESTIVAL, *around Gabriel's Wharf, 56 Upper Ground, SE1 (0171 620 0544). Waterloo/Charing Cross BR/underground*. On various days from *early July to early September* Gabriel's Wharf, a workplace for about 20 craft and designer artists, holds a festival with, typically, live music and dance from around the world, a children's carnival procession, collectors' cars, street theatre, children's workshops and possibly even an open air circus. All year the craftspeople can be seen making sculpture, jewellery, ceramics, fashion etc, from *Tues–Sun 11 am–6 pm*.

DOGGETT'S COAT AND BADGE RACE, *London Bridge, SE1 to Albert Bridge, SW11 (0171 626 3531). July. London Bridge underground*. Thomas Doggett, an 18th-century Irish comedian left a legacy for this half-hour race (the oldest rowing event in the world) to commemorate the anniversay of George I's accession to the throne. It involves six Thames watermen racing for four and a half miles against the tide. The winner receives a distinctive scarlet uniform and silver badge.

CLERKENWELL FESTIVAL, *Clerkenwell Green, EC1 (0171 253 6644). Mid–July, ending on first Sunday after 16 July. Farringdon/Barbican underground*. A week with street entertainment, stalls, music, children's activities and processions.

SWAN UPPING, *Thames (Sunbury-on-Thames to Pangbourne, Berkshire). Mon–Fri, third week in July, 9.30 am–5 pm. Details: 0171 235 1863.* The swans on the Thames are owned by the Queen, and by two City livery companies, the Dyers' Company and the Vintners' Company. This extraordinary 300 year-old ceremony, where boats manned by colourfully dressed oarsmen search for swans for five days, is to establish who owns the cygnets and to mark their beaks accordingly.

VINTNERS' COMPANY PROCESSION, *Upper Thames Street, EC4. On the second Wednesday in July. Details: 0171 236 1863. Blackfriars underground.* Dressed in traditional costume, members of the Vintners' Company proceed from Vintners' Hall in Upper Thames Street to the Church of St James's, Garlickhythe, to celebrate the election of their newly sworn-in master. The Company's wine porters head the party, sweeping the road with birch brooms to clear the way.

DISABILITY ARTS DAY, *Victoria Embankment Gardens, Villiers Street, WC2 (0171 375 0441). Late July. Charing Cross BR/underground.* A cabaret show.

CART MARKING, *Guildhall Yard, EC2 (0171 489 8287). Late July or early August, 11 am. Moorgate BR/under-*

ground. This registration ceremony for horses and carts evolved after increasing concern for traffic congestion – not today, but in the 17th century.

QUEEN MOTHER'S BIRTHDAY GUN SALUTES, *Hyde Park, W2 (Hyde Park Corner underground) or Green Park, SW1 (Green Park underground) at noon (telephone 0171 298 2100 for further details) and the Tower of London, EC3 at 1 pm (Tower Hill underground) on 4 August – or if a Sunday, on the following day.*

SHRI VALLABH NIDHI UK ASIAN FESTIVAL, *Roundwood Park, Harlesden Road, NW10 (0181 900 5659). Willesden Green underground.* Held in *July or August,* this is a Hindu celebration lasting a week or more.

RIDING HORSE PARADE, *Rotten Row, Hyde Park, W1. First Sunday in August around 1 pm. Hyde Park Corner underground.* Over 50 horses and their riders compete in various events.

CHILDREN'S FESTIVAL, *Calthorpe Project Community Garden, 258–274 Gray's Inn Road, WC1 (0171 837 8019). A Sunday in mid- to late-August. King's Cross BR/ underground.* Various events for under- and over-eights which have included such things as play areas, art workshops, karaoke, trapeze workshops and children's bands.

SWISS COTTAGE FESTIVAL, *Swiss Cottage Civic Site, NW3 (0171 586 8731). A Sunday in August or September. Swiss Cottage underground.* Theatre, games, music, inflatables and other street entertainments for all the family.

NOTTING HILL CARNIVAL, *around Ladbroke Grove and Notting Hill, W11 (0181 964 0544). August bank holiday Sunday and Monday, noon–9 pm. Notting Hill Gate underground.* Established in 1965, this is possibly Europe's biggest outdoor festival with thousands of people enjoying several live music stages and sound systems with calypso, house, rap, ragga, Caribbean soca and reggae music, with dancing, costume parades and a procession. Predominantly a West Indian festival with participation from Asian and Latin American communities.

OPEN HOUSE *(0181 341 1371). A weekend usually in early/mid–September* when the public are welcome to visit buildings of particular architectural significance or cultural interest that they would normally not have access to. In the past, buildings as wide ranging as court-houses, a modern monastery, ITN's headquarters and a nuclear bunker have taken part in the scheme.

LIMEHOUSE FESTIVAL, *around Limehouse, E14 (0171 286 6101/0181 874 2787). Limehouse DLR.* Dependent upon the tide, this weekend event is usually held in

September or *October* and has attractions ranging from Chinese dragons, vintage boats, narrow boats and sailing barges, theatre, arts, dance, environmental displays, children's activities, live music, street entertainers and various stalls.

AUTUMN EQUINOX DRUID CEREMONY, *Primrose Hill, NW3. Held in September: details from the Druid Order on 0181 771 0684. Camden Town underground.* This is an ancient ritual by the Order of Druids, celebrating autumn, the season of harvest.

CHINATOWN FESTIVAL, *Gerrard Street, W1 and Newport Place, WC1 (0171 439 3822). Held in September. Leicester Square underground.* Quite like the Chinese New Year Festival but smaller; there are stalls and entertainments including dancing dragons.

COVENT GARDEN MARKET FESTIVAL OF STREET THEATRE, *Covent Garden, WC2 (0171 240 0560). Two weeks in September. Covent Garden underground.* A celebration with various acts including puppeteers, acrobats and stilt-walkers.

ANGEL CANAL FESTIVAL, *City Road Basin, N1 (0171 267 9100). A Sunday in early September, 11 am–6 pm. Angel underground.* A community festival with stalls, music, boat trips and Punch and Judy.

QUEEN'S PARK ENTERTAINMENT DAY, *Queen's Park, Kingswood Avenue, NW6 (0181 969 5661). Generally second Sunday in September. Queen's Park underground.* The community puts on music, games and other entertainments as well as stalls at this well-attended event.

SLOUGH ARM CANAL DAY, *Bloom Park, off Middle Green Road, Slough (0171 286 6101). Usually second Sunday in September. Slough BR.* Various entertainments including Shire-horse rides, morris dancing, clog dancing, music, stalls, story-telling and bouncy castles.

BATTLE OF BRITAIN WEEK, *near 15 September.* A series of events including an RAF fly-past over London, memorials, and on the Sunday, remembrance services at Westminster Abbey and other churches.

GREAT RIVER RACE, *a Saturday in mid-September, beginning between 10 am and 2 pm according to the tide (0181 398 9057).* About 250 oared and paddled boats race the 22 miles from Ham House in Richmond to Island Gardens, the Isle of Dogs. Quite spectacular to watch as a great variety of boats take part including old passenger barges, Hawaiian war canoes, Irish curraghs, Chinese dragon boats and (replica) Viking longships. Many of the boats are 100–150-years old. The start of the race is staggered and it takes nearly two hours for all the boats to leave, and over five hours from the first boat leaving to the last finishing. The race can be seen all along the Thames, but it's most fun to view from the start or finish.

HORSEMAN'S SUNDAY, *Church of St John and St Michael, Hyde Park Crescent, W2 (0171 262 1732). Third Sunday in September: morris dancing at 11 am, service at 11.30 am. Paddington underground.* At the front of the church the vicar, on horseback, blesses over 100 horses in a 30-minute service. The horses head for Hyde Park, and at approximately 1.30 pm show-jumping takes place in the north of Kensington Gardens.

RAISING OF THE THAMES BARRIER, *Unity Way, Woolwich, SE18 (0181 854 1373). Usually in early October. Charlton BR.* This is the best time to see this feat of modern engineering, installed in 1982. From the riverbank, you can watch the ten huge metal gates being raised against the high tide as a commentary explains what is happening. There's a pleasant riverside walk and a children's play area.

PUNCH AND JUDY FESTIVAL, *Covent Garden Piazza, WC2 (0171 240 0930/0171 836 9136). First Sunday in October. Covent Garden underground/Charing Cross BR/ underground.* A nation-wide collection of the traditional ferocious and untamed puppets.

COSTERMONGER'S PEARLY HARVEST FESTIVAL, *St Martin-in-the-Fields, Trafalgar Square, WC2 (0171 930*

0089). First Sunday in October, service 2 pm. Charing Cross BR/underground. Costermongers sold fruit and vegetables on London's streets; their representatives, over 100 cockney Pearly Kings and Queens in their traditional costumes covered with pearl buttons, gather for a harvest thanksgiving, bringing fruit and veg for the poor and old.

HARVEST OF THE SEA THANKSGIVING, *St Mary-at-Hill, Eastcheap, EC3 (0171 626 4184). Second Sunday in October, service 11 am. Monument underground.* Grateful fish-dealers bring their catches to this special service.

SHAKESPEARE IN SPITALFIELDS, *Spitalfields Market, E1 (0171 375 0441). Late October. Liverpool Street BR/underground.* Talented thespians perform Shakespeare.

TRAFALGAR DAY PARADE, *Trafalgar Square, WC2 (0171 928 8978). Sunday nearest to 21 October at 11 am. Charing Cross underground.* Parade made up of hundreds of sea cadets and marching bands, and a commemoration service for Nelson's 1805 victory with wreaths laid at the base of Nelson's column.

STATE OPENING OF PARLIAMENT, *House of Lords, Palace of Westminster, SW1 (0171 219 4272). Also Premium rate information line 0839 123413. Late October or early November, or when a new government comes to power. Queen arrives at Parliament at 11 am. Westminster under-*

ground. The public cannot attend the ceremony (which is televised) but can see the Queen arrive in a state coach, along with the Household Cavalry. Popular, so arrive early. There are gun salutes to mark the occasion at *Hyde Park, W2 (Hyde Park Corner underground)* or *Green Park, SW1 (Green Park underground) at noon (telephone 0171 298 2100 for further details) and the Tower of London, EC3 at 1 pm (Tower Hill underground)*.

BONFIRE NIGHT *(0171 971 0026). Also premium rate information line 0839 123410. 5 November*. All over Britain firework displays with huge bonfires (not all free) are held in parks and open spaces to commemorate Guy Fawkes' 1605 Gunpowder Plot to blow up Parliament. There are usually good displays at *Alexandra Park, Battersea Park, Blackheath, Highbury Fields, Primrose Hill* and *Ravenscourt Park*.

LONDON TO BRIGHTON VETERAN CAR RUN, *starting at Serpentine Road, Hyde Park, W2. (Details: 01753 681736). First Sunday in November, beginning around 7.30 am. Hyde Park Corner underground*. This, the oldest competitive motoring event, first held in 1896, celebrates the end of the requirement for a man with a red flag to walk in front of the car. Crowds of over a million cheer the magnificent pre-1905 cars all along the route, the A23.

ADMISSION OF THE LORD MAYOR ELECT, *Guildhall,*

Gresham Street, EC3 (0171 606 3030). Second Friday in November. Bank/St Paul's underground. Apply to the Keeper's Office for a ticket to see this 20-minute silent ceremony where the retiring Lord Mayor hands over the insignia to the new one.

LORD MAYOR'S SHOW, *the City of London (Details: 0171 606 3030/0171 332 1456). Second Saturday in November, 9 am–5 pm. Bank/Temple underground.* At around *11 am* the new Lord Mayor travels in an 18th-century gilded coach from the Guildhall to the Royal Courts of Justice in the Strand to swear solemn vows, returning by about *2.15 pm.* The streets of the City are taken over by a procession of about 60 floats, 20 marching bands, and street dancers; it all ends with fireworks from a barge on the Thames between Waterloo and Blackfriars bridges.

REMEMBRANCE SUNDAY CEREMONY, *The Cenotaph, Whitehall, SW1. (Details: 0171 730 3488/0171 930 8131). Second Sunday in November, 10.30 am. Westminster underground.* Mourning crowds gather to pay a minute's silent tribute to Commonwealth citizens who lost their lives in the World Wars. Buglers of the Royal Marines sound The Last Post and the Queen, other members of the Royal Family and representatives of Government and the Services lay wreaths. The Bishop of London takes a service of Remembrance.

COCKPIT WORKSHOPS OPEN DAY, *Cockpit Yard, Northington Street, WC1 (0171 831 6761). First or second weekend in December. Holborn underground*. Lots of craft demonstrations to see as 80 or so craftspeople at Cockpit make such things as ceramics, glass, woodwork, metalwork, jewellery and textiles.

ART GALLERIES AND EXHIBITIONS

AFRICA CENTRE, *38 King Street, WC2 (0171 836 1973). Open gallery Mon–Fri 9.30 am–5.30 pm; Sat 11 am–4 pm. Covent Garden underground*. The gallery has pictures and crafts by African artists.

AGNEW'S GALLERIES, *43 Old Bond Street, W1 (0171 629 6176). Admission charge for some exhibitions. Open Mon–Fri 9.30 am–5.30 pm*. Established in 1860, the gallery holds exhibitions featuring, for example, 18th-century drawings, water-colours and Old Masters. Many works can be seen here before ending up in museums.

ARCHITECTURAL ASSOCIATION, *34–36 Bedford Square, WC1 (0171 636 0974). Open Mon–Fri 10 am–7 pm; Sat 10 am–3 pm. Tottenham Court Road underground*. A gallery with absorbing architectural exhibitions.

ARCHITECTURE FOUNDATION, *The Economist Building, 30 Bury Street, SW1 (0171 839 9389). Open Tues,*

Wed, Fri noon–6pm; Thur, Sat, Sun 2–6 pm. Green Park underground. This campaigning charity has regular exhibitions looking at modern architecture and examining how to improve our cities and towns.

THE ARTHOUSE, *140 Lewisham Way, SE14 (0181 694 9011). Open Wed–Sun 11 am–6 pm. New Cross BR/ underground*. Contemporary works.

ASSOCIATION OF PHOTOGRAPHERS GALLERY, *10 Domingo Street, EC1 (0171 608 1441). Open Mon–Fri 9.30 am–6 pm. Barbican underground*. Striking images used in today's newspapers and magazines.

AUSTIN-DESMOND AND PHIPPS, *Pied Bull Yard, 15a Bloomsbury Square, WC1 (0171 242 4443). Open Mon–Fri 10 am–5.30 pm. Holborn underground*. Principally modern British painting is shown at this commercial exhibition space.

THE BARBICAN CENTRE, *Silk Street, EC2 (0171 638 4141). Open Mon–Sat 9 am–11 pm, Sun noon–11 pm. Barbican underground*. Various exhibitions in the Concourse Gallery and the foyer galleries, with displays in the libraries too, in this, the world's largest arts centre under one roof.

BATTERSEA ARTS CENTRE (BAC), *Lavender Hill, SW11 (0171 223 2223). Open Mon 10 am–6 pm; Tues–Sat*

10 am–10 pm; Sun noon–10 pm. Clapham Junction BR.
Exhibitions of contemporary works.

BEN URI ART SOCIETY, *21 Dean Street, W1 (0171 437 2852). Open Mon–Thur 10 am–5 pm; Sun 3–5 pm. Tottenham Court Road underground.* Regular temporary exhibitions displaying works of Jewish interest by Jewish and non-Jewish artists and displaying from the permanent collection including works by Auerbach, Epstein and Bomberg.

BLOND FINE ART, *Canalside Studios, 2–4 Orsman Road, London, N1 (0171 739 4383). Thur–Sun 11 am–6 pm. Highbury and Islington BR/underground.*

BLOOMSBURY WORKSHOP, *12 Galen Place, off Bury Place, WC1 (0171 405 0632). Open Mon–Fri 10 am–5.30 pm. Holborn underground.* There's a gallery displaying paintings, prints, sculptures and sketches by the Bloomsbury Group.

BRIXTON ARTISTS' COLLECTIVE, *35 Brixton Station Road, SW9 (0171 733 6957). Open Mon–Sat 10 am–6 pm. Brixton underground.* A stimulating series of exhibitions mostly by local artists.

CAMDEN ARTS CENTRE, *Arkwright Road, NW3 (0171 435 2643). Open Tues–Thur noon–8 pm; Fri–Sun noon–*

6 pm. Hampstead/Finchley Road underground. Contemporary art.

CAMERAWORK, *121 Roman Road, E2 (0181 980 6256). Open Tues–Sat 1–6 pm. Bethnal Green underground.* Unconventional, challenging exhibitions of contemporary photography.

CHELSEA COLLEGE OF ART AND DESIGN, *Manresa Road, SW3 (0171 351 3844). Open Mon–Sat 9 am–5 pm. Sloane Square underground.* End-of-term exhibitions and occasionally smaller ones at other times, consisting of painting, sculpture, ceramics, graphics and interior design.

CHISENHALE GALLERY, *64–84 Chisenhale Road, E3 (0181 981 4518). Open Wed–Sun 1–6 pm. Bethnal Green/ Mile End underground.* Innovative contemporary art in this huge (64 x 36 feet), stark exhibition space boasting no natural light, just lots of concrete and plain white walls.

CITY RACING, *60 Oval Mansions, Vauxhall Street, Oval, SE11 (0171 582 3940). Open Fri–Sun noon–7 pm. Oval underground.* Young artists working in all mediums.

CONTEMPORARY APPLIED ARTS, *43 Earlham Street, WC2 (0171 836 6993). Open Mon–Sat 10 am–6 pm; Thur until 7 pm. Covent Garden underground.* Ceramics, glass, metal, textiles, furniture, wood, pottery, jewellery and other exhibits.

CORAM GALLERY, *Lamb's Conduit Passage, WCI (0171 404 2040). Mon–Fri 10 am–6 pm. Holborn underground.* This gallery specialises in displaying modern British works.

CORK STREET (AND DERING STREET) AREA, *WI*. It's a good idea to treat the many private art galleries in the Cork Street vicinity *(Green Park/Bond Street underground)* as one entity with many doors. They tend to concentrate upon established modern art, and even if their exhibitions don't stay in the mind the names of these commercial London galleries certainly will. Anthony d'Offay, Annely Juda, Karsten Schubert, Rebecca Hossack ... It seems a mandatory requirement before opening your own gallery that you possess an unusual, posh-sounding name. I suppose trading as Kevin Sydney Smythe Fine Art (Croydon) Ltd just doesn't have the same ring along those up-market Mayfair streets. Opening hours for the galleries are typically *10.30 am–5.30 pm Mon–Fri, 10.30 am–1 pm Sat* unless otherwise stated. Most are closed in *August*. Don't be intimidated by the grand, stark rooms or by a possibly disapproving stare from a member of staff. How do they know you're not a millionaire art buyer just because you've got tatty jeans and an old tee-shirt? The galleries include:

ALAN CRISTEA GALLERY
Cork Street (0171 439 1866). Prints and drawings.

ANNELY JUDA FINE ART
23 Dering Street (0171 629 7578). Modernist work.

ANTHONY d'OFFAY
9, 21 and 23 Dering Street (0171 499 4100). International, often avant-garde, contemporary artists.

ANTHONY REYNOLDS GALLERY
5 Dering Street (0171 499 4100). 20th century works including Warhol.

BERNARD JACOBSON GALLERY
14a Clifford Street (0171 495 8575). Modern British art.

FINE ART SOCIETY
148 New Bond Street (0171 629 5116). Mainly 19th- and 20th-century British works.

GIMPEL FILS
30 Davies Street (0171 493 2488). Modern art.

JASON AND RHODES
New Burlington Place (0171 434 1768).
Contemporary British art.

MARLBOROUGH FINE ART
6 Albermarle Street (0171 629 5161). Shows here have
included Freud, Bacon and Hockney.

RAAB GALLERY
9 Cork Street (0171 734 6444). Specialises in large,
dramatic canvasses.

VICTORIA MIRO
21 Cork Street (0171 734 5082). Minimalist works.

WADDINGTON GALLERIES
5, 11, 12 and 34 Cork Street (0171 437 8611). You can
see work here ranging from up- and-coming
newcomers to Picasso.

CORPORATION OF LONDON ART COLLECTION,
*Guildhall Art Gallery, Aldermanbury, EC2 (0171 606
3030). Open Mon–Fri 10 am–5 pm by appointment*. Telephone or write to see some of the huge collection of art
collected by the Corporation for over 200 years. The
works are situated in various offices and institutions,
and are also in storage.

CRAFTS COUNCIL, *44a Pentonville Road, N1 (0171 278
7700). Open Mon–Thur 10 am–5 pm; Sat 10 am–1 pm,
2–5.30 pm; Sun 2–5.30 pm. Angel underground*. This is
the national body for promoting crafts and the gallery
is a show-case for contemporary pottery, printing, tex-

tiles etc. There's a reference library as well as a general crafts information service.

DRILL HALL ARTS CENTRE, *16 Chenies Street, WC1 (0171 637 8270). Exhibitions can be seen 6–11 pm when shows are playing. Goodge Street underground.* Art exhibition space in the bar area.

DULWICH PICTURE GALLERY, *College Road, SE21 (0181 693 5254). Free admission Fri 10 am–5 pm. West or North Dulwich BR.* 13 rooms displaying over 300 pictures including words by Rubens, Rembrandt, Canaletto, Gainsborough and Van Dyck.

ENGLAND AND CO, *14 Needham Road, W11 (0171 221 0417). Open Tues–Sat 11 am–6 pm. Notting Hill Gate underground.* A small, unpretentious commercial gallery.

FLOWERS EAST, *199–205 Richmond Road, E8 (0181 985 3333)* and FLOWERS EAST AT LONDON FIELDS, *282 Richmond Road, E8 (0181 533 5554). Open Tues–Sun 10 am–6 pm. Bethnal Green underground.* A wide range of mainly British modern artists.

FRITH STREET, *60 Frith Street, W1 (0171 494 1550). Open Tues–Fri 10 am–6 pm; Sat 11 am—4 pm. Tottenham Court Road underground.* Modern British artists displayed in an attractive wood-panelled public gallery.

THE GALLERY, *St John's, Smith Square*, SW1 *(0171 222 1061). Open Mon–Fri 10 am–5 pm. Westminster underground*. A variety of exhibitions by contemporary artists.

GOETHE-INSTITUT GALLERY, *50 Princes Gate, Exhibition Road*, SW7 *(0171 411 3400). Open Mon–Fri 10 am–8 pm; Sat 10.30 am–12.30 pm. South Kensington underground*. German artists and art collections.

GREENWICH THEATRE GALLERY, *Croom's Hill*, SE10 *(0181 858 7755). Open daily 10 am–10 pm. Greenwich BR*. Exhibitions change with each theatre show.

GREENWICH PRINTMAKERS, *1a Greenwich Market*, SE10 *(0181 858 1569). Open Tues–Sun 10 am–5.30 pm. Greenwich BR*.

HAMILTON'S, *13 Carlos Place*, W1 *(0171 499 9493). Open Mon–Fri 10 am–6 pm; Sat 11 am–5 pm. Bond Street underground*. This is the place to go to see work by top photographers including Helmut Newton, Irving Penn and David Bailey.

HARROW ARTS CENTRE, *Uxbridge Road, Hatch End*, HA5 *(0181 428 0124). Open Mon–Fri, and some Sats 9 am–11 pm. Pinner underground*. Modern works from the locality and elsewhere.

HEIFER GALLERY, *3 Calabria Road*, N5 *(0171 226 7380)*.

Open Mon–Fri 10 am–5 pm. Highbury and Islington BR/ underground. Contemporary works.

INSTITUTO CERVANTES, *22 Manchester Square, W1 (0171 935 1518). Open Mon–Thur 9.30 am–6.30 pm; Fri 9.30 am–5 pm. Marble Arch/Bond Street underground.* Regular exhibitions by Spanish artists.

ITALIAN CULTURAL INSTITUTE, *39 Belgrave Square, SW1 (0171 235 1461). Open Mon–Fri 9.30 am–5 pm. Knightsbridge underground.* Regular exhibitions by Italian artists.

IVEAGH BEQUEST, KENWOOD, *Hampstead Lane, NW3 (0181 348 1286). Open daily Apr–Sept 10 am–6 pm; Oct–Mar 10 am–4 pm. Donations gratefully received. Hampstead/Golders Green underground.* Exhibition of 17th- and 18th-century paintings including Gainsboroughs and Rembrandts.

KARSTEN SCHUBERT CONTEMPORARY ART, *42 Foley Street, W1 (0171 631 0031). Open Tues–Fri 10.30 am–5.30 pm; Sat 11 am–5 pm. Goodge Street underground.* An established commercial gallery.

KINGSTON MUSEUM AND ART GALLERY, *Wheatfield Way, Kingston, Surrey (0181 546 5386). Open Mon, Tues, Thur–Sat 10 am–5 pm. Kingston BR.* A variety of exhibitions including those by local artists.

LAUDERDALE HOUSE COMMUNITY ARTS CENTRE, *Waterlow Park, Highgate Hill, N6 (0181 348 8716). Open Tues–Fri 11 am–4 pm. Archway underground*. Two galleries with exhibitions of paintings, photographs and occasionally sculptures by artists from around the world.

LEIGHTON HOUSE, *12 Holland Park Road, W14 (0171 602 3316). Open Mon–Sat 11 am–5.30 pm. Garden open Apr–Sept 11 am–5.30 pm. Donations requested. High Street Kensington underground*. A permanent collection of paintings by Lord Leighton (1803–96) and his contemporaries as well as temporary exhibitions of modern and historic art, and sculptures in the garden.

LISSON GALLERY, *67 Lisson Street, NW1 (0171 724 2739). Open Mon–Sat 10 am–5 pm. Edgware Road underground*. A popular contemporary gallery.

LLEWELLYN ALEXANDER GALLERY, *124–126 The Cut, SE1 (0171 620 1322). Open Mon–Sat 10 am–7.30 pm. Waterloo BR/underground*. A highlight is the annual summer 'Not the Royal Academy' exhibition of works submitted but rejected by the Royal Academy Summer Exhibition.

LYRIC THEATRE, *King Street, W6 (0181 741 2311). Open 10 am–6 pm. Hammersmith underground*. Exhibitions in the foyer.

MALL GALLERIES, *The Mall, SW1 (0171 930 6844). Open*

daily 10 am–5 pm. Charing Cross BR/underground. Exhibitions are free to Westminster residents, and some are free to all. Occasional gallery tours. A varied programme including young unknowns as well as established artists.

MARBLE HILL HOUSE, *Richmond Road, Twickenham, Middlesex (0181 892 5115). Open Oct–Mar Wed–Sun 10 am–4 pm; Apr–Sept daily 10 am–6 pm. Richmond BR/underground, St Margarets BR.* Georgian fine art.

MATT'S GALLERY, *42–44 Copperfield Road, E3 (0181 983 1771). Open during exhibitions Wed–Sun noon–6 pm. Mile End underground.* Not a place of worship for those who follow Matt's cartoons each day in the *Daily Telegraph*, but a gallery displaying contemporary works in a wide spectrum of media by British and foreign artists that have often been specifically designed for the building.

MORLEY COLLEGE GALLERY, *61 Westminster Bridge Road, SE1 (0171 928 8501). Open during exhibitions Mon–Fri 10 am–6 pm, Wed until 8 pm. Lambeth North underground.* Modern British artists from the College and elsewhere.

NATIONAL GALLERY, *Trafalgar Square, WC2 (0171 839 3526). Open Mon–Sat 10 am–6 pm; Sun 2–6 pm; guided tours and lectures daily Mon–Sat. Charing Cross BR/underground.* Much of the history of western art can be found here. The nation's gigantic collection of Western masterpieces from the 13th to early 20th centuries.

Constable, Turner, Monet, Michelangelo, Velazquez, Van Eyck, Van Gogh, da Vinci, Titian, Picasso – they're all there. Regular changing exhibitions. Children's quizzes. The Micro Gallery (the computer information centre in the Sainsbury Wing), can provide you with a personal printed-out tour map that highlights the pictures you most wish to see. Incidentally, just before you enter the gallery, take a look round and you may notice the 185-foot high Nelson's Column in Trafalgar Square, famous for its abundance of tourists, pigeons, demonstrations and general unrest, and a huge free drunken party on New Year's Eve.

NATIONAL MUSEUM OF CARTOON ART, *15–17 St Cross Street, EC1 (0171 405 4717). Open Mon–Fri noon–6 pm. Donations welcomed. Farringdon/Chancery Lane underground.* Cartoons, comic strips and caricatures from Britain and around the world.

NATIONAL PORTRAIT GALLERY, *2 St Martin's Place, WC2 (0171 306 0055). Open Mon–Sat 10 am–6 pm; Sun 2–6 pm. Daily lectures. Donations welcomed. Charing Cross BR/underground.* Paintings, drawings, engravings, sculptures, photographs and cartoons from the 15th century onwards. Most of the prominent figures in British history are represented here. Regular special exhibitions.

OLD BULL ARTS CENTRE, *68 High Street, Barnet, Herts*

(0181 449 0048). Open Mon–Fri 10 am–5.30 pm; Sat, Sun noon–5.30 pm. High Barnet underground. Local, contemporary art including installations, sculpture, photography and painting.

OPEN AIR ART EXHIBITIONS with artists possessing a huge range of talents from atrocious to good are along the railings on the *Piccadilly* side of GREEN PARK, W1 at *weekends; Heath Street*, HAMPSTEAD, NW3 at *weekends June–August;* along railings on the *Bayswater Road* side of HYDE PARK, W2 on *Sundays.*

THE ORANGERY AND THE ICE HOUSE, *Holland Park, off Kensington High Street, W8 (0171 603 1123). Open daily 11 am–7 pm during exhibitions. High Street Kensington underground.* All forms of work are shown at these galleries but check first as they are occasionally closed.

ORLEANS HOUSE GALLERY, *Riverside, Twickenham, Middlesex (0181 892 0221). Open Apr–Sept: Tues–Sat 1–5.30 pm, Sun 2–5.30 pm; Oct–Mar: Tues–Sat 1–4.30 pm, Sun 2–4.30 pm. Donations welcomed. Richmond BR/ underground.* This villa, designed by James Gibbs and built in 1710, has an opulently decorated baroque Octagon Room and is set in a beautiful woodland garden by the river. Varied exhibitions all year. Occasional free events including lectures.

PHOTOFUSION, *17a Electric Lane, Brixton, SW9 (0171*

738 5774). *Open Tues–Sat 10 am–5.30 pm. Brixton under-ground.* Contemporary documentary photography by photographers at home and abroad.

PHOTOGRAPHER'S GALLERY, *5 and 8 Great Newport Street, WC2 (0171 831 1772). Open Tues–Sat 11 am–7 pm. Guided tours by arrangement. Donations welcomed. Leicester Square underground.* Contemporary photography, particularly reportage.

POLISH CULTURAL INSTITUTE, *34 Portland Place, W1 (0171 636 6032). Open Mon–Wed, Fri 10 am–4 pm; Thur 10 am–8 pm. Regent's Park underground.* Regular exhibitions with a Polish theme.

THE PUMP HOUSE, *Battersea Park, Albert Bridge Road, SW11 (0181 871 7530). Open Apr–Sept: Wed–Sun 11 am–6 pm; Oct–Mar: Wed–Sun 11 am–3 pm. Battersea Park BR.* Contemporary works.

PYM'S GALLERY, *9 Mount Street, W1 (0171 629 2020). Open Mon–Fri 9.30 am–6 pm. Marble Arch underground.* 19th and 20th-century Irish art.

REBECCA HOSSACK, *35 Windmill Street, W1 (0171 409 3599). Open Mon–Sat 10 am–6 pm. Tottenham Court Road underground.* A commercial gallery showing a stimulating selection of young artists.

REED'S WHARF GALLERY, *Mill Street, SE1 (0171 252 1802). Open Tues–Fri 10 am–6 pm; Sat 11 am–3 pm. London Bridge BR/underground.* Standing on the river, this bright gallery occupying the ground floor of a 19th-century wharf-house displays established and unknown artists from around the world.

RIBA ARCHITECTURE CENTRE, *66 Portland Place, W1 (0171 580 5533). Open Mon, Wed, Fri 8 am–7 pm; Tues, Thur 8 am–9 pm; Sat 9 am–5 pm. Oxford Circus underground.* Five gallery spaces explore architecture and design, and engineering and landscape design through models and drawings.

RIBA HEINZ GALLERY, *21 Portman Square, W1 (0171 580 5533 ext. 4807). Open Mon–Fri 11 am–5 pm; Sat 10 am–1 pm. Marble Arch underground.* Regular architectural exhibitions.

RIESCO GALLERY, *Croydon Clocktower, Katharine Street, Croydon, CR9 (0181 253 1030). Open Mon–Fri noon–6 pm; Sat, Sun noon–5 pm. East Croydon/West Croydon BR.* A permanent exhibition at the new Clocktower cultural complex.

RIVERSIDE STUDIOS, *Crisp Road, Hammersmith, W6 (0181 741 2255). Open Mon–Sat 10.30 am–11.30 pm; Sun noon–11.30 pm. Hammersmith underground.* Gallery space in the foyer showing a variety of artistic talents.

ROYAL ACADEMY OF ARTS, *Burlington House, Piccadilly, W1 (0171 439 7438). Open daily 10 am–6 pm. Green Park/Piccadilly Circus underground*. The Academy is housed in the huge Burlington House, a grand Palladian mansion, which would be even more impressive if they threw the ugly cars out of the central courtyard and installed some grass. Most *Tuesdays to Fridays* at *1 pm* there are tours of the 18th-century Private Rooms, where works by Royal Academicians are on display. You also get to see Michelangelo's *Taddei Tondo*, his only sculpture in Britain.

ROYAL COLLEGE OF ART, *Kensington Gore, SW7 (0171 584 5020). Open Mon–Fri 10 am–6 pm during exhibitions. Gloucester Road/South Kensington underground*. Varied exhibitions of work in progress during the terms. There are degree shows in *May* and *June*.

ROYAL COLLEGE OF MUSIC PORTRAITS DEPARTMENT, *Prince Consort Road, SW7 (0171 589 3643). Open Mon–Fri 10 am–5.30 pm by appointment only. South Kensington underground*. Music-related paintings, prints, photographs, engravings and statues.

ROYAL FESTIVAL HALL GALLERIES, *South Bank Centre, SE1 (0171 928 3002). Open daily 10 am–10.30 pm. Waterloo BR/underground*. A mixture of styles in a variety of media.

ROYAL NATIONAL THEATRE, *South Bank Centre, SE1 (0171 633 0880). Open Mon–Sat 10 am–11 pm. Waterloo BR/underground*. Exhibitions throughout the foyers.

RUDOLPH STEINER HOUSE, *35 Park Road, NW1 (0171 723 4400). Open Mon–Fri 10 am–5 pm and at other times (variable). Baker Street underground*.

SAATCHI COLLECTION, *98a Boundary Road, NW8 (0171 624 8299). Open Fri, Sat noon–6 pm. Swiss Cottage underground*. One of the country's finest collections, including works by Hockney and Warhol. A large and exciting purpose-built gallery.

ST MARTINS GALLERY, *St Martin-in-the-Fields, Trafalgar Square, WC2 (0171 839 4342). Open Mon–Sat 10 am–8 pm; Sun noon–6 pm. Charing Cross BR/underground*. Artists, who are often present in the gallery, displaying their work against the ancient stone- and brickwork of the church crypt.

SERPENTINE GALLERY, *Kensington Gardens, W2 (0171 402 0343). Open 10 am–6 pm during exhibitions. Lancaster Gate underground*. Innovative contemporary works in a wonderful location – a former tea pavilion within Kensington Gardens.

THE SHOWROOM, *44 Bonner Road, E2 (0181 983 4115)*.

Open Wed–Sun 1–6 pm. Bethnal Green underground. An enterprising contemporary gallery.

SOUTH LONDON GALLERY, *65 Peckham Road, SE5 (0171 703 6120). Open during exhibitions Tues–Fri 11 am–6 pm; Thur 11 am–7 pm; Sat, Sun 2–6 pm. Peckham Rye/Queen's Road BR.* A centre for the arts since 1891, this has six exhibitions annually: often contemporary art including painting, photography, sculpture and video.

SPECIAL PHOTOGRAPHERS' COMPANY, *21 Kensington Park Road, W11 (0171 221 3489). Open Mon–Fri 10 am–6 pm; Sat–11 am–5 pm. Notting Hill Gate underground.* A wide range of styles exhibited, from social documentary to fashion.

STABLES ART GALLERY, *Gladstone Park, Dollis Hill Lane, NW10 (0181 452 8655). Opening times vary. Dollis Hill underground.* A wide range of contemporary artists.

THE STUDIO, *28 Beckenham Road, Beckenham, Kent (0181 663 0103). Open Tues–Sat 11 am–5.30 pm. Clockhouse/Beckenham Junction BR.* The main gallery generally exhibits touring exhibitions, while the Café Bar shows local artists.

TATE GALLERY, *Millbank, SW1 (0171 887 8000). Open Mon–Sat 10 am–5.50 pm; Sun 2–5.50 pm; guided tours*

available daily and regular lectures. Pimlico underground.
Opened in 1897, the gallery houses national collections
of British paintings including Hogarth, Gainsborough,
Reynolds, Constable, Blake, Sargent, and Pre-Raphae-
lites, and 20th-century painting and sculpture from
Impressionism through to post-war work such as Pop
Art, which includes Picasso and Bacon. The Clore
Gallery houses The Turner Collection. There's modern
sculptures and prints by Chagall and Matisse. The
Gallery's displays, covering the 16th century to the
present, change annually.

TODD GALLERY, *1–5 Needham Road, W11 (0171 792
1404). Open Tues–Fri 11 am–6 pm; Sat 11 am–4 pm.
Notting Hill Gate underground*. A large private gallery
specialising in abstract works.

TOM ALLEN ARTS CENTRE, *Grove Crescent Road,
Strateford, E15 (0181 519 6818). Open Mon–Sat during
various art events. Phone for details of opening hours.
Stratford BR/underground*. A small exhibition space
showing work by artists countrywide.

TRICYCLE THEATRE, *269 Kilburn High Road, NW6
(0171 328 1000). Open Mon–Sat 10 am–11 pm. Kilburn
underground*. The gallery's exhibitions change regularly
at this friendly theatre.

TURTLE KEY ARTS CENTRE, *74a Farm Lane, SW6*

(0171 385 4905). Open Mon–Fri 10.30 am–6 pm. Fulham Broadway underground. Although primarily a theatre space, there are occasional contemporary art exhibitions here.

UNIVERSITY COLLEGE ART COLLECTION, *Strang Print Room, South Cloisters, University College, Gower Street, WC1 (0171 387 7050 ext 2540). Open during term-times Mon–Fri 1-2.30 pm. Goodge Street underground.* Temporary exhibitions of the collection, including prints, paintings, sculptures, photographs and books. Of particular note are Old Master etchings, engravings, early English mezzotints, works of the Slade School from the late 19th century (including Stanley Spencer and Augustus John) and a large number of drawings by Flaxman.

WALLACE COLLECTION, *Hertford House, Manchester Square, W1 (0171 935 0687). Open Mon–Sat 10 am–5 pm; Sun 2–5 pm. General tours Sat 11.30 am; Sun 3 pm; Mon–Fri 1 pm; and also Wed 11.30 am. Bond Street underground.* Four generations of the Wallace family collected this remarkable assortment of arms and armour, furniture, clocks, porcelain, sculpture and pictures, including ones by Titian, Gainsborough, Rembrandt and Rubens, and *The Laughing Cavalier* by Frans Hals.

WATERMANS ARTS CENTRE, *40 High Street, Brentford,*

TW8 (0181 847 5651). Open Tues–Sat 11 am–7pm; Sun noon–6 pm. Gunnersbury BR/underground. If you are from the 'Constable cows grazing by a stream' school of art appreciation, the first floor, staircase and foyer galleries may not be for you. With exhibition descriptions in their brochures such as, 'The exhibition will focus on the role of art educationalists and the variety of aesthetics being validated through art schools today ... development of their work in relation to their tutors' aesthetic and the impact of the latter on society and the environment ... from the perceptual via the subjective to the philosophical ...' etc, it's hardly an Athena poster shop.

WHITECHAPEL ART GALLERY, *80 Whitechapel High Street, E1 (0171 522 7878). Open Tues–Sun 11 am–5 pm, Wed until 8 pm. Aldgate East underground.* A lively programme of mainly 20th-century art exhibitions from a leading London art venue.

WOODLANDS ART GALLERY, *90 Mycenae Road, Blackheath, SE3 (0181 858 5847). Open Mon, Tues, Thur–Sat 11 am–5 pm; Sun 2–5 pm. Westcombe Park BR.* Contemporary paintings, prints, sculpture, textiles, ceramics, and photography displayed in a grand house in tranquil grounds.

ZELDA CHEATLE GALLERY, *8 Cecil Court, WC2 (0171 836 0506). Open Tues–Sat 10.30 am–6 pm. Charing Cross*

BR/underground. A distinguished small photographic gallery.

BUDDHISM

LONDON BUDDHIST CENTRE, *51 Roman Road, E2 (0181 981 1225). Open Mon–Fri 10 am–5 pm. Bethnal Green underground*. A drop-in centre that offers *weekday* lunchtime meditation classes *1–2 pm* and a introductory evening on *Wednesdays, 7–9.30 pm*. A voluntary donation is requested for further evenings.

LONDON BUDDHIST SOCIETY, *58 Eccleston Square, SW1 (0171 834 5858). Open Mon–Fri 2–6 pm; Sat 2–5 pm. Victoria underground*. There are a series of lectures on *Tuesdays* at *6.30 pm* introducing Buddhism, with further lectures on many *Wednesdays* at *6.30 pm* whilst on *Saturdays* at *3 pm* there is a meditation class. On some *Sundays* there are all-day meditation sessions.

BUSINESS INFORMATION

BUSINESS INFORMATION SERVICE, *the British Library, 25 Southampton Buildings, Chancery Lane, WC2. Chancery Lane underground*. The library, *open Mon–Fri 9.30 am–9 pm, Sat 10 am–1 pm*, has Britain's most comprehensive collection of business information and also an information line *(0171 323 7454, Mon–Fri 9.30 am–5.30 pm)* that can answer simple business queries such as market figures and company details. They will spend up to 10 minutes on your query before implementing a charge.

CITY BUSINESS LIBRARY, *1 Brewers Hall Garden,* EC2 *(0171 480 7638). Open Mon–Fri 9.30 am–5 pm. Moorgate underground.* A reference library crammed with business reference works including surveys, trade and annual reports, directories and 80 newspapers.

CAREERS INFORMATION

If you are deciding upon a career, THE HANDBOOK OF FREE CAREERS INFORMATION (published by Trotman) is available from your local library and compiles a host of organisations that offer free careers information including booklets, posters and pamphlets and sometimes audio-visual programmes available on free loan. Of use to school pupils, college students, adult jobseekers and- changers, and parents alike.

CHARITY SPONSORSHIP

Choose your challenge – for example a parachute jump – and let people sponsor it for a charity. Part of the money raised pays for your dare and the remainder goes to the nominated charity.

CHRISTMAS

CHRISTMAS LIGHTS, *Oxford Street, W1 (0171 629 1234); Regent Street and Bond Street, W1 (0171 629 1682). Oxford Circus/Bond Street underground. Also Covent Garden, WC2 (0171 836 9136; also premium rate information line 0839 123418). Covent Garden underground. Lights switched on early- to mid-November until Twelfth Night.* The lights along these streets help create a festive air, even though Christmas goods are on sale the moment summer ends. The *W1* switching on 'ceremony' by a celebrity can be very crowded so it's best to go later, when you can also take in the Christmas lights in neighbouring *St Christopher's Place* and *Carnaby Street, W1.* There are also lights to admire or bemoan else-where, such as *Kensington High Street, W8, Knightsbridge, SW1* and *Blackheath Village, SE3.*

SANTA is installed, from *mid-November*, at HARRODS, *Knightsbridge, SW1 (0171 730 1234) Knightsbridge underground*; SELFRIDGES, *Oxford Street, W1 (0171 629 1234) Marble Arch/Bond Street underground* and HAMLEYS, *188 Regent Street, W1 (0171 734 3161).*

LONDON CHRISTMAS PARADE, *begins Piccadilly, W1. A*

Sunday in late November. Piccadilly Circus underground.
An American-style parade of floats, dancers, marching
bands, clowns, jugglers, stilt-walkers and cartoon characters leave the Royal Academy of Arts, to travel along
Piccadilly Circus, Regent Street and Oxford Street
before arriving at Marble Arch 90 minutes or so later.

GREAT CHRISTMAS PUDDING RACE, *Covent Garden,*
WC2 (0181 446 4226). Early December. Covent Garden
underground.

BROADGATE ARENA, *Broadgate Centre, Eldon Street,*
EC2 (0171 588 6565). Liverpool Street BR/underground.
Stages live performance of music, drama and dance and
Christmas events.

CHRISTMAS TREE, *Trafalgar Square, WC2. Early Decem-*
ber. Charing Cross BR/underground. Every year since 1947
the citizens of Oslo in Norway have given the citizens
of London a Christmas tree as an expression of gratitude
for Britain's help in World War II. There are regular carol
concerts *(4pm–10pm)* around the tree until Christmas Eve.

Of the many CAROL SERVICES and other special
Christmas events taking place, the following churches
are particularly recommended: ST BARTHOLOMEW'S,
West Smithfield, EC1 (0171 606 5171); ST MARTIN-IN-
THE-FIELDS, *Trafalgar Square, WC2 (0171 930 1862);*
SOUTHWARK CATHEDRAL, *Montague Close, SE1 (0171*

407 3708); WESTMINSTER ABBEY, *Dean's Yard, SW1 (0171 222 5152).* ST. JAMES'S, *Piccadilly, W1 (0171 734 4511)* typically has a children's Carol Concert, advent cards and possibly a passion play during December.

PETER PAN CUP SWIMMING RACE, *The Serpentine, Hyde Park, W2 (01753 544441). December 25, approximately 8 am. Lancaster Gate/Knightsbridge underground.* Around 25 brave/mad swimmers participate in a small, festive race.

NEW YEAR'S EVE CELEBRATIONS, *Trafalgar Square, W1. From 9 pm on 31 December. Charing Cross BR/ underground.* A huge party to see in the new year, with Auld Lang Syne sung by a choir of thousands. Not for those who particularly cherish their space, and the widespread drunkenness can be quite threatening. The all-important midnight chime of Big Ben is invariably drowned out by the deafening revelry, but at least public transport home is free this night.

WATCHNIGHT SERVICE, *St Paul's Cathedral, Ludgate Hill, EC4 (0171 248 2705). New Year's Eve, 11.30 pm. St Paul's underground.* A lovely and particularly well-attended service.

CHURCHES

Of the many churches in London, a number are architectural gems. There are 38 churches in the City of London alone and each of these is worthy of a visit. (There were a mammoth 97 before the Fire of London in 1666.) Here's a selection of these tranquil havens:

ALL-HALLOWS-BY-THE-TOWER, *Byward Street, EC3. Tower Hill underground*. Although only the red-brick tower escaped damage during the Blitz, preserved in the tiny crypt are Roman paving, remains of Saxon crosses and an arch of a Saxon church built on this site in 675 AD.

ALL SAINTS, *7 Margaret Street, W1. Oxford Circus underground*. Of the many churches built in the capital during the 19th century, this atmospheric building stands out for the variety of coloured bricks used for decorative effect and the granite, alabaster and marble in the interior.

BROMPTON ORATORY, *Brompton Road, SW3. South Kensington underground*. Built in heavy Renaissance style in 1884 and boasting a nave that is 50-feet wide, this flamboyant Catholic church has an interior rich in marble and mosaics.

CHELSEA OLD CHURCH, *Cheyne Walk, sw3. Sloane Square underground.* Dating from 1157 but extensively rebuilt since then, and containing a rich collection of monuments. Here Henry VIII is believed to have married wife no. 3, Jane Seymour, soon after Anne Boleyn's execution.

CHRIST CHURCH, *Commercial Street, e1. Aldgate East underground.* The 225-foot triangular spire of this Hawksmoor church dominates the area, Spitalfields.

ST ALFEGE, *Greenwich High Road, se10. Greenwich BR.* Built in 1714, this is one of the best examples of a Nicholas Hawksmoor church. There's murals by James Thornhill, carvings by Grinling Gibbons and a memorial to General Woolfe, whose statue is in nearby Greenwich Park.

ST ANNE, LIMEHOUSE, *Commercial Road, e1. Westferry/ Limehouse DLR.* Hawksmoor, a pupil of Wren, was clearly influenced by his teacher. This Baroque church he designed in 1712 has an immense tower as well as a magnificent organ built for the 1851 Great Exhibition.

ST ANNE AND ST AGNES, *Gresham Street, ec2. St Paul's underground.* One of the churches rebuilt by Wren after the Great Fire of London in 1666, and restored after damage sustained during World War II. A spacious interior with a central vault boasts elegant columns and various antiquities.

ST BARTHOLOMEW-THE-GREAT, *West Smithfield, EC1. Barbican/St Paul's underground*. London's oldest parish church and one of its few examples of Norman architecture; remains include a half-timbered 13th-century gateway and inside are huge Romanesque pillars.

ST CLEMENT DANES, *Strand, WC2. Charing Cross BR/ underground*. A church has been here since the 9th century and was rebuilt in the 1680s by Wren and again after World War II. It became the memorial church of the Royal Air Force, and crests of hundreds of air squadrons are in the nave and aisles. The bells in the 115-foot tower could be the ones mentioned in the at least 500-year-old nursery rhyme 'Oranges and Lemons'. They play out that tune, although ST CLEMENT'S EASTCHEAP, *Clement's Lane, EC4 (Monument underground)*, another Wren church, with beautiful 17th-century woodwork, might instead be the church referred to in the rhyme.

ST ETHELREDA, *Ely Place, EC1. Chancery Lane underground*. Built in 1291, this is the oldest pre-Reformation Roman Catholic church in the capital. There's a huge vaulted undercroft with medieval roof timbers and a pre-Reformation model of Ely Place.

ST GEORGE, *Bloomsbury Way, WC1. Holborn/Tottenham Court Road underground.* The great Georgian architect Nicholas Hawksmoor gave St George's a striking Corinthian portico supported by six columns and an unusual pyramid-style steeple crowned by a statue of George I in a Roman toga. Inside, the neo-classical design is enhanced by fine gilded plasterwork.

ST GEORGE THE MARTYR, *Borough High Street, SE1. Borough underground.* Rebuilt by architect John Price in 1736, this is a handsome church rich in historical and literary connections. Little Dorrit was married here in Dickens' novel. The churchyard, now a peaceful garden, was the site of the Marshalsea debtors' prison where Dickens' father was imprisoned, and a wall survives.

ST GILES CRIPPLEGATE, *Fore Street, EC2. Barbican/Moorgate underground.* A Norman church originally stood on this site, where Oliver Cromwell married in 1620 and poet John Milton is buried.

ST JAMES'S, *Piccadilly, W1. Piccadilly Circus underground.* A busy Wren church with a splendid galleried interior and altar, organ case and font carved by Grinling Gibbons. The spire, replaced in 1968, is made of fibreglass, of all things. There's a pretty paved memorial garden with a small outdoor craft market.

ST MARGARET'S, WESTMINSTER, *Parliament Square,*

SW1. *Westminster underground*. Few visitors to Westminster Abbey also take time to discover its neighbour,
St Margaret's, which is the official church of the House
of Commons. It has many monuments and beautiful
stained glass and has enjoyed a prestigious following:
Chaucer and Caxton were parishioners, while Churchill,
Milton and Pepys married here. Sir Walter Raleigh is
buried here.

ST MARTIN-IN-THE-FIELDS, *Trafalgar Square, WC2.
Charing Cross BR/underground*. The fields have long
gone, but James Gibbs' imposing church has a magnificent Corinthian portico and a soaring steeple to admire
as well as a spacious galleried interior with Grinling
Gibbons woodwork, Venetian glass and a vaulted crypt.

ST MARY ABCHURCH, *Abchurch Lane, off Cannon
Street, EC4. Cannon Street BR/underground*. The quiet
exterior masks the magnificence of the interior with its
marvellous painted dome and Grinling Gibbons lime-
wood reredos in yet another impressive restored Wren
church.

ST MARY-LE-BOW, *Cheapside, EC2. Bank underground*.
Standing out from the drab office blocks, this is the
Wren-designed church, also known as Bow Church,
where to be a true Cockney you have to be born within
earshot of its 'Bow bells'. The bells sounded the wake-
up call and evening curfew for the locality from the

14th to 19th centuries. Only the handsome tower and steeple survived World War II. The interior is unremarkable, but beneath the church there is an interesting Norman crypt, incorporating the walls of a Saxon church.

ST MARY-LE-STRAND, *Strand, WC2. Aldwych underground.* This church has stained-glass windows – stained by the traffic as well as the creative urges of glaziers of long past, for it is marooned on an island on one of London's busiest roads. Risk a visit at your peril. Recitals are invariably augmented by car horns. Designed by James Gibbs in 1717, it is a good example of the Baroque style.

ST PAUL'S, *Bedford Street, Covent Garden, WC2. Covent Garden underground.* Designed by Inigo Jones in 1633 and boasting a magnificent portico overlooking Covent Garden's piazza, this is known as 'the actor's church'. The interior features theatrical memorials. Eliza Dolittle met Professor Higgins here in Shaw's play *Pygmalion*, and the film of it, *My Fair Lady*.

CITY FARMS

In the last 15 years or so, city farms (on the defence in their own small way against the great urban decay) have sprung up in the most unlikely of places such as rubbish dumps, abandoned industrial sites and other unloved, forgotten wastelands.

They are working farms, where the animals have to pay their way, but that doesn't stop them offering great recreational and educational opportunities, bringing the countryside and its activities to urban people. Many have regular events such as jumble sales, fun days, dog shows, barn dances, pig racing and sheep fairs.

They all have characters of their own. For example, Stepping Stones is a friendly, cosy little place where those running the farm are much in evidence, whereas Mudchute has more the appearance of an abandoned, segregated field with the livestock left alone and allowed to roam. Well, allowed to roam by London standards, anyway.

All these farms are run by volunteers, so if you would like a more lingering taste of the countryside and don't object to learning about animal care and some agriculture-related skills like building and horticulture, get in touch with your nearest.

BROOKS FARM, *Skelton's Lane Park, Skelton's Lane, E10 (0181 539 4278). Open summer: Tues–Sun 10.30 am–5.30 pm; winter: Tues–Sun 9.30 am–4.30 pm. Leyton Midland BR*. Donkeys, pigs, sheep, cows, ducks and chickens.

CORAM'S FIELDS, *93 Guildford Street, WC1 (0171 837 6138). Open daily 9 am–7 pm. Russell Square underground*. Animals include goats, sheep, pigs, rabbits, ducks and hens. Adults only admitted if accompanied by a child.

DENE CITY FARM, 39 *Windsor Avenue, Merton Abbey, SW19 (0181 543 5300). Open Tues–Sun 9 am–5 pm. Donation box. Morden Road BR*. Opened in late 1994 on a meadow in the National Trust's Morden Hall Park, the farm stocks the usual ingredients, including sheep, geese, chickens, calves and the odd field.

FREIGHTLINERS FARM, *Paradise Park, Sheringham Road, N7 (0171 609 0467). Open Tues–Sun 9 am–1 pm, 2–4.30 pm. Holloway Road underground/Highbury and Islington BR/underground*. A small, busy Islington farm, the oldest in the capital, with livestock including cows, geese, goats, ducks, pigs and bees.

HACKNEY CITY FARM, *1a Goldsmith's Row, E2 (0171 729 6381). Open Tues–Sun 10 am–4.30 pm. Donation box. Bethnal Green underground*. Originally a brewery, this small, friendly farm of only $1\frac{1}{2}$ acres with goats, sheep, pigs, cows, hens, chickens, turkeys, rabbits, ducks, bees and a butterfly tunnel even manages to fit in a beautiful, peaceful flower garden.

KENTISH TOWN CITY FARM, *1 Cressfield Close, Grafton Road, NW5 (0171 916 5421). Open Tues–Sun 9 am–5.30 pm. Chalk Farm/Kentish Town underground*. Five acres with horses, pigs, goats, rabbits, cows, sheep, ducks and chickens. Milking and feeding twice daily.

MUDCHUTE PARK AND FARM, *Pier Street, E14 (0171*

515 5901). Open daily 9 am–5 pm. Mudchute DLR. On a site covering over 30 acres, this is a peaceful spot amongst the towering buildings of Docklands. There are sheep, goats pigs, cattle and the odd horse and pony, with gardens, as well as a riding arena (not free). There's an agricultural show in August.

NEWHAM CITY FARM, *King George Avenue, E16 (0171 476 1170). Open Tues–Sun 10 am–5 pm summer; 10 am– 4 pm winter. Prince Regent DLR.* The east of the capital almost seems to have the monopoly on city farms. Despite the abundance of them in the area, Newham manages to enjoy over 50,000 visitors annually. There are horses, pigs, goats, sheep, chickens, ducks and a llama.

SPITALFIELDS COMMUNITY FARM, *Weaver Street, E1 (0171 247 8762). Open Tues–Sun 9 am–6 pm summer; 10 am–5 pm winter. Shoreditch underground.* Though little, this working farm has a good range of animals, including goats, pigs, sheep, cows and donkeys.

STEPPING STONES FARM, *Stepney Way, E1 (0171 790 8204). Open Tues–Sun 9.30 am–6 pm. Stepney Green underground.* Stepping Stones manages to evoke a real country farm atmosphere despite being overshadowed by tower blocks. Crammed into a relatively small space, as well as the usual cows, pigs, sheep, geese, chickens, rabbits and ducks, there's a wildlife pond, a play area with toys and books, a ferret, a donkey and guinea pigs. The latter make excellent slippers when hollowed out.

SURREY DOCKS FARM, *Rotherhithe Street, SE16 (0171 231 1010). Open Tues–Sun 10 am–5 pm (but check as often closed Fridays or for lunch 1–2 pm). Donation boxes. Surrey Quays/Rotherhithe underground.* By the Thames and dominated by Canary Wharf, there's a blacksmith's forge, a wind turbine, an orchard, wild area, vegetable garden, herb garden, riverside walk, duck pond and a room to observe their bees in addition to the goats, pigs, donkeys, geese, turkeys and other animals at this farm of just two-and-a-half acres. There are training projects for people with learning difficulties and various events through the year including a summer playscheme for the over–8s.

THAMESIDE PARK CITY FARM, *40 Thames Road, Barking, Essex (0181 594 8449). Open daily 10 am–5 pm. Barking BR/underground.* There are goats, sheep, horses, chickens, ducks and geese.

VAUXHALL CITY FARM, *24 St Oswald's Place, SE11 (0171 582 4204). Open Tues–Thur, Sat, Sun 10.30 am–5 pm. Vauxhall underground.* Tiny but well-stocked with animals.

WELLGATE COMMUNITY FARM, *Collier Row Road, Romford, Essex (017087 47850). Open Mon–Fri 9.30 am–3.30 pm; Sat, Sun 9.30 am–12.30 pm. Donation* *box. Chadwell Heath BR.* Under two acres but with goats, sheep, pigs, geese, ducks, chickens, turkeys, rabbits and guinea pigs.

CLOAKROOMS *Left-Luggage*

BANK OF ENGLAND MUSEUM, *Threadneedle Street, EC2 (entrance in Bartholomew Lane) (0171 601 5545). Open Mon–Fri 10 am–5 pm; also Sun 11 am–5 pm from Easter–Sept. Bank underground.* Anything 'within reason' can be deposited.

THE BARBICAN CENTRE, *Silk Street, EC2 (0171 638 4141). Open Mon–Sat 9 am–11 pm; Sun noon–11 pm. Barbican underground.* There is generally no problem leaving packages and bags.

BRITISH MUSEUM, *Great Russell Street, WC1 (0171 636 1555). Open Mon–Sat 10 am–5 pm; Sun 2.30–6 pm. Goodge Street/Tottenham Court Road/Russell Square underground.* Coats, hats, umbrellas and small hand luggage may be deposited.

MUSEUM OF MANKIND, *6 Burlington Gardens, W1 (0171 323 8043). Open Mon–Sat 10 am–5 pm; Sun 2.30–6 pm. Piccadilly Circus underground.* No large bags, suitcases or backpacks.

NATIONAL GALLERY, *Trafalgar Square, WC2 (0171 839 3526). Open Mon–Sat 10 am–6 pm; Sun 2–6 pm. Charing Cross BR/underground.* No packages or bags.

NATIONAL PORTRAIT GALLERY, *2 St Martin's Place, WC2 (0171 306 0055). Open Mon–Sat 10 am–6 pm; Sun 2–6 pm. Charing Cross BR/underground.* Small parcels, boxes, bags, umbrellas and walking sticks are acceptable, whilst suitcases and rucksacks are not.

PUBLIC RECORD OFFICE MUSEUM, *Chancery Lane, WC2 (0181 876 3444). Open Mon–Fri 10 am–5 pm. Refundable £1 coin required for locker. Chancery Lane underground.* Articles up to suitcase size are permitted.

ROYAL FESTIVAL HALL, *South Bank Centre, SE1 (0171 928 3002). Open daily 10 am–10.30 pm. Waterloo BR/underground.* No restrictions.

ROYAL NATIONAL THEATRE *South Bank Centre, SE1 (0171 633 0880). Open Mon–Sat 10 am–11pm. Waterloo BR/Underground.* No restrictions.

TATE GALLERY, *Millbank, SW1 (0171 887 8000). Open*

Mon–Sat 10 am–5.50 pm; Sun 2–5 pm. Pimlico underground. 'Anything that's not alive is allowed . . .'

VICTORIA & ALBERT MUSEUM, *Cromwell Road, SW7 (0171 938 8500). Open Mon noon–5.50 pm; Tues–Sun 10 am–5.50 pm. South Kensington underground.* No luggage may be left, only coats, umbrellas etc.

COMICS

The Redan Company publish a number of comics for young children such as Fireman Sam, Rosie and Jim, Thomas the Tank Engine and Mr Men. To receive a free copy, send a self-addressed envelope that is at least 253 x 305mm, with a 29p stamp (or the current 100g postage rate) affixed, to *London for Free comic offer, The Redan Company, 29 St John's Lane, EC1M 4BJ.*

CONSUMER INFORMATION

The monthly consumer magazine WHICH? regularly places advertisements in the national press offering three or four months' subscription for free, and these contain around 40 consumer reports on goods and services, finding out whether they are good value for money. You fill out a direct debit mandate to take up the offer, and this has to be cancelled by a specified date if you do not wish to continue receiving the magazine or be charged. I took up the offer for my own consumer test and unfortunately found that in my view, at the normal price of nearly £5 for each copy of the magazine, it was not good value for money.

CONTRACEPTION AND ABORTION

Advice, contraceptives and abortions are free to British citizens on the National Health Service, EU residents and foreigners working or studying in Britain. Two doctors must agree to a woman having an abortion.

Condoms and other contraception, leaflets and advice are available for the asking from FAMILY PLANNING CLINICS. The FAMILY PLANNING ASSOCIATION at 27 *Mortimer Street, W1 (0171 636 7866) Goodge Street underground,* can specify your nearest one. Don't be too choosy: requests for a box of fluorescent ribbed passion-fruit flavoured sheaths will probably not be accommodated.

BROOK ADVISORY CENTRES give advice and contraception, although each branch sets an age limit for free contraception. The branch at *233 Tottenham Court Road, W1 (0171 323 1522) open Mon–Thur 9 am–7.30 pm, Fri 9.30 am–3 pm* can specify your nearest centre.

COSMETICS AND PERFUMES

Almost all of the big cosmetics companies (especially the more expensive brands) provide free samples of their products from time to time – whatever their consultants may say. How else are they going to get you hooked into regularly buying their over-priced, over-packaged products?

The department stores stocking their good often also provide free skincare and make-up consultations, free make-overs and occasional special events including product launches. It's worth getting on a cosmetic company's register – give your name and address to the beauty consultant – so that you hear of forthcoming promotional events where further samples are often given.

There are plenty of shops to choose from. In central London there's DEBENHAMS, DH EVANS, JOHN LEWIS and SELFRIDGES in *Oxford Street, W1 (Marble Arch/Bond Street/Oxford Circus underground)* and nearby is FENWICK in *Bond Street* and DICKENS AND JONES in *Regent Street;* HARRODS *and* HARVEY NICHOLS *in Knightsbridge, SW1 (Knightsbridge underground)*; PETER JONES, *Sloane Square, SW1 (Sloane Square underground)*; BARKERS OF KENSINGTON, *Kensington High Street, W8 (High Street Kensington underground)* and ARMY AND NAVY, *Victoria Street, SW1 (Victoria BR/underground)*. Also larger branches of BOOTS THE CHEMIST.

So, if one sales assistant has no samples – or is unwilling to give any – there are plenty of other outlets to try.

These department stores stock a wide range, such as Chanel, Prescriptives, Estée Lauder, Clarins, Clinique and Lancôme. Most companies are quite forthcoming in offering samples although a short consultation may be necessary first. The samples usually last for at least a week and are very handy for the handbag or travel-bag.

If you like a dash of fragrance and are on the way to a party, a quick walk around the perfume counters won't go amiss. The use of several scents at the same time acts as a very effective insect repellent.

CYCLING

If you enjoy watching cycling, CYCLE TRACKS, *Eastway Cycle Circuit, Temple Mills Lane,* E15 *(0181 534 6085) open Mon–Sun to dusk*, has regular events including time trials, cyclo-cross and mountain bike races.

HERNE HILL CYCLE STADIUM, *Burbage Road,* SE24 *(0171 737 4647) Opening hours vary. Herne Hill BR.* Admission is sometimes free to spectators at this, the only velodrome in London, where a variety of races are held. Ring for details.

DENTAL TREATMENT

NHS dental care is only free to British citizens receiving Income Support or Family Credit, those on an NHS low income scheme, the under-17s and those under 19 studying full-time, women over 60, men over 65 and pregnant women and women who have had a baby in the last twelve months (but pregnant women can only get this if they were pregnant when the treatment started).

An exception is GUY'S HOSPITAL DENTAL SCHOOL *St Thomas Street, SE1 (0171 955 5000). Open 8.45 am– 3.30 pm Mon–Fri*. Dental treatment is free to all but although emergency treatment is dealt with at the walk-in surgery, there is a long waiting list for some dental work.

Emergency treatment (free to all) is available from:

EASTMAN DENTAL HOSPITAL *256 Gray's Inn Road, WC1 (0171 837 3646). Open 8.30 am–10 pm Mon–Fri.* Walk-in dental surgery, no appointment necessary.

KING'S COLLEGE HOSPITAL *Denmark Hill, SE5 (entrance in Caldecot Road) (0171 737 4000). Open 9 am–5 pm Mon–Fri* but best to turn up *before 9 am* for the morning surgery or *before 1 pm* for the afternoon surgery to have a chance of receiving emergency treatment.

LONDON HOSPITAL DENTAL INSTITUTE *New Road, Whitechapel,* EI *(0171 377 7000). Open Mon–Fri 8.30 am–5 pm* but you are advised to appear at *8.30 am* to have a good chance of treatment.

DISABLED INFORMATION

ARTSLINE *(0171 388 2227)* provides free information for the disabled on cultural and entertainment events. It can forward free individual guides covering such things as restaurants and theatres, but requests postage costs.

THE BRITISH SPORTS ASSOCIATION FOR THE DISABLED *(0171 490 4919)* gives advice and information on suitable sport activities for people with disabilities.

You can collect a free 'London Disability Guide' from the GREATER LONDON ASSOCIATION FOR DISABLED PEOPLE (GLAD) at *336 Brixton Road,* SW9 *(0171 274 0107). Open Mon–Fri 9 am–5 pm. Brixton underground.* They will post a copy if postage costs are paid, and the guide is also available in large print, tape and braille formats.

LONDON TRANSPORT'S UNIT FOR DISABLED PASS-

ENGERS *(0171 918 3312)* has a free guide, 'Access to the Underground'.

TRIPSCOPE *(0181 994 9294)* can help with general enquiries.

DRINK

I once met a man, clearly inebriated, who showed me a surprisingly complex map he had drawn up on the back of an old wine list. It showed the route he had worked out (and which he took most weeks) linking a formidable number of off-licences that held Saturday afternoon wine-tastings. Obviously, in the interests of public sobriety, it cannot be reproduced here. Nevertheless, the following off-licences and wine merchants have tastings, which may include wines, beers, whiskies and even champagnes:

MAJESTIC WINE WAREHOUSES have a most agreeable wine-tasting system: eight to ten wines are on offer at the special wine-tasting counter *every day* throughout opening hours *(Mon–Sat 10 am–8 pm; Sun 10 am–6 pm)* and there are occasional themed tasting weekends too. Branches at: *Albion Wharf, Hester Road, SW11; Arch 84, Goding Street, SE11; 12 Balham Hill, SW12; 40 Brighton Road, Surbiton; 229 The Broadway, SW19; 36 Cambridge Road, Kingston; 166 Campden Hill Road, W8; 9 Catford*

Hill, SE6; 63 Chalk Farm Road, NW1; 86 East Barnet Road, New Barnet; 107 Fortis Green, N2; 165 Goldhawk Road, W12; 123 Greenwich South Street, SE10; 42 Hastings Road, W13; 125 High Road, Bushy Heath; 60 High Street, E11; 2 Holloway Road, N7; 421 New King's Road, SW6; 91 Pelham Street, SW7; Unit 2, 226 Purley Way, Croydon.

ODDBINS usually have tastings on *Saturdays* from *2–5 pm*, but on *Fridays* in the City. There are branches at *17 Battersea Bridge Road, SW11; 64 Belsize Lane, NW3; 21 Bellevue Road, SW17; 7 Borough High Street, SE1; 47 Brewer Street, W1; 219 Brompton Road, SW3; 25 Charlotte Street, W1; 56 Church Road, SW13; 167 Clapham High Street, SW4; 57 Cranleigh Parade, Sanderstead; 11 Curzon Street, W1; 2 Denbigh Street, SW1; 91 Dulwich Village, SE21; 23 Earlham Street, WC2; 264 Earl's Court Road, W8; East Croydon Station; 65 Ebury Street, SW1; 41a Farringdon Street, EC4; 56 Friars Stile Road, Richmond Hill; 142 Fulham Road, SW10; 795 Fulham Road, SW6; 7 George Street, W1; 4 Great Portland Street, W1; 2 Harwood Road, SW6; 14 Heath Road, Twickenham; 822 High Road, N12; 318a High Holborn, WC1; 52 High Street, Beckenham; 26 High Street, Bromley; 173 High Street, Hampton Hill; 58 High Street, NW3; 42 High Street, Sutton; 223 Kensington High Street, W8; 23 Kew Road, Richmond; 55 and 209 King's Road, SW3; 55 Kingston Hill, Kingston; 4 Lauderdale Parade, W9; 538 London Road, North Cheam; 5 London Street, EC3; 195 Lower Richmond Road, SW15; 32 Marylebone High Street, W1; 3 Nelson Road, SE10; 38 New King's Road,*

SW6; 66 and 141 Notting Hill Gate, W11; 74 Old Brompton Road, SW7; 43 Queenstown Road, SW8; 105 Queensway, W2; 14 Ridgway, SW19; 95 Rosendale Road, SE21; 137 St Margaret's Road, Twickenham; 78 Southampton Row, WC1; 5 Station Parade, Richmond; 395 The Strand, WC2; 2 Stratford Road, W8; 27 Temple Fortune Parade, NW11; 26 Tranquil Vale, SE3; 64 and 101 Upper Street, N1; 58a Victoria Road, Surbiton; 135 Victoria Street, SW1; 98 Wandsworth Bridge Road, SW6; 12 Westbourne Grove, W2; 15 High Street, West Wickham; 115 White Hart Lane, SW15.

WINE RACK generally have wine-tastings every *Saturday* and *Sunday*. There are branches at 71 *Abbeville Road, SW4; 90 Alexandra Park Road, N10; 5 Bellevue Road, SW17; 786 Finchley Road, NW11; 809 Fulham Road, SW6; 278 Fulham Road, SW10; 52 Greyhound Road, W6; 756 High Road, N12; 6 High Street, SW13; 88 High Street, SW19; 4 Lupus Street, SW1; 173 New King's Road, SW6; 96 Park Hall Road, SE21; 108 Pitshanger Lane, W5; 2 Ranleagh Road, W5; 57 St Helens Gardens, W10; 51 St John's Wood High Street, NW8; 75 Station Road, E4; 22 Totteridge Lane, N20; 43 Tranquil Vale, SE3; 191 Upper Richmond Road West, SW14, 11 Walton Street, SW3* and 169 *West End Lane, NW6*. At their 32 *Goswell Road, EC1* branch the tastings are on *Thursdays* and *Fridays*.

Branches of NICOLAS are happy for visitors to try their wines on *Saturday afternoons*. They are at 71 *Abingdon Road, W8; 6 Fulham Road, SW3; 157b Great Portland*

Street, W1; 98 Holland Park Avenue, W11; 17 Kensington Church Street, W8; 10 Kew Green, Kew; 282 Old Brompton Road, SW5; 75 St John's Wood High Street, NW8; 11 Sheen Road, Richmond.

In addition branches of VICTORIA WINES have regular tastings, usually at least once a month, and these can vary from just one wine to a whole range of drinks. It's best to ring the wine department at head office *(01483 715066)* or to phone your local branch (details from *Yellow Pages*).

A number of branches of UNWINS have regular tastings, usually on *Saturdays*. Ring your local branch for details. Head office *(01322 272711)* can provide their number, or look in *Yellow Pages*.

Beer lovers will welcome the existence of THE BITTER EXPERIENCE, *129 Lee Road, SE3*, which has about 200 beers in stock. They always have from four to eight draught beers available for sampling.

Alternatively, if the idea of drinking alcohol disagrees with you, go on a water-based pub crawl with your local temperance movement.

ENGLISH HERITAGE

Safeguarding England's historic buildings and ancient monuments, English Heritage has several London sites where there is no admission fee:

ELTHAM PALACE, *Court Yard, SE9 (0181 854 2242). Open Thur and Sun 10 am–4 pm Oct–Mar; 10 am–6 pm Apr–Sept. Eltham/Mottingham BR*. This 13th-century royal palace, largely rebuilt from the 15th century, boasts a great hall with a hammer-beam roof and a bridge over a moat.

KENWOOD, THE IVEAGH BEQUEST, *Hampstead Lane, NW3 (0181 348 1286). Open daily 10 am–4 pm Nov–Mar; 10 am–6 pm Apr–Oct. Golders Green underground*. Kenwood, a splendid neo-classical mansion remodelled *c.* 1765 by Robert Adam, sits on the edge of Hampstead Heath and contains one of England's most impressive collections of paintings including artists such as Rembrandt, Vermeer, Hals, Reynolds, Turner and Gainsborough as well as an 18th-century jewellery collection and the highest quality antique furniture. Just three miles from central London, Kenwood's beautiful landscaped park has sloping lawns and a lake.

LONDON WALL, *near Tower Hill underground station, EC3*. Adjacent to the station is the best preserved section of the Roman Wall, which was heightened in the Middle Ages. The wall enclosed 330 acres, stretching from Blackfriars to where the Tower of London now stands.

MARBLE HILL HOUSE GARDENS, *Richmond Road, Twickenham, Middlesex (0181 892 5115)*. *Richmond BR/underground, St Margaret's BR*. Sixty-six acres of parkland that surround an impressive Palladian villa (for which there is an admission charge).

WINCHESTER PALACE, SOUTHWARK, *Clink Street, SE1 (0171 222 1234)*. *London Bridge BR/underground*. An unusual circular window features in the remains of this 13th-century town house later damaged by fire.

FASHION

HARRODS, *Knightsbridge, SW1 (0171 730 1234)*. Throughout the year fashion workshops are held, often in association with magazines such as *Marie Claire*, *Harpers & Queen* and *Vogue*. Telephone for details.

There are also occasional fashion shows with a complimentary drink at SELFRIDGES, *Oxford Street, W1 (0171 629 1234)*.

FILM AND VIDEO

BRITISH LIBRARY, *Great Russell Street, WC1 (0171 412 7222/0171 636 1544). Open Mon–Sat 10 am–5 pm; Sun 2.30–6 pm. Russell Square underground.* Regular videos on weekday afternoons in the Seminar Room.

BRITISH MUSEUM, *Great Russell Street, WC1 (0171 636 1555). Donations welcomed. Open Mon–Sat 10 am–5 pm; Sun 2.30–6 pm. Russell Square underground.* Regular weekday film-showings.

INSTITUTO CERVANTES, *22 Manchester Square, W1 (0171 935 1518). Open Mon–Thur 9.30 am–6.30 pm; Fri 9.30 am–5 pm. Marble Arch/Bond Street underground.* Telephone for details of films put on by this institute created to promote Spanish culture.

MUSEUM OF MANKIND, *6 Burlington Gardens, W1 (0171 323 8043). Open Mon–Sat 10 am–5 pm, Sun 2.30–6 pm. Piccadilly Circus underground.* Videos of up to an hour long about different cultures around the world shown *Tues–Fri 1.30 pm, 3 pm.*

NATIONAL GALLERY, *Trafalgar Square, WC2 (0171 839 3526). Open Mon–Sat 10 am–6 pm; Sun 2–6 pm. Charing Cross BR/underground.* Films on artists and schools of art on *Mondays* at *1 pm.*

TATE GALLERY, *Millbank, SW1 (0171 887 8000). Open Mon–Sat 10 am–5.50 pm; Sun 2–5.50 pm. Pimlico underground.* Regular film-showings each week.

WHITECHAPEL ART GALLERY, *Whitechapel High Street, E1 (0171 522 7878). Open Tues–Sun 11 am–5 pm; Wed until 8 pm. Aldgate East underground.* Regular art-orientated film- and video-screenings.

FOOD FROM STREET MARKETS

When a stock-take of the kitchen indicates the need for a shopping expedition for vegetables, fruit and flowers, the only acceptable time to hit the local market is when the stall-holders are packing up at the end of the day. It is then that you can often help yourself to a surprising variety of left-overs.

Granted, it's a bit of a jump from a visit to the supermarket, where you can obtain exotic pre-trimmed, pre-scrubbed produce flown in the day before from Asia or Africa, wrapped in cellophane and weighed to the gramme, with a nice but rather over-careful sell-by date on the label – a label which invariably includes helpful cooking instructioins like 'boil' or 'wash before use'. They sure make you pay for all these extras.

It seems sacrilege to let the bin men throw away the muddle of food left behind by the market traders. It may be too ripe to be possible to sell the next day, or a

Food Information ▬▬▬

bit bruised, or simply too much trouble for them to pick up. Yet much of it is perfectly good to eat, and can easily be washed or peeled.

You have to get the timing right, however. Strike as the stalls pack up or soon after, before the street cleaners appear. Don't be too greedy and help yourself to fruit or vegetables that are soft enough for the city dirt to have worked its way in; and meat or fish are probably best left well alone.

I visited Lewisham Street Market, SE13, as it was closing at around 5.30 pm on a weekday and picked up a carrier bag full of discarded fruit and vegetables. All of it was fresh and undamaged. You just have to be sure the produce *is* discarded – a couple of oranges standing alone on the pavement a few feet away from the stalls are unlikely to be claimed by anyone, but helping yourself to a pound of lychees on a stall that *looks* deserted could end you up with problems. When in doubt, ask.

FOOD INFORMATION

The Ministry of Agriculture, Fisheries and Food has produced a series of colourful FOODSENSE leaflets covering food allergies, additives, safety, labelling, pesticides, nutrition, radiocactivity and chemicals in food, natural toxicants and healthy eating. Write to *Foodsense, SE99 7TT*, or ring the order line *(0645 556000)* and ask for all the leaflets, which total over 150 pages packed with photographs and information.

TESCO and SAINSBURY'S regularly bring out full-colour recipe cards, available at their stores. There are usually several cards available at any time, so it's easy to build a collection. They're hard-wearing and laminated and will therefore survive spillages and manhandling in the kitchen.

FOOD PLANTS

London offers a wealth of food that are delicious, healthy and free, in the form of wild plants. They're all there for the taking, but you need to know where they are and when to find them.

If you are not experienced at gathering wild food plants, you will need a comprehensive field guide to accurately identify the different species, and to know what to avoid, such as carcinogenic *bracken*, *dog's mercury*, which can damage internal organs when ingested, the aptly named *fool's parsley, hemlock, buttercups, mistletoe, black, green, woody and deadly nightshade*, the deadly *water dropworts*, and some varieties of fungi such as the deadly poisonous *destroying angel, panther cap* and *death cap*. Despite such hazards, proportionally very few plants pose a health risk and taking care over identification is all that is required.

Use restraint when gathering: don't be so enthusiastic you single-handedly remove the wild plant harvest for the whole borough, and only take small amounts of what you are picking from each plant, to enable it to survive your onslaught. Leave some food for the wild animals and birds. Avoid searching at the sides of busy roads or areas that may have been treated with weed killers or insecticides. When trying out a new food, eat it in moderation at first in case it disagrees with you.

FOOD FOR FREE *(Richard Mabey, Collins)* is a good introduction to the subject and has colour illustrations of over 240 species of food plant, noting where to find them and at what time of year, but also offering guidance on picking and preparation, and culinary and nutritional tips. It describes any special preparations that may be required to make a plant palatable. Also, there's THE OXFORD BOOK OF FOOD PLANTS *(Oxford University Press)*, FREE FOR ALL *(Ceres, Thorsons Publishers)* and a number of books wholly concerned with mushroom gathering, a pastime which has, well, mushroomed in popularity in recent years. Maybe it's a revolt against the growth of pre-packed and convenience foods, products that are identical wherever in Britain you buy them. See MUSHROOMS IN THE WILD *(Ian Tribe, Orbis)*, and THE MUSHROOM HUNTER'S FIELD GUIDE *(Alexander Smith, University of Michigan Press)*.

Food plants have many uses. They can be used in

salads, soups, as a side vegetable, as teas, herbal remedies, puddings, pies, jams, purées, jellies, beers, wines and as additions to casseroles. They add new flavours, scents and textures to the kitchen. Unlike many commercial foodstuffs, most are likely to be free from agricultural chemicals but, even so, they should be thoroughly washed before use.

Examples of food plants include *common sorrel*, which is quite easy to find on grassland and heaths. Although hardly used here, it appears in many French dishes. Rich in vitamin C, its sharp flavour goes down well in soups and salads, although the high acid content can aggravate conditions like stomach ulcers, rheumatism and arthritis. Five hundred years ago the pretty woodland flower known as *wood sorrel* was a popular ingredient for salads and sauces, though it should be used in small quantities.

Lamb's lettuce, or *cornsalad*, pre-washed in plastic bags, sells at a very grand price in supermarkets as a posh alternative to the standard salad fare. Yet it is no more than another common edible weed.

You could make a soup from *red*, *white* and *stinging nettles* or stir-fry *shepherd's purse* and *wintercress*. *Cleavers*, plentiful in woodland and hedges, can be boiled briefly in salted water as an interesting alternative to spinach or greens. Infused with boiling water, it makes a refreshing mild diuretic tea, slightly tasting of cucumber. The ripe seeds can even be ground and used as a substitute for coffee.

The Wildlife and Countryside Act does not allow the digging up of wild plants by the root unless on your own land or with the landowner's permission. But if you have *dandelion* in your garden the roots make another coffee substitute, and the Japanese use them as a side vegetable. The leaves, cooked, make a spinach-like vegetable and if chopped, a salad. They combine well with *chickweed*. Makes a change from boring old lettuce, cucumber and tomato.

Wild garlic, found in woods and hedgebanks, is a mild replacement for spring onion or garlic and is excellent chopped up raw and added to sandwiches, salads, sauces and soups. Lightly boiling the leaves of *ground elder* yields a spicy flavour.

Good alternatives to spinach or greens include *common orache* and *bladder campion*. There's also *Fat-Hen*, which also has a somewhat less appealing name, *dungweed*. It contains more vitamin B1, iron and protein than cabbage. The roots must not be eaten.

The large array of fungi available includes the ugly but delicious *horn of plenty* the *wood hedgehog*, the nutty-tasting *fairy-ring champignon*, the *chanterelle* which smells of apricots, the rich tasting and common *honey fungus*, the milder *oyster mushroom* (which is commonly sold in supermarkets) and the sometimes enormous *puffball*. All can be prepared in a great variety of ways.

Trees provide nuts (for example *walnut, sweet chestnut, hazel, beech*) and fruit (sour *bullace, sloes, crabapples, rowan-berries and elder*). But a bowl of *elderberries* cannot hope to compete with *blackberries*, *raspberries* and *wild strawberries*.

As an alternative to visiting a wood or heath, the local rubbish tip may have crops such as potatoes, tomatoes or marrows scattered about that emanated from seeds from household dustbins.

FOOD SHOPS

BARSTOW AND BARR, 24 *Liverpool Road*, N1 *(0171 359 4222). Open Mon noon–8 pm; Tues–Fri 10 am–8 pm; Sat 9 am–6 pm; Sun 10 am–2 pm. Angel underground.* You are welcome to try a small selection from this shop's stock of over 100 cheeses, and also Provence olives. There's another branch at *Unit 90, Camden Lock, Chalk Farm,* NW7 *(0171 428 0488). Open Sat, Sun 11 am–5.30 pm. Camden Town underground.*

THE CHEESEBOARD, 26 *Royal Hill,* SE10 *(0181 305 0401). Open Mon–Wed, Fri, Sat 9 am–5 pm; Thur 9 am–1 pm. Greenwich BR.* A huge range of cheeses available for tasting, many obscure. If you buy some, don't complain, as one old gentleman did, that your Red Leicester is orange.

FRATELLI CAMISA, 53 *Charlotte Street,* W1 *(0171 255 1240). Open Mon–Sat 9 am–6 pm. Goodge Street underground.* Various cold meats, olives, cheeses etc.

HAND MADE FOOD, *40 Tranquil Vale, Blackheath SE3 (0181 297 9966). Open Mon–Fri 9 am–7 pm; Sat 9 am–5.30 pm; Sun 10 am–2 pm. Blackheath BR.* Like many delicatessens and specialist food shops, Hand Made Food is happy for everything from its fresh food range to be tasted, if this privilege is not abused. A nice touch is the children's toys available to play with for younger visitors not particularly engrossed by the merits of extra virgin olive oils or obscure salami.

HARRODS, *Knightsbridge, SW1 (0171 730 1234). Open Mon, Tues, Sat 10 am–6 pm; Wed–Fri 10 am–7 pm. Knightsbridge underground.* When tastings and product launches occur, a whisk through the huge Food Hall sampling the varied fare can effortlessly procure you an impressive calorie intake.

HARE KRISHNA RESTAURANT, *9 Soho Street, W1 (0171 437 3662). Open Mon–Sat 11 am–7.30 pm. Tottenham Court Road underground.* The management does not mind giving away its delicious vegetarian food as it believes it provides spiritual benefit but consistent abusers of its system and, in the words of a spokesman, 'the intoxicated and hardcore tramps' are not admitted.

THE HIVE, *53 Webbs Road, SW11 (0171 924 6233). Open Mon–Sat 10 am–6 pm. Clapham South underground/Clapham Junction BR.* A honey-lover's paradise! Sample some of the 40 or so types of honey on sale. A further attraction is an observation glass beehive installed in the shop.

NEAL'S YARD DAIRY, *Short's Gardens, WC2 (0171 379 7646). Open Mon–Sat 9 am–7 pm; Sun 10 am–5 pm. Covent Garden underground.* Cheeses from Britain and Ireland principally.

RIPPON CHEESE STORES, *26 Upper Taschbrook Street, SW1 (0171 931 0628). Open Mon–Fri 9 am–6.30 pm; Sat 9 am–5 pm. Pimlico underground.* Quite a choice with over 550 cheees on offer.

ROCOCO, *321 King's Road, SW3 (0171 352 5857). Open Mon–Sat 10 am–6.30 pm. Sloane Square underground.* This is *the* place for chocolate, from modest kid's bars to unspeakably delicious truffles made from the world's rarest cocoa bean. Try a sample or two – at your peril . . .

ROSSLYN DELICATESSEN, *56 Rosslyn Hill, NW3 (0171 794 9210). Open Mon–Sat 8.30 am–8.30 pm; Sun 8.30 am–5 pm. Hampstead underground.* Most weekends there's free tastings of a particular product, but otherwise cheeses, meats, pâtés and olives can usually be tried at other times.

FOOTBALL

CHELSEA FOOTBALL CLUB, *Stamford Bridge, Fulham Road, SW6 (0171 385 0710) Fulham Broadway underground*. To go behind the scenes – 'you see what you don't see, if you see what I mean,' explained the spokeswoman – book a place with 'Chelsea in the Community' at the number above. Ground tours are usually on *Fridays* at *11 am* and last around an hour and a half.

MILLWALL FOOTBALL CLUB, *The Den, Zampa Road, SE16 (0171 232 1222). South Bermondsey BR*. Request in writing to go on a tour of the grounds, which lasts around an hour and a half.

FREQUENT EVENTS

Pageantry can be seen daily in London:

CEREMONY OF THE KEYS, *Tower of London, EC3 (0171 709 0765). Daily 9.30–10.05 pm. Special pass required: write to the Resident Governor, Queen's House, HM Tower of London, EC3 enclosing a stamped self-addressed envelope. Tower Hill underground.* A 700-year-old routine of locking up the Tower of London, home to the Crown

Jewels, where the Sentry and the Chief Warder have an historic verbal exchange.

CHANGING OF THE GUARD:
BUCKINGHAM PALACE, *SW1. April to mid-August daily 11.25 am; late August to March alternate days 11.25 am. St James's Park underground*. This famous 40-minute ceremony that takes place inside the railings of the palace is London's most popular regular event so arrive in good time for a good view of it.

HORSE GUARDS, *Horse Guards Parade, Whitehall*, SW1 *(0171 930 1793). Mon–Sat 11 am, 4 pm; Sun 10 am, 4 pm. St James's Park underground/Charing Cross BR/underground.* A less crowded, scaled-down version lasting 25 minutes.

FUN-FAIRS

Popular fun-fair sites include:
ALEXANDRA PARK, *Muswell Hill*, N22. *Wood Green underground;* BATTERSEA PARK, *Albert Bridge Road*, SW11. *Sloane Square underground*; BLACKHEATH COMMON, SE3. *Blackheath BR*; HAMPSTEAD HEATH, NW3. *Hampstead underground.*

Fairs are typically held on *Good Friday to Easter Monday* and on the *Spring (May)* and *August Bank Holiday weekends, Fri–Mon.*

GARDENING

If you have gardening skills but nowhere to practice them, the CALTHORPE PROJECT COMMUNITY GARDEN, *258–274 Gray's Inn Road, WC1 (0171 837 8019) King's Cross BR/underground*, is happy for volunteers to help out in their acre of gardens. Regular helpers can look after their own section of garden single-handed.

HACKNEY CITY FARM, *1a Goldsmith's Row, E2 (0171 729 6381). Open Tues–Sun 10 am–4.30 pm. Bethnal Green underground*. Includes a large garden where volunteers can help plant and grow things and learn about propagating new plants, organic controls and companion planting.

HORNIMAN GARDENS, *100 London Road, Forest Hill, SE23 (0181 699 2339). Open 8 am–dusk. Forest Hill BR*. Horticultural demonstrations are held about once a month on Wednesday afternoons from March to September and occasionally on Sunday afternoons too.

LONDON WILDLIFE GARDEN CENTRE, *28 Marsden Road, SE15 (0171 252 9186). Open Tues, Wed, Thur, Sun 11 am–4 pm. Donations welcomed. East Dulwich BR*. This London Wildlife Trust centre promotes wildlife gardening and appreciation of wildlife in your garden. There are lots of gardening ideas, including a visitor centre, demonstration areas, a nursery, wildlife gardens with a pond, meadows and woods, and even beehives, a sensory/herb garden, and a demonstration building featuring such innovations as a roof insulated by installing plants on it and recycled newspapers in the walls. Events include four open days a year as well as talks, workshops, training programmes and clubs for 5–8 year olds and 8–16 year olds with environmental activities such as fossil hunting, tree planting and making a nature film.

GYMNASIUM EQUIPMENT

PRIMROSE HILL, *NW3*. *Chalk Farm/Camden Town underground*. There has been an open-air gymnasium here since Victorian times, and nowadays there is a choice of around 20 different types of exercise equipment.

VICTORIA PARK, *Victoria Park Road, E9 (0181 985 1957)*. *Mile End underground*. A fitness trail with some gym equipment.

WINN'S COMMON, *Plumstead, SE18*. *Plumstead BR*. Has a small selection of outdoor gym equipment.

WEST HAM PARK, *Upton Lane, E7*. *Plaistow under-*

ground. Has a keep-fit trail with a few items of gym equipment.

HAIRCUTS

LONDON COLLEGE OF FASHION, *20 John Prince's Street, W1 (0171 514 7482/0171 514 7400). Open Mon–Fri 10 am–5 pm during term-times. Oxford Circus underground*. Ladies and men are both welcome. Call to make an appointment.

TONI AND GUY HAIRDRESSING ACADEMY, *16 West Central Street, WC1 (0171 240 7899). Tottenham Court Road/Holborn underground*. Appointments available for women on weekdays at *10 am* and *2 pm*.

TONI AND GUY LONDON ACADEMY, *33 St Christophers' Place, W1 (0171 486 4733) Bond Street underground*. Competent students trained in 'the Tony and Guy specific way of cutting hair' – whatever that is – have appointments available for men on *weekdays* at *10 am* and *2 pm*.

HITCH-HIKING

Bear in mind that hitching can be dangerous and therefore do not hitch alone.

BRIGHTON *via M23 and A23:* hitch at Purley Way, Croydon by Denning Avenue *(Waddon BR).*

BRISTOL *via M4:* wait at Great West Road, w4, near Hammersmith Bridge *(Hammersmith underground).*

CAMBRIDGE *via M11:* hitch from Eastern Avenue, Ilford *(Redbridge underground).*

DOVER *via M2 and A2:* start from the A102(M) round-about with Woolwich Road, SE10 *(Westcombe Park BR).*

FOLKESTONE *via M20:* start from Sidcup Road, SE9 at junction with Court Road (Mottingham BR).

NORTHAMPTON *via M1:* starting point is Staples Corner, NW2 *(Brent Cross underground).*

OXFORD *via M40:* hitch from Western Avenue, W3 at Horn Lane junction *(Acton Main Line BR).*

SOUTHAMPTON *via M3:* begin at Chertsey Road,

Twickenham, at roundabout with Whitton Road (*Twickenham BR*).

LECTURES, TALKS AND DISCUSSIONS

THE ALBANY CENTRE, *Douglas Way, SE8 (0181 692 0231). Open Mon–Sat 10 am–6 pm. New Cross BR/underground*. There are poetry readings, and occasional tours of the theatre explaining the workings backstage, from lighting to sound.

ARCHITECTURAL ASSOCIATION, *34–36 Bedford Square, WC1 (0171 636 0974). Open Mon–Fri 10 am–7 pm; Sat 10 am–3 pm. Tottenham Court Road underground*. Weekly afternoon and evening lectures.

ARCHITECTURE FOUNDATION, *The Economist Building, 30 Bury Street, SW1 (0171 839 9389). Open Tues, Wed, Fri noon–6 pm; Thur, Sat, Sun 2–6 pm. Green Park underground*. This campaigning charity has urban-planning debates.

BRITISH LIBRARY, *Great Russell Street, WC1 (0171 412 7222). Open Mon–Sat 10 am–5 pm; Sun 2.30–6 pm. Russell Square underground*. Regular talks and slide lectures related to the collection, and also special events (details from the *Events Box Office* on *0171 412 7760*).

BRITISH MUSEUM, *Great Russell Street, WC1 (0171 636 1555)*. *Open Mon–Sat 10 am–5 pm; Sun 2.30–6 pm. Donations welcomed. Russell Square underground. Weekday* lectures at *1.15 pm*, gallery talks *Tues–Sat 11.30 am* and talks at other times from *Sat–Tues*.

CAMDEN ARTS CENTRE, *Arkwright Road, NW3 (0171 435 2643)*. *Open Tues–Thur noon–8 pm; Fri–Sun noon–6 pm. Finchley Road underground*. Artists give informal talks about their works on display. Ring for details.

ECOLOGY CENTRE, *45 Shelton Street, WC2 (0171 379 4324)*. *Open Mon–Fri 10 am–6 pm. Covent Garden underground*. Occasional talks.

EXPLORE WORLDWIDE, *Venue: Baden-Powell House, Cromwell Road, SW7 (01252 344161)*. *Gloucester Road underground*. This travel company offers informative two-hour slide lectures every two weeks or so and although the shows obviously mention the holidays they sell, there's an opportunity to learn about other lands. Different cultures and ancient sites around the world, hiking in mountain regions, wildlife and natural history etc., are all covered. Ring for a ticket.

GEFFRYE MUSEUM, *Kingsland Road, E2 (0171 739 9893)*. *Open Tues–Sat 10 am–5 pm; Sun 2–5 pm. Old Street underground*. Talks on *Saturdays* at *2 pm* and *3.30 pm* and other talks related to special exhibitions.

GREENWICH BOROUGH MUSEUM, *232 Plumstead High Street, SE18 (0181 855 3240). Plumstead BR*. Afternoon talks given once a month on a wide range of subjects.

GRESHAM COLLEGE, *Barnard's Inn Hall, EC1 (0171 831 0575). Open Mon–Fri 9.30 am–5 pm. Chancery Lane underground*. Request a free programme detailing the year's lectures, which tend to run from *September* to *November* and *February* to *May*, when there could be anything from two or three a month to nearly 20. The lectures are on astronomy, divinity, geometry, law, music, physic and rhetoric, the subjects that the founder, City merchant Sir Thomas Gresham, insisted upon when establishing the college in 1597. Nowadays the College also delivers lectures on commerce and occasionally other subjects such as literary London.

GUILDHALL SCHOOL OF MUSIC AND DRAMA, *Silk Street, Barbican, EC2 (0171 628 2571). Barbican/Moorgate underground*. Occasional talks on aspects of music and drama.

HOLLAND PARK, *Illchester Place, Kensington, W8. (0171 602 9483). Holland Park underground*. Summer talks about the wildlife and history of the park are given at the Ecology Centre.

INSTITUTO CERVANTES, *22 Manchester Square, W1 (0171 935 1518). Open Mon–Thur 9.30 am–6.30 pm; Fri 9.30 am–5 pm. Marble Arch/Bond Street underground.* Ring for details of lectures and talks with a Spanish theme.

ITALIAN CULTURAL INSTITUTE, *39 Belgrave Square, SW1 (0171 235 1461). Open Mon–Fri 9.30 am–5 pm. Knightsbridge underground.* Regular lectures on Italian themes.

MUSEUM OF LONDON, *150 London Wall, EC2 (0171 600 3699). St Paul's underground.* Regular lunch-time lectures and gallery talks.

MUSEUM OF MANKIND, *6 Burlington Gardens, W1 (0171 323 8043). Open Mon–Sat 10 am–5 pm; Sun 2.30–6 pm. Touch sessions for the blind by arrangement. Donations welcome. Piccadilly Circus underground.* Occasional lectures and talks, or even music performances.

NATIONAL GALLERY, *Trafalgar Square, WC2 (0171 839 3526). Charing Cross BR/underground.* Lunch-time lectures every day except *Sun*.

NATIONAL PORTRAIT GALLERY, *2 St Martin's Place, WC2 (0171 306 0055). Open Mon–Sat 10 am–6 pm; Sun 2–6 pm. Donations welcomed. Charing Cross BR/underground.* Daily lectures.

POLISH CULTURAL INSTITUTE, *34 Portland Place, W1 (0171 636 6032). Open Mon–Wed, Fri 10 am–4 pm; Thur 10 am–8pm. Regent's Park underground.* Regular lectures with a Polish theme.

RIVERSIDE STUDIOS, *Crisp Road, Hammersmith, W6 (0181 741 2255). Open Mon–Sat 10.30 am–11.30 pm; Sun noon–11.30 pm. Hammersmith underground.* Occasional talks and discussions.

ROYAL INSTITUTION, *21 Albermarle Street, W1 (0171 409 2992). Green Park underground.* Generally once a term (or three times a year), the Institution organises a free lunch-time talk on a general scientific subject. Ring to join the free mailing list.

ROYAL SOCIETY OF ARTS, *8 John Adam Street, WC2 (0171 930 5115). Charing Cross BR/underground. Lectures are usually at 6 pm on weekdays. Seat reservations and a lecture programme for the year available from the Lecture Booking Office by letter or on 0171 930 9286.* Early booking is advisable for these popular lectures by members on a broad range of topical themes such as art, architecture, commerce, industry, science and the media. There are also occasional lectures for children.

ST MARY-LE-BOW, *Cheapside, EC2 (0171 248 5139). Bank underground.* During the academic year on *Tuesdays* at *1.05 pm* the rector talks to a prominent figure (such as an actor or politician) about current affairs, their personal outlook, where the universe ends etc. Admission is on a first come, first served basis.

SCIENCE FOR LIFE, *The Wellcome Building, 183 Euston Road, NW1 (0171 611 8727/8888). Open Mon–Fri 9.45 am–5 pm; Sat 9.45 am–1 pm. Euston BR/underground*. Occasional talks and debates.

SCIENCE MUSEUM, *Exhibition Road, SW7 (0171 938 8080). Free admission daily 4.30–6 pm. South Kensington underground*. Occasional talks.

TATE GALLERY, *Millbank, SW1 (0171 887 8000) Open Mon–Sat 10 am–5.50 pm; Sun 2–5.50 pm. Pimlico underground*. Daily lectures.

VALENCE HOUSE MUSEUM, *Becontree Avenue, Dagenham (0181 595 8404). Open Tues–Fri 9.30 am–1 pm, 2–4.30 pm; Sat 10 am–4 pm. Chadwell Heath BR*. Lectures about the collection from time to time.

VICTORIA & ALBERT MUSEUM, *Cromwell Road, SW7 (0171 938 8638). Open Mon noon–5.50 pm; Tues–Sun 10 am–5.50 pm. Donation requested. South Kensington underground*. Apart from the daily gallery talks and tours, there are also occasional special lectures.

WALLACE COLLECTION, *Hertford House, Manchester*

Square, W1 *(0171 935 0687). Open Mon–Sat 10 am–5 pm; Sun 2–5 pm. Bond Street underground.* General tours daily and occasional specialist lecture tours.

WATERMANS ARTS CENTRE, *40 High Street, Brentford, TW8 (0181 847 5651). Open Tues–Sat 10.30 am–11 pm; Sun 10.30 am–10.30 pm. Gunnersbury BR/underground.* Occasional talks.

WHITECHAPEL ART GALLERY, *Whitechapel High Street,* E1 *(0171 522 7878). Open Tues–Sun 11 am–5 pm, Wed until 8 pm. Aldgate East underground.* Occasional talks.

WILLIAM MORRIS GALLERY, *Lloyd Park, Forest Road, Walthamstow,* E17 *(0181 527 3782). Open Tues–Sat 10 am–1 pm, 2–5 pm; and first Sun in each month, 10 am–noon, 2–5 pm. Walthamstow Central BR/underground.* Occasional lectures relating to William Morris and the arts and crafts movement.

LIBRARIES

Details of a selection of various libraries follow, where you are free to browse or study. Included are some big libraries with comprehensive collections and also some of London's libraries with specialist collections.

To find out where your standard local borough

libraries are, consult the Yellow Pages. If you haven't got a copy, you'll find one at your local library. Yes, what a conundrum.

Many people use their library just to read the newspapers and magazines provided. Libraries are often also a good source of information concerning events, services, organisations and courses in the area.

Many local libraries hold children's activities in the school holidays, which could be anything from pottery or dance workshops to puppet shows and story-telling.

THE BARBICAN LIBRARY, *The Barbican Centre, Silk Street, EC2 (General library: 0171 638 0569; children's library: 0171 628 9447). Open Mon–Fri 9.30 am–5.30 pm (Tues until 7.30 pm); Sat 9.30 am–12.30 pm. Barbican underground.* The City's leading lending library. Membership (if you wish to borrow) is open to those living, working or studying in the City of London and to regular visitors to the centre.

BATTERSEA REFERENCE LIBRARY, *Altenburg Gardens, SW11 (0181 871 7467). Open Mon–Fri 9 am–9 pm; Sat 9 am–5 pm. Clapham Junction BR.* Contains special collections on William Blake, Edward Thomas, building and architecture, and the occult.

BRITISH MUSIC INFORMATION CENTRE, *10 Stratford Place, W1 (0171 499 8567). Open Mon–Fri noon–5 pm. Bond Street underground.* The Centre offers an information service on contemporary classical British music using their extensive collection of recordings, scores, videos and other materials.

CATHOLIC CENTRAL LIBRARY, *47 Francis Street, SW1 (0171 834 6128). Open Mon–Fri 10 am–5 pm; Sat 10 am–1.30 pm. Victoria BR/underground.* Specialises in Catholicism, unsurprisingly.

ECOLOGY CENTRE, *45 Shelton Street, WC2 (0171 379 4324) Open Mon–Fri 10 am–6 pm. Covent Garden underground.* Library with a green theme.

FINSBURY REFERENCE LIBRARY, *245 St John Street, EC1 (0171 278 7343). Open Mon, Thur 9.30 am–8 pm; Tues, Sat 9.30 am–5 pm; Fri 9.30 am–1 pm. Angel/Farringdon underground.* Specialises in art, design, photography and the Sadlers Wells collection.

GEFFRYE MUSEUM, *Kingsland Road, E2 (0171 739 9893). Open Tues–Sat 10 am–5 pm; Sun 2–5 pm. Old Street underground.* Reference library and furniture trade archive.

GOETHE-INSTITUT LIBRARY, *50 Princes Gate, Exhibition Road, SW7 (0171 411 3400). Open Mon–Thur 10 am–8 pm; Sat 10.30 am–1 pm. South Kensington underground.* A collection concerning Germany.

GUILDHALL LIBRARY, *Aldermanbury, off Gresham Street, EC2 (0171 606 3030). Open Mon–Sat 10 am–5 pm. Bank/Moorgate underground.* An unrivalled collection of books, illustrations, maps, prints and manuscripts about London. There's an exhibition room of famous books and manuscripts.

HOMERTON LIBRARY, *Homerton High Street, E9 (0181 985 8262). Open Mon 10 am–5 pm; Tues 10 am–7 pm; Thur 1–7 pm; Fri 10 am–6 pm; Sat 9 am–12.30 pm, 1.30 pm–5 pm. Homerton BR.* Special collections on Australasia and the Americas.

HORNIMAN MUSEUM, *London Road, Forest Hill, SE23 (0181 766 7663). Open Tues–Sat 10.30 am–6 pm; Sun 2–6 pm. Telephone for appointment. Forest Hill BR.* Reference library concerned with the museum's exhibits.

IMPERIAL COLLEGE AND SCIENCE MUSEUM LIBRARIES, *Imperial College Road, SW7 (0171 938 8234). Open Mon–Fri 9.30 am–9 pm; Sat 9.30 am–5.30 pm. South Kensington underground.*

INSTITUTO CERVANTES, *22 Manchester Square, W1 (0171 935 1518). Open Mon–Thur 9.30 am–6.30 pm; Fri 9.30 am–5 pm. Marble Arch/Bond Street underground.* An extensive Spanish library.

ITALIAN CULTURAL INSTITUTE LIBRARY, *39 Bel-*

grave Square, SW1 (0171 235 1461). Open Mon–Fri
9.30 am–5 pm. Knightsbridge underground.

KEATS HOUSE, Keats Grove, Hampstead, NW3 (0171 435
2062) Open Apr–Oct: Mon–Fri 10 am–1 pm, 2–6 pm; Sat
10 am–1 pm, 2–5 pm; Sun 2–5 pm; Nov–Mar: Mon–Fri
1–5 pm; Sat 10 am–1 pm, 2–5 pm; Sun 2–5 pm. Library
by prior arrangement. Hampstead underground. Donations
requested. A library concerned with the life and work of
the Romantic poet.

KENSINGTON CENTRAL LIBRARY, Phillimore Walk,
W8 (0171 937 2542). Open Mon, Tues, Thur, Fri
10 am–8 pm; Wed 10 am–1 pm; Sat 10 am–5 pm. High
Street Kensington underground. Specialises in genealogy,
heraldry and folklore.

LIMEHOUSE LIBRARY, 638 Commercial Road, E14 (0171
987 3183). Open Mon, Tues, Thur 9 am–8 pm; Wed, Fri
9 am–5 pm; Sat 9 am–12.30 pm, 1.30–5 pm. Limehouse
DLR. Has special sections on French, Portuguese and
German literature.

MAIDA VALE LIBRARY, Sutherland Avenue, W9 (0171
798 3659) Open Mon–Fri 9.30 am–7 pm; Sat
9.30 am–5 pm. Maida Vale underground. Special sections
on social justice and criminology, and military history.

MAP LIBRARY, Department of Geography, University

College London, 26 Bedford Way, WC1 (0171 387 7050 ext 5537). Open Mon–Fri 9 am–1 pm, 2–5 pm but telephone in advance. Russell Square/Euston Square/Warren Street underground. If it's maps you want, this is the place to see them. Also over 600 atlases to complete the collection.

MARX MEMORIAL LIBRARY, *37 Clerkenwell Green, EC1 (0171 253 1485). Open to visitors Mon–Thur 1–6 pm. Farringdon underground.* A huge collection of political and social literature.

MARYLEBONE LIBRARY, *Marylebone Road, NW1 (0171 798 1037). Mon–Fri 10 am–7 pm; Sat 9.30 am–5 pm. Baker Street underground.* The location of the library ensures there is a special section on Sherlock Holmes, in addition to ones on medicine and dentistry.

MAYFAIR LIBRARY, *25 South Audley Street, W1 (0171 798 1391). Open Mon–Fri 9.30 am–7 pm; Sat 9.30 am–1 pm. Bond Street underground.* Special collections of literature in European and other languages.

MUSEUM OF LONDON, *150 London Wall, EC2 (0171 600 3699). Open Tues–Sat 10 am–5.50 pm. Telephone for appointment. St Paul's underground.* Has a wide range of books about London.

MUSEUM OF MANKIND, *6 Burlington Gardens, W1 (0171*

636 1555 ext 8043). Open Mon–Sat 10 am–5 pm; Sun 2.30–6 pm. Donations welcome. Piccadilly Circus underground. Large reference library.

NATIONAL MARITIME MUSEUM, *Romney Road, SE10 (0181 858 4422). Open Mon–Fri 10 am–5 pm. Proof of I.D. required. Greenwich/Maze Hill BR.* Has one of the biggest reference libraries relating to all things maritime.

NATIONAL SOUND ARCHIVE, 29 *Exhibition Road, SW7 (0171 589 6603). Open Mon–Fri 10 am–5 pm and to 9 pm Thur. South Kensington underground.* Library of catalogues, periodicals, etc., and listening service.

NATURAL HISTORY MUSEUM, *Cromwell Road, SW7 (0171 938 9123). Open Mon–Fri 10 am–5 pm. Proof of I.D. required. South Kensington underground.* Large reference library.

NEWSPAPER LIBRARY, *Colindale Avenue, NW9 (0181 200 5515). Open to over-18s Mon–Sat 10 am–5 pm. Proof of identity with signature required. Colindale underground.* If you want to see the Battle of Waterloo edition of *The Times*, or other editions of newspapers and periodicals, this branch of the British Library is the place to come.

ORDER OF ST JOHN REFERENCE LIBRARY, *St John's Gate, St John's Lane, EC1 (0171 253 6644). Open by appointment only, Mon–Fri 10 am–5 pm; Sat 10 am–4 pm. Farringdon/Barbican BR/underground.* Literature relating to the Order of St John.

PHOTOGRAPHER'S GALLERY, *5 and 8 Great Newport Street, WC2 (0171 831 1772). Open Tues–Sat 11 am–7 pm. Donations welcomed. Leicester Square underground.* Reference library.

POETRY LIBRARY, *Royal Festival Hall, South Bank Centre, SE1 (0171 921 0943). Open daily 11 am–8 pm. Waterloo BR/underground.* A collection of 20th-century poetry.

POLISH CULTURAL INSTITUTE LIBRARY, *34 Portland Place, W1 (0171 636 6032). Open Mon–Wed, Fri noon–3 pm. Regent's Park underground.* A relatively small library with around 4000 books concerned with aspects of Poland.

ROYAL GEOGRAPHICAL SOCIETY, *Lowther Lane, Kensington Gore, SW7 (0171 589 5466). Open Mon–Fri 10 am–1 pm, 2–5 pm. South Kensington underground.* The excellent library of this society dedicated to exploration is open to non-members by appointment.

RUDOLF STEINER HOUSE, *35 Park Road, NW1 (0171 723 4400). Open Mon–Fri 11 am–1 pm, 2–5 pm. Baker Street underground.* Works of and about Steiner, which visitors are welcome to browse and study. Steiner (1861–1925) was an Austrian philosopher who developed his own spiritual and mystic teaching designed to develop the whole human being.

ST BRIDE PRINTING LIBRARY, *St Bride Institute, Bride Lane, EC4 (0171 353 4660). Open Mon–Fri 9.30 am–5.30 pm by appointment. St Paul's underground.* This reference library covering the history of printing has original wooden printing presses from the 1800s on display. The librarian may even have time to explain how they worked.

SCIENCE REFERENCE AND INFORMATION SERVICE, *25 Southampton Buildings, Chancery Lane, WC2 (0171 323 7494). Open Mon–Fri 9.30 am–9pm; Sat 10 am–1 pm. Chancery Lane underground.* Special collections include patents, inventions, markets and products, industry and technology.

SHOREDITCH LIBRARY, *Pitfield Street, N1 (0171 739 6981). Open Mon, Tues, Fri 10 am–5 pm; Thur 1–7 pm, Sat 9 am–5 pm. Old Street underground.* Special collections on small manufacturing industries.

SWISS COTTAGE LIBRARY, *88 Avenue Road, NW3 (0171 413 6533). Open Mon, Thur 10 am–7 pm; Tues, Fri 10 am–6 pm. Swiss Cottage underground.* Has an Ordnance Survey map collection as well as *The Times* newspaper from 1785 on microfilm.

WELLCOME INSTITUTE HISTORY OF MEDICINE LIBRARY, *The Wellcome Building, 183 Euston Road, NW1 (0171 611 8888). Open Mon, Wed, Fri 9.45 am–5.15 pm; Tues, Thur 9.45 am–7.15 pm; Sat 9.45 am–1 pm. Euston BR/underground.* A large collection on the history of medicine.

WELLCOME TRUST INFORMATION SERVICE LIBRARY, *The Wellcome Building, 183 Euston Road, NW1 (0171 611 8888). Open Mon–Fri 9.45 am–5.00 pm. Euston BR/underground.* Wholly concerned with medicine, it keeps up-to-date with medical research and advances.

WESTMINSTER CENTRAL REFERENCE LIBRARY, *35 St Martin's Street, WC2 (0171 798 2034). Open Mon–Fri 10 am–7 pm; Sat 10 am–5 pm. Charing Cross BR/underground.* A comprehensive library that includes international telephone directories, maps, special collections on theatre, cinema, ballet, art, antiques and architecture, and a register of British companies.

WILLIAM MORRIS GALLERY, *Lloyd Park, Forest Road, Walthamstow, E17 (0181 527 3782). Open Tues–Sat 10 am–1 pm, 2–5 pm; and first Sun in each month, 10 am–noon, 2–5 pm. Walthamstow Central BR/under-*

ground. The archive and reference library are open by appointment.

THE LIFE OF A LIGGER: THERE IS SUCH A THING AS A FREE LUNCH

If you have the ruthlessness, ingenuity, confidence, cheeky personality and possibly the stupidity required, you can turn the art of getting something for nothing, or getting in where you're not invited, into something approaching a full-time occupation.

This behaviour, known as 'ligging', 'blagging', or 'free-loading', is an especially popular pastime with many members of the media industry, who are almost required to master the art as part of their basic training.

And there's no end to it. With persistence, if you're able to pass yourself off as a half-competent hack travel writer, there are enough newspapers, magazines, airlines, ferry companies, car hire firms, tour operators and tourist offices out there to sponsor your international trips whether your piece actually appears in a publication or not.

But you need to be impudent enough to do it. If you possess this quality, one opportunity leads to another. You could, say, drop in on a freebie function such as the preview of a Cork Street art exhibition (which are usually on Tuesdays) by entering when the signing-in book is unattended or at the same time as a group of others that you see are about to walk in.

Over the food and wine most generously provided by your host, you could get talking to a friend of a celebrity having a party later in the evening. What a coincidence it is, you exclaim, that you know the celebrity too (not letting on that the time you met him was when you obtained his autograph, before we went into decimalisation). Obviously, your new acquaintance concludes that it would be ludicrous for you not to attend the party. You realise that this means you won't be able to slip anonymously into a press screening of that big film you've been anxiously awaiting, that's showing in an hour in a preview theatre in Wardour Street.

At the shindig you meet a commissioning editor of a national broadsheet (don't worry, there are a lot about – some papers almost have more editors and executives than readers) who is so merry by way of intoxication that he'd commission a pot of paint, never mind you, the London-based theatre/food/sports reporter (delete according to freebies not required) for the Philadelphia Examiner/Arctic Airways In Flight Magazine/Prague Gazette. And so on ...

At the door of a promotional party, the best way to deal with the PR people in existence to weed out sycophants like you, is to make one of them think they've met you before. Public relations is all about meeting people all of the time, and they probably wouldn't know you from Adam even if they *had* once met you. So it's best to start the conversation by asking 'How are you? You've lost some weight/changed your hair. I suppose it's been a while'. Unless the PR person is absolutely *sure* you're an imposter, she's hardly going to risk causing a scene by ejecting you at such an important occasion.

If you know or know of someone who's a member of a London club, needless to say it would be very wrong to sign yourself in there under their name, which means, of course, that they will be approached for the payment of the bill you ran up whilst on the premises. (It's well to bear in mind that you may later be approached by the fraud squad.)

When playing golf, try starting at the sixth hole and finishing at the fifth and you'll have no need to bother the management for the payment of green fees.

Each time you see a printing shop, call in and say you want to get some invitations printed, and ask whether they have any samples. Help yourself to any that are for future parties, weddings, conferences and other functions that appeal, explaining that you need them to facilitate the design of your own invitation.

It's best to visit restaurants in groups of at least 11 if the service charge is 10% and groups of 13 if the service charge is 12.5%. Get the group to agree beforehand to split the bill equally, saying that dissecting it with a calculator after the meal is so very tacky. When the bill comes, stress to the other members of the party how important it is to add 10%/12.5% to the total. This takes care of your share of the costs. It's a bit rotten to deprive the waiter or waitress of a tip, but at least you get a good meal for nothing.

If you are in employment, by loosely defining your job title, you can again get something for nothing. Suppose, for example, that you work as teaboy at a rock magazine. Then, even if only one of the ten record companies you approach for a review copy of the latest release by a favoured band doesn't make enquiries to find that coffee-making and rubbish-bin-emptying takes up the bulk of your work-load, at least you've been sent one free CD and with any luck they'll be keen to send you more.

Opportunities are all around. If a crowd is walking into a house, good liggers will always join them. There are endless excuses were they to be caught out. I mean, can *you* read half the house numbers clearly in a darkened street? It's best to go in brandishing a bottle of wine, which you can instantly return to the car on the pretext of having left your lights on by mistake. When you return to the celebrations, if someone asks who you're with, you can simply say John, Jane or David – there's always someone of that name present.

Ligging is only at the expense of your conscience and perception of morality. And at least if you go too far, accommodation will be free too – a spell in prison.

MAGAZINE AND NEWSPAPERS

There's a wealth of free literature available in London without you having to search out the local library – which has probably been closed down anyway, or at best had half the books thrown out to make way for racks of videos (invariably decrepit 70s TV serials like *Colditz* and *Poldark*), condensed talking books (not so often for the blind, but for the bone idle) and CDs (usually *The Best of Chicago* or *Bread*, plus *Rumours* and *Hotel California* and a couple of Bob Dylan recordings from his boring phase because all the best stuff is always out on loan).

You'll be awash with that up-market type of magazine (that really only exists to help flog expensive apartments), which is thrust through your letter-box if you have a desirable enough address. If you don't, you'll have to make do with the more down-market titles stuffed in your face first thing in the morning at central train stations and from various other sources.

Yet these can be surprisingly good. For a number of years many people have bought *The Spectator* primarily to read Jeffrey Bernard's column, 'Low Life'. It is reprinted in MIDWEEK magazine, along with articles and listings. Probably the best written of the capital's free publications, many of the contributors also write for or go on to write for the national media. It is distributed from *8–10 am* at major rail and underground stations on *Mondays* and *Thursdays* and also from dispensers.

GIRL ABOUT TOWN and MS LONDON are also distributed from *8–10 am* at major rail and underground stations on *Mondays* and also from dispensers. They are aimed at young working women, and if you disregard the dubious adverts for bargain-basement hen night venues and cocktail bars, there are often good articles about relationships, careers and fashion and film interviews and reviews.

CAPITAL GAY is a *weekly* magazine with news, reviews, features (often provocative) and listings, available from most gay venues, some bookshops and health centres.

THE PINK PAPER is another free gay *weekly* newspaper, covering national news and information, available from gay venues and a number of gay and straight bookshops.

There are also several free *weekly* newspapers available from central London street dispensers (in *The Strand, WC2*, and *Earl's Court Road, SW5*, for example) such as NEW ZEALAND NEWS UK, SOUTHERN CROSS and SA TIMES, which apart from the occasional vaguely interesting travel article are chiefly only of interest to their targeted audiences, namely New Zealanders, Australians and South Africans respectively.

TRAVELLER MAGAZINE is a *weekly* magazine also available from central London street dispensers and also with a bias towards Australian and New Zealand readers with its inclusion of news pages concerning those countries. But the travel features and London listings make it of interest to the general reader.

TRAILFINDER MAGAZINE is another publication available from central street dispensers and is published three times a year. Although it promotes a travel agency, in each issue it includes six or seven travel articles and excellent colour photography to accompany them.

Although HEALTH SHOPPER, available from many health food shops *bi-monthly*, has 'news' items promoting new products relating to healthy living, it also contains features about how to improve diets and lifestyles and lots of depressing statistics confirming the dangers of consuming unhealthy foods – which seems to be anything that isn't a free-range organic carrot that's been fed lentils and vitamin supplements.

MAKE-OVERS AND BEAUTY CARE

THE BODY SHOP *(head office: 01903 731500)* has over 40 branches around London and these offer free make-overs (or if you wish, just selected items such as eyes or lips), appliction tips and advice; some also give skincare, handcare and footcare demonstrations. Full make-overs take around 20–30 minutes, but if you are in a hurry they can provide express make-overs in 10 minutes. Unlike some stores, if you do not like wearing much make-up the staff will not apply a whole bucket's-worth to your face. An appointment is often necessary, and it's usually best to avoid lunch-times and Saturdays. There are branches at: *The Ashley Centre, King Shade Walk, Epsom; Bentalls Centre, Kingston upon Thames; Brent Cross Shopping Centre, NW4; 464 Brixton Road, SW9; Broadway Shopping Centre, Bexleyheath; Broadwalk Shopping Centre, Station Road, Edgware; 56 The Broadway, W5; 15 Brompton Road, SW3; 22 Cheapside, EC2; 1 Church Street, Enfield; Covent Garden Market, WC2; Exchange Shopping Centre, Ilford; 50a George Street, Richmond; 32 Great Marlborough Street, W1; 7 Hampstead High Street, NW3; Heathrow Airport, Hounslow; 18 High Holborn, WC1; 85 High Road, N22; 128 High Street, Bromley; 180 High Street, Hounslow; 115 High Street, Sutton; 137 Kensington High Street, W8; 8 King's Mall, King's Street, W6; 54 King's Road, SW3; Lewisham Shopping Centre, SE13; Liverpool Street Station, EC2; 23 Long Acre, WC2; 64, 268 and 374 Oxford Street, W1; Piccadilly Circus, W1; 194 Portabello Road, W11; 80 Powis Street, SE18; 77 Putney High Street, SW15; Queen's Road, SW19; 11 St Ann's Road, Harrow; 9 Stratford Centre, E15; Surrey Quays Shopping Centre, SE16; 407 Upper Richmond Road West, SW14; 7 Upper Street, N1; Victoria Station, SW1; 113 Victoria Street, SW1; Whiteleys Shopping Centre, Queensway, W2; Whitgift Centre, Croydon.*

Some department stores offer occasional free make-overs and beauty care – see the Cosmetics and Perfumes section for more details.

MARKETS

Some of London's street markets, such as Brixton and Brick Lane, are dominated by particular ethnic groups and therefore serve as an excellent introduction to the diversity of peoples living in the capital. The oldest markets, such as Brick Lane, Petticoat Lane and Portobello Road, preserve some of London's history while reflecting the changing times and fashions.

Many markets can be a great experience even if you have no intention of buying anything. Some sell unusual or interesting wares, while others, though selling the ordinary and drab, reflect the economic fortunes of the area or simply add real colour and personality to their neighbourhoods.

BERMONDSEY (NEW CALEDONIAN) MARKET, *Bermondsey Square, SE1. Open Fri 5 am–1 pm. London Bridge BR/underground, Borough/Elephant and Castle underground*. Brisk business occurs at this antique dealers' market consisting of hundreds of stalls with an overwhelming variety of goods, best seen before dawn when scores of torches flicker as buyers examine the goods.

BERWICK STREET MARKET, *Berwick Street, WI. Open Mon–Sat 9 am–5 pm. Tottenham Court Road underground.* Dating back to the 1840s, this busy, boisterous general food market survives (retaining much of its character) despite the huge volume of both pedestrian and vehicular traffic, and adds colour to daytime Soho.

BRICK LANE MARKET, *EI, E2. Sun from 5.30 am–1 pm. Aldgate/Shoreditch underground.* A real East End experience as Brick Lane and nearby streets come alive with stalls selling almost anything at this big, ramshackle Cockney/Jewish-dominated market. You also witness the realities of London's poor: an old man waiting patiently in hope of selling a handful of trinkets, a lady standing forlornly with a few bits of bric-à-brac.

BRIXTON MARKET, *around Atlantic Rd SW9. Open Mon, Tues, Thur–Sat 8.30 am–6 pm; Wed 8.30 am–1 pm. Brixton BR/underground.* This large, lively, exotic, general market has an Afro-Caribbean flavour, with reggae music reverberating around the railway arches and the biggest choice of African and Caribbean food in Europe. From goat meat, calf heads and exotic fish to mango, yam and okra. The presence of Rastafarian priests and the smell of incense complete the exotic atmosphere you can be assured is a world away from Harvey Nic's.

CAMDEN MARKET, *Camden High Street/Chalk Farm Road, NWI. Open Thur–Sun 9 am–5 pm. Camden Town/Chalk*

Farm underground. Busiest and best at the weekend, there are several markets in the area offering great variety, such as INVERNESS STREET, a local food market, and the weekend STABLES and CAMDEN CANAL MARKETS with collectables, as well as the indoor ELECTRIC BALL-ROOM MARKET. CAMDEN LOCK, where it all began, occupies renovated warehouses. The summer months are enhanced by street theatre, music and art shows.

CAMDEN PASSAGE, *Upper Street, N1. Most stalls open Tues–Sat 10 am–5 pm. Market times are Wed 7 am–2 pm and Sat 9 am–3.30 pm. Angel underground*. This market, located in Islington, changes from a civilised antiques market on Wednesday (with books on Thursday) to a lively flea market on Saturday.

CHAPEL MARKET, *Chapel Street, N1. Open Tues, Wed, Fri, Sat 9 am–4 pm; Thur, Sun 9 am–1 pm. Angel underground*. A friendly local market that has existed for over 100 years.

CHURCH STREET MARKET, *NW8, W2. Open Tues–Sat 9 am–5 pm. Edgware Road underground*. Church Street has had a market since the 1840s. Nowadays this lively local facility sells anything from bric-à-brac, groceries and clothes to antiques. Nearby BELL STREET MARKET, also in Lisson Grove *open Sat 9.30 am–5 pm)* is smaller yet chaotic.

COLUMBIA ROAD MARKET, *Columbia Road, E2. Open*

Sun 8 am–12.30 pm. Shoreditch underground. Lots of plants and flowers on display.

COVENT GARDEN MARKET, *The Piazza, WC2 (0171 836 9136). Daily 9 am–4 pm. Covent Garden underground*. Stalls with crafts, over-priced junk and antiques.

GABRIEL'S WHARF, *56 Upper Ground, SE1 (0171 620 0544). Open Tues–Sun 11 am–6 pm. Waterloo BR/underground*. Has colourful craft workshops with a small crafts market on *Fridays 11 am–3 pm*. Gabriel's Wharf also has riverside walks.

GREENWICH MARKETS, *College Approach, Stockwell Street and Greenwich High Road, SE10. Open Sat, Sun 9 am–5 pm. Greenwich BR*. The success of these antiques, clothes, books, music and crafts markets has done much to exacerbate the parking and pollution problems in Greenwich centre in recent years.

KENSINGTON MARKET, *Kensington High Street, W8. Mon–Sat 9.30 am–6 pm. High Street Kensington underground*. Either packed with great fashion, or full of seedy trash, according to your view and age.

LEADENHALL MARKET, *Gracechurch Street, EC3. Open Mon–Fri 8 am–5 pm. Bank underground*. Built in 1881, this picturesque Victorian covered market in the City, with its impressive ironwork façade with stalls for various foods, is especially lively at lunch-time.

LEATHER LANE, *EC1. Open Mon–Fri 11 am–2 pm. Chancery Lane/Farringdon underground.* An old Cockney market.

NORTHCOTE ROAD MARKETS, *Northcote Road, SW11. Antiques market open Mon–Sat 10 am–6 pm; Sun noon–5 pm. General market Mon, Tues, Thur–Sat 9 am–5 pm; Wed 9 am–1 pm. Clapham Junction BR.* A mix of nationalities here, as well as goods on sale, from a covered antiques market, juggling equipment and uni-cycles to Halal butchers and West Indian greengrocers.

PETTICOAT LANE, *Middlesex and Wentworth Streets, E1. Open Sun 9 am–2 pm; partially open Mon–Fri 10 am–2.30 pm. Liverpool Street/Aldgate underground.* London's most famous market, and over 200 years old. With over a thousand stalls on Sundays, it's a real experience, packed with people and goods from the humdrum to the bizarre.

PORTOBELLO ROAD, *W11. Open Mon–Sat 9 am–5 pm. Notting Hill Gate/Ladbroke Grove underground.* Several markets merged into one, crammed with junk, books, clothing, jewellery and antiques and some interesting shops around it all, especially around the Westway flyover. There's a cosmopolitan atmosphere with all ages and nationalities, best on Saturdays when it's busiest and when there's often street performers and buskers.

A small crafts market with home-made jewellery, knitwear and ethnic crafts, toys, hats, etc. (although garish souvenirs have increasingly been emerging) is at the churchyard of ST MARTINS-IN-THE-FIELDS, *Trafalgar Square, WC2. Open Mon–Sat 11 am–5 pm. Charing Cross BR/underground*. ST JAMES'S, *Piccadilly, W1 (Piccadilly Circus underground)* also has a small outdoor craft market in the pretty paved garden *Fri, Sat 10 am–5 pm*.

SHEPHERD'S BUSH MARKET, *Uxbridge/Goldhawk Road W12. Shepherd's Bush underground*. Lock-ups, stalls and shops with Asian and African clothes and foods.

MEDICAL TREATMENT

In an emergency, telephone 999 (free of charge) and ask for an ambulance.

Medical treatment under the National Health service is free to:
Nationals of members of the European Union: Austria, Belgium, Denmark, Finland, France, Germany, Greece,

Italy, the Irish Republic, Luxembourg, the Netherlands, Portugal, Spain and Sweden;

Also nationals of Bulgaria, the Czech and Slovak Republics, Gibraltar, Hungary, Iceland, Malta, New Zealand, Norway, Russia, the former Soviet Union republics apart from the Baltic States, and former Yugoslav republics;

Residents of Australia, Barbados, the British Virgin Islands, the Falkland Islands, Hong Kong, Montserrat, Poland, Romania, St Helena, the Turks and Khakis Islands (although treatment is limited to problems arising during a visit to Britain, not pre-existing conditions);

NATO personnel;

Anyone who at the time of treatment has been in the UK for the previous 12 months;

Students and trainees whose course requires them to be employed for more than 12 weeks during their first year;

People with HIV/AIDS at a clinic for the treatment of sexually transmitted diseases. Treatment is limited to a diagnostic test and associated counselling.

Those living in the UK for a settled purpose for more than six months may be accepted as ordinarily resident and not be liable to charges.

There are no NHS charges for district nursing, health visiting, midwifery, ambulance transport and family-planning services.

DOCTORS

If you are a British citizen visiting or working in London temporarily, you can go to any general practitioner (GP). You will probably have to show your medical card or fill in a 'lost medical card' form. Overseas students may register with an NHS GP.

GREAT CHAPEL STREET MEDICAL CENTRE, *13 Great Chapel Street, W1 (0171 437 9360). Open Mon, Tues, Thur 11 am–12.30 pm; Mon–Fri 2–4 pm.* A free walk-in surgery for anyone without a doctor.

PRESCRIPTIONS

Prescriptions are free to children under 16, those under 19 in full-time education, women over 60, men over 65, pregnant women and women who have had a baby in the previous twelve months, people receiving War Pensions, those with certain medical conditions (for example diabetes and epilepsy), people on Income Support, Family Credit or an NHS low income scheme.

SIGHT TESTS, GLASSES AND LENSES

Children under 16, young people under 19 studying full-time, people with diabetes, people who have glaucoma or who are aged 40 or over and the child, brother, sister or parent of a person with glaucoma, those who are registered blind or partially sighted or need at least one exceptionally powerful lens, or are a patient of the Hospital Eye Service, and those on Income Support,

Family Support or an NHS low income scheme are entitled to a free eye test. Financial help with buying glasses or contact lenses is possible – ask your optician or a benefits agency office.

WIGS AND FABRIC SUPPORTS
Children under 16, young people under 19 studying full-time and those on Income Support, Family Support or an NHS low income scheme are also entitled to these.

EMOTIONAL AND MENTAL HEALTH
JUST ASK *46 Bishopsgate, EC2 (0171 628 3380). Open Mon–Thur 10am–9pm; Fri 9am–5pm. Closed in August.* Free counselling to those under 30 earning under £10,000.

MIND *Granta House, 15–19 Broadway, Stratford E15 (0181 519 2122). Open Mon–Fri 9.15am–5.15pm.* Gives general and legal advice and can refer callers to local support groups.

THE SAMARITANS have 24-hour helplines (0171 734 2800/0181 301 1010) for emotional problems and various drop-in London centres.

MUSEUMS AND COLLECTIONS

AGE EXCHANGE REMINISCENCE CENTRE, *11 Black-heath Village, SE3 (0181 318 9105). Open Mon–Fri 10 am–5.30 pm. Blackheath BR*. The past explored via a reconstructed 1930s shop and temporary exhibitions.

ALFRED DUNHILL MUSEUM, *60–61 Burlington Arcade, W1 (0171 499 9566). Open Mon–Fri 9.30 am–5 pm by appointment. Piccadilly Circus underground*. The history of the firm with examples of motoring accessories, watches, pipes, lighters and pens made by Dunhill.

BADEN-POWELL MUSEUM, *Queen's Gate, SW7 (0171 584 7030). Open daily 8 am–8 pm. South Kensington/ Gloucester Road underground*. Memorabilia, mementoes and pictures tell the story of scouting, which Lord Baden-Powell began in 1907.

BANK OF ENGLAND MUSEUM, *Threadneedle Street, EC2 (entrance in Bartholomew Lane) (0171 601 5545). Open Mon–Fri 10 am–5 pm; also Sun 11 am–to 5 pm from Easter–Sept. Bank underground*. Housed within the Bank of England itself in the heart of the City of London, the museum covers a history of the Bank from 1694 to the high-tech of today. There are interactive videos and displays including a modern dealing desk, ancient gold bars, banknotes and coins and Roman pottery and mosaics uncovered when the bank was rebuilt.

BARNET MUSEUM, *31 Wood Street, Barnet, EN5 (0181 449 0321). Open Tues–Thur 2.30–4.30 pm; Sat 10 am– noon, 2.30–4.30 pm. High Barnet underground*. A small but lively museum about the story of the Barnet district, including relics of the Battle of Barnet in 1471, one of the last of the Wars of the Roses.

BETHNAL GREEN MUSEUM OF CHILDHOOD, *Cambridge Heath Road, E2 (0181 980 2415). Open Mon–Thur, Sat 10 am–5.30 pm; Sun 2.30–6 pm, children's workshops Sat 11 am and 2 pm. Bethnal Green underground*. This branch of the Victoria & Albert Museum has toys, dolls, teddy bears, nursery furniture, children's clothes, puppets, games and costumes. There are over 40 dolls' houses alone and there'd be more if they could get the planning permission. Also temporary exhibitions. There are children's activities in the school holidays.

BEXLEY MUSEUM, *Hall Place, Bourne Road, Bexley (01322 526574). Open Mon–Sat 10 am–5 pm; Sun (summer only) 2–6 pm. Bexley BR*. Amongst the displays are ones on natural history, archaeology and geology in the locality. Also featured are some Roman pottery and a collection of butterflies, as well as temporary exhibitions, usually concerning the Bexley area.

BLACK CULTURAL ARCHIVES MUSEUM, *378 Coldharbour Lane, SW9 (0171 738 4591). Museum open Mon–Sat 10 am–6 pm, archives by appointment. Brixton BR/underground*. Exploring the history of black people in Britain from Roman times onwards, augmented by regular temporary exhibitions.

BRITISH DENTAL ASSOCIATION MUSEUM, *64 Wimpole Street, W1 (0171 935 0875 ext 209). Open Mon–Fri 10 am–3 pm. Oxford Circus/Bond Street underground*. If you're brave enough, come and see equipment and re-created surgeries presenting the history of dentistry in Britain.

BRITISH LIBRARY, *Great Russell Street, WC1 (0171 636 1544). Open Mon–Sat 10 am–5 pm; Sun 2.30–6 pm. Russell Square underground*. The exhibition galleries house beautiful collections of manuscripts and books. The Manuscript Saloon holds manuscripts of historical and literary interest, famous autographs, maps, heraldry, music and bibles, including King John's Magna Carta (1215) and Handel's Messiah. There's also the populist-sounding 'manuscript of the month'. There are illuminated manuscripts from the 7th through to the 17th century, and the King's Library, built in 1826 for the books of George III, features displays of oriental illuminated manuscripts and printed books. There are also temporary exhibitions. For a tour of the world-famous, spectacular, domed Round Reading Room with its 25 miles of shelving (half of that needed to house the works of Barbara Cartland alone) *Mon–Fri 2.15 pm* and *4.15 pm* – obtain a ticket from Reader Admissions on the day only.

BRITISH MUSEUM, *Great Russell Street, WC1 (0171 636 1555). Open Mon–Sat 10 am–5 pm; Sun 2.30–6 pm. Lectures and gallery talks Tues–Sat and films Tues–Fri. Donations welcomed. Goodge Street/Tottenham Court Road/Russell Square underground.* Founded in 1753, this, the capital's most popular sight (attracting over 6 million visitors annually) and one of the world's great museums, shows the works of man from prehistoric times onwards. There are permanent displays of antiquities from Egypt, Greece and Rome, and there are prehistoric, Romano-British, Medieval, Renaissance, modern and oriental collections. There are temporary exhibitions of coins, medals, prints and drawings. Also featured are the Rosetta Stone, the Elgin Marbles, Egyptian mummies, and a children's trail through the museum. If you need a break from the endless exhibits (over 6 million of them), grassy RUSSELL SQUARE, WC1, is nearby.

BROMLEY MUSEUM, *The Priory, Church Hill. Bromley BR6 (01689 873826). Open Mon–Wed, Fri and Sat 9 am–5 pm. Orpington BR.* Uncovering how people lived in the Bromley area from prehistoric times to the present, including such items as Saxon jewellery and a typical 1930s dining room.

BRUCE CASTLE MUSEUM, *Lordship Lane, Tottenham, N17 (0181 808 8772). Open Tues–Sun 1–5 pm, guided tours by arrangement with curator. White Hart Lane BR/ Wood Green underground.* Standing in Bruce Castle Park, this Elizabethan/Jacobean/Georgian building with its 16th-century tower has a museum concerned with local and postal history.

BT TELECOMMUNICATIONS MUSEUM, *145 Queen Victoria Street, EC4 (0171 248 7444). Open Mon–Fri 10 am–5 pm. Blackfriars BR/underground.* The past, present and future of telecommunications is displayed with working exhibits, films, interactive videos, hands-on activities, and models and pictures from early telegraphs to satellites, from a Victorian telegraph office to digital technology.

BURGH HOUSE, THE HAMPSTEAD MUSEUM, *New End Square, NW3 (0171 431 0144). Open Wed–Sun noon–5 pm. Hampstead underground.* This Queen Anne house has displays on the history of Hampstead including local residents such as D. H. Lawrence as well as prints by Constable.

CHARTERED INSURANCE INSTITUTE MUSEUM, *20 Aldermanbury, EC2 (0171 606 3835 ext 3274). Open Mon–Fri 9 am–5 pm. Moorgate/St Paul's underground.* A small museum with display cases illustrating the history of insurance. The exhibits include antique fireman's gear, a Victorian fire engine and a large collection of fire-marks, signs used in the past to indicate that a building was insured.

CHURCH FARM HOUSE MUSEUM, *Greyhound Hill, NW4 (0181 203 0130). Open Mon, Wed–Sat 10 am–1 pm, 2–5.30 pm; Tues 10 am–1 pm; Sun 2–5.30 pm. Hendon Central underground.* A fascinating museum of domestic and local history and the decorative arts within an old gabled farmhouse built in 1659, with a period scullery, kitchen and dining-room, and changing exhibitions. SUNNY HILL PARK is behind the museum.

CLOCKMAKERS' COMPANY MUSEUM, *The Clockroom, Guildhall Library, Aldermanbury, EC2 (0171 606 3030). Open May–Sept daily 10 am–5 pm; Oct–Apr Mon–Sat 10 am–5 pm. Bank/Moorgate underground.* To illustrate 500 years of timekeeping, there are 700 exhibits dating from as far back as the 14th century including the first electric clock, a gas-powered clock, royal timepieces and marvellous grandfather clocks. Try and visit on the hour, at noon if possible.

CRYSTAL PALACE MUSEUM, *Cottage Yard, Anerley Hill, Sydenham, SE19 (0181 676 0700). Open Sun 11 am–5 pm. Donation requested. Crystal Palace BR.* This small museum explores the history of Sir Joseph Paxton's Victorian Crystal Palace.

CUMING MUSEUM, *155–157 Walworth Road, SE17 (0171 701 · 1342) Open Tues–Sat 10am–5pm. Elephant and Castle BR/underground.* Southwark's history from Roman times is unravelled, including special displays on Dickens, Shakespeare, and superstition through the ages plus temporary exhibitions.

EPPING FOREST DISTRICT MUSEUM, *39–41 Sun Street, Waltham Abbey, EN9 (01992 716882). Open Fri–Mon 2–5pm; Tues noon–5pm.* A couple of 16th-century timber-framed buildings containing displays on local history from the Stone Age on. A Victorian gallery has three shops and a police station of the period. There are also temporary exhibitions and a Tudor herb garden.

ERITH MUSEUM, *Erith Library, Walnut Tree Road, Erith, Kent (01322 336582). Open Mon, Wed, Sat 2.15–5pm. Erith BR.* A small museum concerned with the history of Erith.

FORTY HALL MUSEUM, *Forty Hill, Enfield, Middlesex (0181 363 8196). Open Thur–Sun 11am–5pm. Enfield Chase BR.* An imposing Carolean mansion with elaborate Jacobean ceilings, which as a museum struggles for a unified theme. Among other exhibits it houses 17th- and 18th-century furniture, local history and ecology displays, childhood momentoes and an exhibition of the history of advertising and packaging.

FREEMASONS' HALL MUSEUM, *Freemason's Hall, WC2 (0171 831 9811). Open Mon–Fri 10am–5pm; most Sats 10.30am–1pm. Tours (including the Grand Temple) 11am, noon, hourly from 2pm–6pm. Holborn/Covent Garden underground*. Although Freemasons have a reputation for secrecy, they have no qualms about opening their headquarters, the Grand Lodge, to the public. There are collections including jewellery, medals and regalia associated with Masonic ritual. The huge marble and jade temple is majestic.

GEFFRYE MUSEUM, *Kingsland Road, E2 (0171 739 9893). Open Tues–Sat 10am–5pm; Sun 2–5pm. Old Street underground*. This grand building was named after the Lord Mayor of London in 1685, Sir Robert Geffrye, who bequeathed almshouses and a chapel for the poor. The museum is primarily concerned with interior design and presents (with tremendous attention to detail) fascinating room displays showing homes from before 1600 to the 1950s. There are also attractive gardens with mature trees and a restful walled herb garden *(open Apr–Oct)* providing further botanical interest. In the summer there are activities for children such as treasure hunts, juggling and face-painting, and music in the museum or garden.

GRANGE MUSEUM OF COMMUNITY HISTORY, *Neasden Lane, NW10 (0181 908 7432). Open Mon–Fri 11am–5pm; Sat 10am–5pm. Neasden underground*.

Dating from around 1700, the building was originally part of a farm and now has exhibitions about the local area, the London Borough of Brent. There are temporary displays, a local history library and period rooms including a reconstructed draper's shop. Visitors may picnic in the enclosed garden and conservatory and there's a children's play area.

GREENWICH BOROUGH MUSEUM, 232 *Plumstead High Street, SE18 (0181 855 3240). Open Mon 2–7 pm; Thur–Sat 10 am–1 pm, 2–5 pm. Plumstead BR.* Displays include a history of the borough, local geology and archaeology and a wildlife gallery plus temporary exhibitions.

GUNNERSBURY PARK MUSEUM, *Gunnersbury Park, Popes Lane, W3 (0181 992 1612). Open Mar–Oct: Mon–Fri 1–5 pm, Sat, Sun 1–6 pm; Nov–Feb: daily 1–4 pm. Guided tours bookable in advance. Donation requested. Acton Town underground.* This early 19th-century mansion within the park has a collection of topographical items, transport displays with coaches of the Rothschild family, costume, toys and archaeology relating to the locality, the boroughs of Ealing and Hounslow. There are temporary exhibitions too. As well as the surrounding park, which houses other historic buildings, Kensington Cemetery is adjacent.

HACKNEY MUSEUM, *Central Hall, Mare Street, E8 (0181 986 6914). Open Tues–Fri 10 am–12.30 pm, 1.30–5 pm,*

Sat 1.30–5 pm. Bethnal Green underground/Hackney Central BR. Explores the local history of the area's cosmopolitan population from Viking times.

HARROW MUSEUM AND HERITAGE CENTRE, *Headstone Manor, Pinner View, HA2 (0181 861 2626). Open Wed–Fri 12.30 pm–5 pm; Sat, Sun 10.30 am–5 pm. Harrow and Wealdstone BR/underground*. This medieval site has, as well as the museum with regular temporary exhibitions, a moat and grounds with plenty of wildlife.

HARROW SCHOOL OLD SPEECH ROOM GALLERY, *Church Hill, Harrow-on-the-Hill, Middlesex (0181 869 1205). Open in term-times Thur–Tues 2.30–5 pm; during holidays Mon–Fri 2.15–5 pm. Harrow-on-the-Hill underground*. Antiquities collected by this famous school, including works by old Harrovians such as Byron and Churchill.

HOGARTH'S HOUSE, *Hogarth Lane, Great West Road, W4 (0181 994 6757). Open Apr–Sept: Mon, Wed–Sat 11 am–6 pm, Sun 2–6 pm; Oct–Mar: Mon, Wed–Sat 11 am–4 pm, Sun 2–4 pm; but closed first two weeks in Sept, last three weeks in Dec. Guided tours available. Turnham Green underground*. English engraver and painter William Hogarth (1697–1764) lived in this 17th-century house for his last 15 years to get some peace and quiet but nowadays even an estate agent couldn't convince you that this patch of London is tranquil, being the place to be if you like traffic congestion since it is conveniently situated for the start of the M4 and the Hammersmith flyover. Engravings, drawings and other mementoes are on display, and there's a pretty garden.

HONEYWOOD HERITAGE CENTRE, *Honeywood Walk, Carshalton, Surrey (0181 773 4555). Free admission Thur 10 am–1 pm. Carshalton BR.* Sutton's history displayed in a 17th-century house, including a children's room with Edwardian toys and an audio-visual display.

HORNIMAN MUSEUM, *London Road, Forest Hill, SE23 (0181 699 1872/2339). Open Mon–Sat 10.30 am–5.30 pm; Sun 2–5.30 pm. Forest Hill BR.* A varied and ever-interesting collection including an aquarium and a large collection of musical instruments that can be heard, touched and played, with occasional demonstrations and interactive videos. There's ethnographical and natural history displays, a library, lectures, concerts and special exhibitions. Horniman Gardens is on the same site and worth a visit.

HUNTERIAN MUSEUM, *Royal College of Surgeons of England, 35–43 Lincoln's Inn Fields, WC2 (0171 405 3474). Open Mon–Fri 10 am–5 pm by appointment only. Donations welcomed. Holborn/Temple underground.* A medical museum that began with eminent 18th-century research surgeon John Hunter's huge collection of

anatomical pathological and zoological specimens and
that has since been enlarged. It examines how the body
adapts to changes, those caused by accident or disease
and reproduction and birth. There are fossils and the
results of experiments, as well as skeletons of a giant, a
dwarf and some infamous 19th-century murderers. The
ODONTOLOGICAL MUSEUM and the WELLCOME
MUSEUMS OF PATHOLOGY AND ANATOMY are also
at the College.

IMPERIAL WAR MUSEUM, *Lambeth Road, SE1 (0171 416
5000). Free admission daily 4.30–6 pm. Lambeth North
underground/Waterloo BR/underground*. The nation's
museum of 20th-century war is imaginative and lively
and includes planes, tanks and various weapons and
also a simulated air raid or, if you'd prefer, an exhibit
providing the experience of trench warfare.

ISLINGTON MUSEUM GALLERY, *268 Upper Street, N1
(0171 354 9442). Open Wed–Fri 11 am–3 pm; Sat 10 am–
5 pm; Sun 2–4 pm. Highbury and Islington underground*.
Temporary exhibitions, lasting around six weeks, relating to the area.

KEATS HOUSE, *Keats Grove, Hampstead, NW3 (0171 435
2062). Open Apr–Oct: Mon–Fri 10 am–1 pm, 2–6 pm; Sat
10 am–1 pm, 2–5 pm; Sun 2–5 pm; Nov–Mar: Mon–Fri
1–5 pm; Sat 10 am–1 pm, 2–5 pm; Sun 2–5 pm; guided
tours by appointment. Hampstead underground. Donations*

requested. This Regency house, where tragic Romantic poet John Keats lived and wrote 'Ode to a Nightingale' as well as many other works, has letters, manuscripts and relics, and mementos of his love for his next-door neighbour, Fanny Brawne.

KEW PUBLIC RECORDS OFFICE, *Ruskin Avenue, Richmond (0181 876 3444). Open Mon–Fri 9.30 am–5 pm. Kew Gardens BR/underground.* There are regular exhibitions using items from the huge collection of national archives from the Norman Conquest onwards.

KINGSTON MUSEUM AND ART GALLERY, *Wheatfield Way, Kingston, Surrey (0181 546 5386). Open Mon, Tues, Thur–Sat 10 am–5 pm. Kingston BR.* An Edwardian museum depicting the area's past, with a special exhibition featuring clothes and momentoes of important Kingston residents.

KODAK MUSEUM, *Headstone Drive, Harrow, Middlesex (0181 863 0534). Open Mon–Fri 9.30 am–4.30 pm; Sat, Sun 2–6 pm. Harrow and Wealdstone BR.* Thousands of exhibits telling the history of photography and cinematography.

LEIGHTON HOUSE, *12 Holland Park Road, W14 (0171 602 3316). Open Mon–Sat 11 am–5.30 pm. Garden open Apr–Sept 11 am–5.30 pm. Donations requested. High Street Kensington underground.* An extraordinary opulent and exotic Victorian house built in 1866 for the then President of the Royal Academy, Frederic, Lord Leighton, by George Aitchison. The stunning domed Arab Hall, with its unusual, rare middle-eastern tiles, mosaic floor and even a fountain and pool, was added in 1879. This really is the ultimate opposite of a Wimpey showhouse new home. There are a variety of works on display and a tranquil garden.

LIFETIMES, *Croydon Clocktower, Katharine Street, Croydon, CR9 (0181 253 1030). Free admission Wed 4.45–6 pm. East/West Croydon BR*. Part of the new Croydon Clocktower cultural complex, Lifetimes is based upon the experiences of Croydon people from 1830 to the present day and there are reconstructions and models (many belongings lent by local people), changing displays, a 'hands on' room and touch-screen computers. The organisers claim that there's so much information it would take over two days to see and hear it all.

LIVESEY MUSEUM, *682 Old Kent Road, SE15 (0171 639 5604). Open Mon–Sat 10 am–5 pm. Elephant and Castle BR/underground*. A small and friendly children's museum. There's a toddlers play area, and older children appreciate the push-button exhibits. Parking in the local side streets is free, which is a rarity these days.

LONDON GAS MUSEUM, *Twelvetrees Crescent, E3 (0171*

987 2000 ext 3344). Open 9 am–4 pm by appointment. Bromley-by-Bow underground. A small museum examining the history of the gas industry, including life before gas, early gas works, how gas is processed and stored, and how natural gas was found. There is a collection of gas appliances.

MARTINWARE POTTERY COLLECTION, *Southall Library, Osterly Park Road, Southall, Middlesex (0181 574 3412). Open Tues, Thur, Fri 9 am–7.45 pm; Wed, Sat 9 am–5 pm. Southall BR.* This collection of slightly eccentric pottery made by the Martin family from 1873 to 1923 is housed in an annexe of the reference library and includes a variety of tiles, jugs, pots and other items. Bigger examples of their work are displayed at the Pitshanger Manor Museum.

MUSEUM OF ARTILLERY, *the Rotunda, Repository Road, Woolwich SE18 (0181 316 5402). Open Mon–Fri 1–4 pm; guided tours by prior arrangement. Donations requested. Woolwich Dockyard BR.* A collection of artillery is housed in this circular structure designed by John Nash, from a Napoleonic cannon to modern-day weapons.

MUSEUM OF GARDEN HISTORY, *St Mary-at-Lambeth, Lambeth Palace Road, SE1 (0171 261 1891). Open Mon–Fri 11 am–3 pm; Sun 10.30 am–5 pm; closed from second Sun in Dec to first Sun in Mar. Donations requested.*

Waterloo BR/underground. As well as exhibits relating to garden history there is a re-created 17th-century garden.

MUSEUM OF LONDON, *150 London Wall, EC2 (0171 600 3699). Free admission Tues–Sun 4.30–5.30 pm. Barbican/ St Paul's underground.* Claiming to be the largest and most comprehensive city museum in the world, it tells the story of London and its people from the first hunter-gatherers of 400,000 years ago, to the city being founded by the Romans around 50 AD, and to the 1500-square-kilometre metropolis of today. There are displays of the homes and workplaces of Londoners, of fine and applied arts and the products of science and industry. There are sculptures, a Victorian shop, a barber's shop, a 1930s car, the Lord Mayor's state coach, Selfridge's lift and a display on the Great Fire.

MUSEUM OF MANKIND, *6 Burlington Gardens, W1 (0171 323 8043). Open Mon–Sat 10 am–5 pm; Sun 2.30–6 pm. Donations welcome. Piccadilly Circus underground.* The ethnography section of the British Museum, this is a comprehensive collection representing old and new cultures from around the world. It provides a fascinating insight into the life-styles of other societies.

MUSEUM OF THE ORDER OF ST JOHN, *St John's Gate, St John's Lane, EC1 (0171 253 6644). Open Mon–Fri 10 am–5 pm; Sat 10 am–4 pm; with half-hour guided tours Tues, Fri and Sat 11 am and 2.30 pm. Donation requested.*

Farringdon/Barbican BR/underground. The museum is housed in a gatehouse built in 1504 that was the entrance to the medieval priory of the Order of St John of Jerusalem, which founded St John's Ambulance amongst its charitable deeds. There is a collection of books dating from 1425, armour, paintings, ceramics, furniture, silver and medical instruments, insignia and other treasures of the Knights of St John. There are also displays looking at the people and personal memorabilia of St John Ambulance including its role in the Boer and World Wars. The 17th-century elaborate model of Jerusalem's Holy Sepulchre is well worth a look despite being very politically incorrect: it's carved from ebony, ivory and mother-of-pearl. There is also a 12th-century crypt.

MUSEUM OF ZOOLOGY AND COMPARATIVE ANAT-OMY, *Medowar Building, Department of Biology, University College London, Gower Street, WC1 (0171 419 3564). Open Mon–Fri 10.30 am–5 pm by appointment with the curator. Euston Square/Russell Square/Goodge Street underground*. Opened in 1928, the collections cover the whole of the animal kingdom with many rare and extinct specimens including one of only five known Quaqqa skeletons, a type of zebra extinct since the 1850s.

NATIONAL ARMY MUSEUM, *Royal Hospital Road, SW3 (0171 730 0717). Open daily 10 am–5.30 pm. Sloane*

Square underground. The history of the British, Indian and Colonial forces from 1485 with reconstructions of the life of a soldier through the years and from the jungles of Burma to the deserts of Sudan. There's a model of the Battle of Waterloo using over 70,000 model soldiers, Florence Nightingale's jewellery, items removed from the Gulf War battleground just after it ended, and even the skeleton of Napoleon's horse. The audio-visual displays, relics, personal mementoes, uniforms and weapons, portraits and prints are augmented by temporary exhibitions and events. A visit combines well with a look at the Great Hall and Chapel of the ROYAL HOSPITAL and it's grounds, RANELAGH GARDENS.

NATIONAL ART LIBRARY, *First floor, Victoria & Albert Museum, Cromwell Road, SW7. (0171 589 6371) Open Mon noon–5 pm, Tues–Thur 10 am–5 pm. Donation requested. South Kensington underground.* Although located within the V&A, the Library pre-dates it by 15 years. There are regular exhibitions from the collection, which exceeds one million books and manuscripts covering the history of art. It includes some of the most beautiful books ever produced including medieval bibles, publications with illustrations by Bonnard and Matisse, and books by Beatrix Potter.

NATIONAL MARITIME MUSEUM, *Romney Road, SE10 (0181 858 4422). Open Mar–Oct: Mon–Sat noon–6 pm,*

Sun 2–6 pm; Nov–Feb: Mon–Sat 10 am–5 pm, Sun 2–5 pm. Greenwich/Maze Hill BR. Free admission (except special exhibitions) to residents of Greenwich and Lewisham boroughs: either Greenwich's Greenwich Card or Lewisham's Vantage Card (available from local libraries) is required as proof. Endless boats, model boats, boat relics and the world's biggest collection of marine art trace Britain's history of the sea. A new interactive gallery (check opening times) with such distractions as levers to pull, a crane to operate, ships to dock and morse messages to send, is a big hit with children. Also at the museum is Inigo Jones' QUEEN'S HOUSE, which was the first building in the Palladian style in Britain and therefore a substantial influence on the country's architecture.

NATIONAL POSTAL MUSEUM, *King Edward Building, King Edward Street, EC1 (0171 239 5420). Open Mon–Fri 9.30 am–4.30 pm; guided tours by prior arrangement Tues–Thur 10 am–noon, 2–4 pm. St Paul's underground.* Probably the world's best collection of British postage stamps, including the world's first, the Penny Black. It would be best to set aside more than a day here if you want to see all 250,000+ stamps. Artefacts such as scales, model mail coaches, paintings, letter-boxes etc. Special exhibitions.

NATIONAL SOUND ARCHIVE, *29 Exhibition Road, SW7 (0171 589 6603/412 7430). Open Mon–Fri 10 am–5 pm and to 9 pm Thur. South Kensington underground.* The audio section of the British Museum, this collection reflects the development of recorded sound from early wax cylinders onwards. Ring to make an appointment to listen from a choice of thousands and thousands of recordings including folk, classical, popular and ethnic music from around the world as well as speech and drama.

NATURAL HISTORY MUSEUM, *Cromwell Road, SW7 (0171 938 9123). Free admission Mon–Fri 4.30–5.50 pm; Sat, Sun 5–5.50 pm. South Kensington underground.* Now incorporating the former Geology Museum (its earth-quake simulator is the main attraction there), this is impressive both inside and out, a magnificent Victor-ian cathedral-like building, but with absorbing up-to-date displays and an unrivalled collection of animals, plants, minerals and fossils. Galleries concentrate upon one subject, such as ecology, the environment or dinosaurs.

NORTH WOOLWICH OLD STATION MUSEUM, *Pier Road, E16 (0171 474 7244). Open Mon–Wed and Sat 10 am–5 pm; Sun 2–5 pm. North Woolwich BR.* A restored Victorian station building with trains, time-tables, a 1920s' ticket office, models, photographs, station signs and a turntable pit. Occasional films. Working locomotive *first Sunday each month* from *Apr–Oct.*

ODONTOLOGICAL MUSEUM, *Royal College of Surgeons of England, 35–43 Lincoln's Inn Fields, WC2 (0171 405 3474). Open Mon–Fri 10 am–5 pm by appointment only. Donations welcomed. Holborn/Temple underground.* In examining the history of odontology and dentistry, there is an excellent collection of comparative pathology, 19th-century preparations of skulls and teeth by the father of British dentistry, Sir John Tomes, and early extraction instruments and dentures. There are examples of 'phossy jaw', a phenomenon which was caused by the phosphorous used in manufacturing matches in the last century, and which led to the 'Match Girl Strike' in the 1880s. The HUNTERIAN MUSEUM and the WELLCOME MUSEUMS OF PATHOLOGY AND ANATOMY are also at the College.

OLD ROYAL OBSERVATORY, *Greenwich Park, SE10 (0181 858 4422). Open Mar–Oct: Mon–Sat noon–6 pm, Sun 2–6 pm; Nov–Feb: Mon–Sat 10 am–5 pm, Sun 2–5 pm. Greenwich/Maze Hill BR. Free admission (except special exhibitions) to residents of Greenwich and Lewisham boroughs: either Greenwich's Greenwich Card or Lewisham's Vantage Card (available from local libraries) is required as proof.* Founded in 1675 by Charles II, this is home to Greenwich Mean Time and the zero meridian line. You can admire the fine views of London from here while standing with one foot in the East and one foot in the West of the globe. At *1 pm daily* the red ball on the top of the building descends, the original reason for this being to enable sailors on the river to set their watches. There's a fine collection of telescopes and related astronomic displays.

PASSMORE EDWARDS MUSEUM, *Romford Road, Stratford, E15 (0181 534 0276). Open Wed–Fri 11 am–5 pm; Sat 1–5 pm; Sun 2–5 pm. Stratford BR/DLR underground.* Displays on local archaeology, geology, natural and social history.

PAVLOVA MEMORIAL MUSEUM, *Ivy House, North End Road, NW11. Open Sat 2–5 pm. Golders Green underground.* Ivy House was home to the great Russian ballerina Anna Pavlova from 1912 to 1931 and it now has a small collection of memorabilia.

PERCIVAL DAVID FOUNDATION OF CHINESE ART, *53 Gordon Square, WC1 (0171 387 3909). Open Mon–Fri 10.30 am–5 pm. Donations welcomed. Euston Square/ Goodge Street underground.* Hundreds of examples of Chinese ceramics from the 9th to 18th centuries, the Song, Yuan, Ming and Qing dynasties.

PETRIE MUSEUM OF EGYPTIAN ARCHAEOLOGY, *Egyptology Department, by Bloomsbury Science Library, University College London, Gower Street, WC1 (0171 387 7050 ext 2884). Open Mon–Fri 10 am–noon, 1.15–5 pm, but closed for four weeks in the summer. Donations requested. Goodge Street/Warren Street underground.* A collection begun in 1884 by Victorian archaeologist Sir Flinders Petrie, the father of Egyptian archaeology, with additions by his colleagues and successors, exhibited to show the development of Egyptian culture, technology and day-to-day life. On display is pottery, jewellery, toys and the world's oldest dress. The museum reckons to have the biggest and finest collection of ancient Egyptian antiquities in any university in the world. Shouldn't it be an Egyptian university claiming that?

PITSHANGER MANOR MUSEUM, *Mattock Lane, W5 (0181 567 1227). Open Tues–Sat 10 am–5 pm. Ealing Broadway underground.* Although there is a changing display of Martinware pottery, it could be argued that this isn't strictly a museum in the usual sense unless you count the Grade I-listed house itself as the exhibit. Set in a park, the house has plasterwork from the mid-18th century and it is interesting from an architectural point of view to see what neo-classical architect Sir John Soane did to the building at the start of the 19th century, when he turned it into a Regency villa.

POLISH INSTITUTE MUSEUM, *20 Princes Gate, SW7 (0171 589 9249). Open Mon–Fri 2–4 pm; first Sat in month 10 am–4 pm. South Kensington/Knightsbridge underground.* A large collection covering Polish history and culture with an emphasis on the Second World War.

PRINCE HENRY'S ROOM, *17 Fleet Street, EC4 (0181 294 1158). Open Mon–Sat 11 am–2 pm. Temple underground.* Built in 1611, this is one of the few City buildings to escape the Great Fire of 1666 and the Blitz of World War II. Named after James I's eldest son, it now holds memorabilia relating to diarist Samuel Pepys.

PUBLIC RECORD OFFICE MUSEUM, *Chancery Lane, WC2 (0181 876 3444). Open Mon–Fri 10 am–5 pm. Chancery Lane underground.* Of the millions of documents from government departments from the 11th century onwards housed here, records displayed include the first national census, the Domesday Book (1086), medieval charters, Shakespeare's will, the Gunpowder Plot papers and details of the funeral of the 'Grand Old' Duke of York. Telephone before visiting, as the museum is moving to Kew, although at the time of going to press the date had not been decided.

PUPPET CENTRE, *Battersea Arts Centre, Lavender Hill, SW11 (0171 228 5335). Open Mon–Fri 2–6 pm. Clapham Junction BR.* Around 50 of the Centre's collection of 500 puppets are on display at any one time as well as related memorabilia.

RAGGED SCHOOL MUSEUM, *46–48 Copperfield Road, E3 (0181 980 6405). Open Wed, Thur 10 am–5 pm; and first Sun of month 2–5 pm. Donations appreciated. Mile End underground.* Dr Barnardo founded the ragged schools for disadvantaged children. This canal-side warehouse was once one, and has captivating exhibitions on East End life including a typical Victorian classroom. There are children's activities in the school holidays.

ROYAL ARTILLERY REGIMENTAL MUSEUM, *Old Royal Military Academy, Academy Road, Woolwich, SE18 (0181 854 2242 ext 5628). Open Mon–Fri 12.30–4.30 pm; Sat, Sun 2–5 pm; (Nov–Mar: Sat, Sun 2–4 pm); guided tours by arrangement. Donations requested. Woolwich Dockyard BR.* Telling the history of the Royal Artillery from its formation in 1716 to the present with displays including weapons, uniforms and other militaria.

ROYAL HOSPITAL CHELSEA MUSEUM, *Royal Hospital Road, SW3 (0171 730 5282). Open Mon–Fri 10 am–noon, 2–4 pm; Sat 2–4 pm. Sloane Square underground.* Charles II founded this hospital for veteran soldiers and it remains the home of over 400 Chelsea Pensioners with their distinctive scarlet coats and tricorne hats. The small museum has pictures (including Van Dyck's famous picture of Charles I and family), medals and uniforms connected with the Royal Hospital as well as a chapel, a great hall and neat, pretty grounds, RANELAGH GARDENS.

ROYAL LONDON HOSPITAL MUSEUM AND ARCHIVE, *St Augustine with St Philip's Church, Newark Street, E1 (0171 377 7000 ext 3364). Open Mon–Fri 10 am–4.30 pm.*

Whitechapel underground. Located in the basement of a fine 19th-century church that is now a medical library, the development and role of the hospital is illustrated.

ROYAL MILITARY SCHOOL OF MUSIC MUSEUM, *Kneller Hall, Kneller Road, Twickenham (0181 898 5533 ext 8630). Open by appointment only Mon–Fri 9 am–6 pm. Hounslow/Whitton BR.* Housed in a huge Jacobean-style mansion that also holds the Army's music academy, the small museum has historic musical instruments including a double-bass made in 1650, uniforms of bandsmen of the British Army, and other associated items.

RUGBY FOOTBALL UNION MUSEUM, *Gate 7, Rugby Football Union Stadium, Rugby Road, Twickenham (0181 892 8161) Open Mon–Fri 9.30 am–1 pm, 2.15–5 pm. Twickenham BR.* The history of the game is, alas, displayed rather unimaginatively.

ST BRIDE'S CHURCH CRYPT MUSEUM, *St Bride's Church, Bride Lane, off Fleet Street, EC4 (0171 353 1301). Open daily 9 am–5 pm; guided tours by appointment. St Paul's underground.* The 'parish church of the press' or the 'Cathedral of Fleet Street', this is the eighth church on the site since the sixth century. The museum holds many relics including Roman remains, medieval walls and historic printing presses, and houses a library concerned with printing techniques. The 226-foot church spire inspired the modern-day wedding cake when a local baker modelled his wedding cakes on it and was then copied by others. That the church is called St Bride's is a coincidence.

SALVATION ARMY INTERNATIONAL HERITAGE CENTRE, *117–121 Judd Street, WC1 (0171 387 1656). Open Mon–Fri 9.30 am–3.30 pm; Sat 9.30 am–noon. King's Cross BR/underground.* Recounting the story of this religious movement set up by William Booth in 1865 to help the poor. There is an hour-long recorded commentary available.

SCIENCE FOR LIFE, *The Wellcome Building, 183 Euston Road, NW1 (0171 611 8727/8888). Open Mon–Fri 9.45 am–5 pm; Sat 9.45 am–1 pm. Euston BR/underground.* A new, absorbing interactive exhibition for all the family that teaches science in an interesting and exciting way. Occasional special events.

SCIENCE MUSEUM, *Exhibition Road, SW7 (0171 938 8080). Free admission daily 4.30–6 pm. South Kensington underground.* An enormous museum (seven floors) devoted to science and technology. Exhibitions include the exploration of space, fire-fighting, nuclear physics, computing, chemistry and medicine. There's a real lunar command module, locomotives and aircraft. Children especially love the endless push-button exhibits and can also solve at first hand scientific problems that have been posed by the equipment in the Launch Pad area. The garden in the basement is particularly popular.

SIR JOHN SOANE'S MUSEUM, *13 Lincoln's Inn Fields, WC2 (0171 405 2107). Open Tues–Sat 10 am–5 pm. Lecture tours Sat 2.30 pm. Donation box. Holborn underground.* Built 1812 and recently restored, this beautiful, unusual museum was architect Soane's house and displays his eccentric collection of plasterwork, paintings, models of buildings – and chillingly, of tombs complete with skeletons – as well as drawings, antiquities, sculptures and books from around the world that took nearly half a century to assemble and which 50,000 people visit annually. The items displayed are staggering in volume and variety and even hold the attention of very young children, who find a surprise around every corner, or a new alcove crammed with more treasures. Soane bequeathed his collection to the nation on the understanding that nothing was removed or changed.

VALENCE HOUSE MUSEUM, *Becontree Avenue, Dagenham (0181 595 8404). Open Tues–Fri 9.30 am–1 pm, 2–4.30 pm; Sat 10 am–4 pm. Chadwell Heath BR.* A mainly 17th-century moated manor house with local artefacts including Stone and Iron Age implements and Anglo-Saxon weapons and jewellery, as well as displays of 17th- and 20th-century interiors.

VESTRY HOUSE MUSEUM, *Vestry Road, Walthamstow,*

E17 (0181 509 1917). Open Mon–Sat 10 am–1 pm, 2–5 pm. Walthamstow Central BR/underground. Housed within an 18th-century workhouse, there are many original features such as a Victorian police cell and displays on local domestic life 100 years ago. Exhibits displaying lifestyles from the Stone Age onwards.

VICTORIA & ALBERT MUSEUM, *Cromwell Road, SW7. (0171 938 8500). Open Mon noon–5.50 pm; Tues–Sun 10 am–5.50 pm. One hour introductory guided tours daily at 11 am, noon, 2 pm and 3 pm except Mon, when they are at 12.15 pm, 2 pm and 3 pm. Also occasional children's tours. Gallery talks and study sessions concentrating on a particular aspect of the collection are every day at 2.30 pm. Donation requested. South Kensington underground.* An exciting museum, possibly the world's greatest of fine and applied arts, with around four million exhibits from all periods and areas of the world. Ten acres of gallery space display sculpture, jewellery, enamels, weapons, silver, miniatures, water-colours, musical instruments, furniture, pottery, glass, a dress collection and changing exhibitions and displays. A good panoramic view of London is obtainable from the Constable Gallery in the Henry Cole Wing.

VINTAGE WIRELESS MUSEUM, *23 Rosendale Road, SE21 (0181 670 3667). Open by appointment only Mon–Sat 11 am–7.30 pm. Donation requested. West Dulwich BR.*

Not only radios here but also the first ever TV set, telephones and thousands of other items.

WELLCOME MUSEUMS OF PATHOLOGY AND ANATOMY, *Royal College of Surgeons of England, 35–43 Lincoln's Inn Fields, WC2 (0171 405 3474). Open Mon–Fri 10 am–5 pm by appointment only. Donations welcomed. Holborn/Temple underground.* For those with a strong stomach there is a collection of dissections displaying the human anatomy, skeletons through man's lifetime and other teaching specimens. The HUNTERIAN MUSEUM and the ODONTOLOGICAL MUSEUM are also at the College.

WILLIAM MORRIS GALLERY, *Lloyd Park, Forest Road, Walthamstow, E17 (0181 527 3782). Open Tues–Sat 10 am–1 pm, 2–5 pm; and first Sun in each month, 10 am–noon, 2–5 pm. Walthamstow Central BR/underground.* Socialist designer William Morris lived in this delightful 18th-century house with its own grounds from 1848 to 1856 and his furniture, wallpapers and fabrics are on display as well as ceramics, furniture and other works by associates including Rossetti and Burne-Jones, and pictures and sculptures by Rodin.

WILLIAM MORRIS SOCIETY, *Kelmscott House, 26 Upper Mall, W6 (0181 741 3735). Open Thur, Sat 2–5 pm. Hammersmith underground.* Designer and author Morris lived here at the end of his life and on display are memorabilia, examples of his work and a printing press used to publish his work.

WIMBLEDON SOCIETY'S MUSEUM, *The Village Club, Ridgeway, 26 Lingfield Road, SW19. Open Sat 2.30–5 pm. Wimbledon underground.* A little museum about the history of the area that's run by volunteers.

MUSIC

Pubs and bars included in the listing below have generously agreed to allow people to visit and hear the live music they put on for free, but as they can only afford to do so regularly if people buy drinks, please don't take liberties by setting up camp at the bar when doors open and demanding pints of tap-water at 20-minute intervals until closing time, or there'll be a much-diminished music section to any future editions of this book.

Of course, London's streets, pedestrian subways and underground stations (especially in the centre of town) produce a variety of BUSKERS of all abilities. If you're not familiar with the tradition, the idea is to show support for the music by donating a few coins as you walk by – unless they're playing yet another untuned rendition of *Tambourine Man* or *Waterloo Sunset* in which case it's correct form to instead *remove* the money the busker has collected and punch him squarely in the face for good measure.

ALEXANDRA PALACE AND PARK, *Wood Green, N22 (0181 365 2121)*. *Wood Green underground/Alexandra Palace BR*. Live music in the form of Grove Shows *every third Sunday in the month*.

THE BARBICAN CENTRE, *Silk Street, EC2 (0171 638 4141)*. *Barbican/Moorgate underground*. Jazz, classical, contemporary, blues, medieval, even Russian gypsy music ... It's all here, generally on *weekday evenings 5.30–7 pm* and *Sundays 12.30–2.30 pm* at the Performance Platform on the ground floor.

BLACKHEATH CONCERT HALLS, *23 Lee Road, SE3 (0181 463 0100)*. *Blackheath BR*. Usually *once a month* from 7.30–10.30 pm on a *Thursday*, there's a Jazz Play-In, a jam session hosted by a professional trio.

BOTTOMLINE, *58 Shepherd's Bush Green, W12 (0181 740 1304)*. *Shepherd's Bush underground*. Free admission to hear occasional bands at this popular pub.

BRIXTON ARTISTS' COLLECTIVE, *35 Brixton Station Road, SW9 (0171 733 6957)*. *Open Mon–Sat 10 am–6 pm*. *Brixton underground*. Occasional cultural events *(donation requested)* featuring music and also possibly visual arts, poetry and acting.

CHURCH LUNCH-TIME CONCERTS, A number of the City's many churches organize lunch-time concerts, usually beginning at approximately *1–1.15pm* on *weekdays* and lasting under an hour. The City of London Information Centre, *St Paul's Churchyard,* EC4 *(0171 606 3030)* can give details of the day's concerts and their publication, *City Events,* gives monthly details. Some other churches around London also put on lunch-time concerts. The standards are almost always high for these performances, which range from solos to chamber orchestras. Although they are free, donations are often requested.

ALL SOULS
Langham Place, W1 *(0171 580 3522). Oxford Circus underground.* Occasional free concerts, especially organ recitals.
ST ANNE AND ST AGNES
Gresham Street, EC2 *(0171 373 5566). St Paul's underground. Mon and Fri* at *1.10pm.* Also other events such as Bach, jazz and Lutheran choral vespers.
ST BRIDE'S
Fleet Street, EC4 *(0171 353 1301) Blackfriars BR/underground.* Frequent concerts at *1.15pm.*
ST GEORGE'S HANOVER SQUARE
2a Mill Street, W1 *(0171 629 0874). Oxford Circus underground.* Recitals usually on *Thur.*

ST GILES CRIPPLEGATE
Barbican, EC2 (0171 606 3630). Barbican/Moorgate underground. Small-scale classical works.

ST JAMES'S
Piccadilly, W1 (0171 734 4511). Piccadilly underground. Thur, Fri and also many *Weds* and *Sats* at *1.10 pm.* Big on Baroque.

ST LAWRENCE JEWRY
Gresham Street, EC2 (0171 600 9478). Bank underground. Piano recitals on *Mondays* at *1 pm* and organ recitals on *Tuesdays* at the same time.

ST MARGARET'S
Broad Sanctuary, SW1 (0171 222 6382). Westminster underground. Occasional choirs *weekdays 1–2 pm*

ST MARGARET'S
Lothbury, EC2 (0171 606 8330). Bank underground. Wednesdays/Thursdays at *1.10 pm.*

ST MARTIN-IN-THE-FIELDS
Trafalgar Square, WC2 (0171 930 0089). Charing Cross BR/underground. At least two performances a week.

ST MARTIN-WITHIN-LUDGATE
Ludgate Hill, EC4 (0171 248 6054). St Paul's underground. Wednesdays at *1.15 pm.*

ST MARY-LE-BOW
Cheapside, EC2 (0171 248 5139). St Paul's underground. Medieval and Renaissance works on *Thursdays* at *1.05 pm.*

ST MARY-LE-STRAND
Strand, WC2 (0171 836 3126). Aldwych underground.

ST MICHAEL'S
Cornhill, EC3 (0171 626 8841). Bank underground.
Organ recitals on *Mondays*.
ST OLAVE'S
Hart Street, EC3 (0171 488 4318). Tower Hill
underground. Wednesdays and *Thursdays* at *1.05 pm*.
ST SEPULCHRE-WITHOUT-NEWGATE
Holborn Viaduct, EC1 (0171 248 1660). Chancery Lane
underground.
SOUTHWARK CATHEDRAL
Montague Close, SE1 (0171 407 2939). London Bridge
BR/underground. Usually an organ recital on
Mondays and a music recital on *Tuesdays 1.10–2 pm*.

COWLEY ARMS, *485 High Street, E11 (0181 539 1330).*
Wanstead underground. This pub has live music on
Friday, Saturday and *Sunday evenings* as well as *Sunday*
lunch-times.

CRYSTAL PALACE TAVERN, *108 Tanner's Hill, SE8*
(0181 692 1536). New Cross BR/underground. Evening
performances ranging from blues to pop, r&b to punk.

THE DEWDROP, *58 Stewarts Road, SW8 (0171 627 1909).*
Battersea Park/Wandsworth Road BR. This public house
has blues one *evening* a week. Phone for details.

FIDDLER AND FIRKIN, *14 South End, Croydon (0181*
680 9728). East Croydon. A pub with anything from

rock and pop to funk and soul on a couple of *weekend evenings*.

GEFFRYE MUSEUM, *Kingsland Road, E2 (0171 739 9893/ 8368). Old Street underground*. In the summer there is occasional music in the museum or garden.

GEORGE AND DRAGON, *208 High Street, Epping, Essex (01992 573671). Epping underground*. Live music *four evenings a week* ranging from jazz to rock, folk and r&b.

GREENWICH PARK, *SE10 (0181 858 2608). Greenwich/ Maze Hill BR*. From *late June to late August* there are band performances usually *Sun 3–4.30 pm, 6–7.30 pm* at the bandstand. Also from *Tues–Sun* from *12.30 pm mid-June to early Sept* typically, there's light music played by duos at the cafeteria.

GREENWICH THEATRE, *Croom's Hill, SE10 (0181 858 7755). Greenwich BR*. Jazz every *Sunday lunch-time* in the bar area.

GUILDHALL SCHOOL OF MUSIC AND DRAMA, *Silk Street, Barbican, EC2 (0171 628 2571). Barbican/Moorgate underground*. There is a rich selection of regular classical concerts and recitals – often two or three a day – during term-times, as well as other events such as modern music concerts, jazz concerts and open rehearsals at the school or other venues. Telephone for a programme of events.

HAMPSTEAD HEATH, *NW3 (0181 348 9930/9945). Hampstead underground. Sunday afternoon* band performances on the bandstands at Parliament Hill and Golders Hill in the summer vary from brass, steel and jazz bands and light orchestras.

HARROW ARTS CENTRE, *Uxbridge Road, Hatch End, HA5 (0181 428 0124). Pinner underground.* Jazz at *lunchtime* on the *last Sunday in the month.*

HARROW MUSEUM AND HERITAGE CENTRE, *Headstone Manor, Pinner View, HA2 (0181 861 2626). Donations welcomed. Harrow and Wealdstone BR/underground.* Jazz, blues and music from the 30s to 50s in the 16th-century timber-framed Tithe Barn, *12.30–2 pm, Sunday* lunch-times.

HORNIMAN GARDENS, *100 London Road, Forest Hill, SE23 (0181 699 2339/1872). Forest Hill BR. Summer Sunday* band concerts in the bandstand.

HYDE PARK, *W1, W2, SW7 (0171 298 2100). Hyde Park Corner/Marble Arch underground.* From *mid-June* to *early September* there is live cafeteria music; on *Sunday afternoons* from *late June* to *late August* there are bandstand concerts; and occasional further musical recitals and concerts.

INSTITUTO CERVANTES, 22 *Manchester Square, W1 (0171 935 1518). Open Mon–Thur 9.30 am–6.30 pm, Fri 9.30 am–5 pm. Marble Arch/Bond Street underground.* Occasional concerts put on by this Spanish Institute – telephone for details.

ITALIAN CULTURAL INSTITUTE, 39 *Belgrave Square, SW1 (0171 235 1461). Open Mon–Fri 9.30 am–5 pm. Knightsbridge underground.* Telephone for details about concerts organised by this body that promotes Italian culture.

KENSINGTON GARDENS, *W2, W8 (0171 298 2100). Lancaster Gate/High Street Kensington underground. Early evening* classical recitals *June–August* at the bandstand.

KING'S HEAD, *115 Upper Street, N1 (0171 226 0364). Angel underground. Evening* performances of pop, rock and jazz – often acoustic solo performers and duos – at this Islington pub.

LAUDERDALE HOUSE COMMUNITY ARTS CENTRE, *Waterlow Park, Highgate Hill, N6 (0181 348 8716). Archway underground.* Occasional concerts, usually classical music.

THE MAPLE TREE, 52 *Maple Road*, SE20 (0181 778 8701). *Anerley BR*. This public house presents Irish music on *Saturday evenings*.

MORLEY COLLEGE, 61 *Westminster Bridge Road*, SE1 (0171 928 8501). *Donation requested. Lambeth North underground*. Regular *Tuesday* lunch-time concerts at 1 pm, including piano recitals, duets and trios.

PARADISE BAR, 460 *New Cross Road*, SE14 (0181 692 1530). *New Cross underground*. Usually *once or twice* a *week*, there is no admission charge to see a wide range of bands in the *evenings* including dance, folk and rock.

PIE AND KILDERKIN, 7 *Devonshire Road*, SE23 (0181 699 2072). *Forest Hill BR*. r&b and rock are presented at this pub.

POLISH CULTURAL INSTITUTE, 34 *Portland Place*, W1 (0171 636 6032). *Open Mon–Wed, Fri 10 am–4 pm; Thur 10 am–8 pm. Regent's Park underground*. Telephone for details of Polish music concerts organised by the institute.

PRINCE OF ORANGE, 189 *Greenwich High Road*, SE10 (0181 858 7349). *Greenwich BR*. The *evening* music styles at this pub include soul, blues and jazz.

QUEEN'S PARK, *Kingswood Avenue*, NW6 (0181 969

5661). *Queen's Park underground. Sunday* bandstand concerts *Aug/Sept* typically ranging from jazz and swing to Caribbean and brass.

REGENT'S PARK, NW1 *(0171 486 7905). Regent's Park/ Camden Town underground.* From *May* to *late August* there is live cafeteria music, weekend bandstand concerts and occasional musical recitals.

RICHMOND PARK, *Holly Lodge, Richmond, Surrey (0181 948 3209). Richmond BR/underground.* From *late June* to *early September* there is light music performed most days at Pembroke Lodge at lunch-times and in the early afternoons.

ROYAL ACADEMY OF MUSIC, *Marylebone Road,* NW1 *(0171 873 7373). Baker Street underground.* There are about 10 orchestral concerts, chamber music performances and recitals each week during term-times, but tickets are required in advance for larger, particularly popular performances.

ROYAL COLLEGE OF MUSIC, *Kensington Church Street,* SW7 *(0171 591 4380). South Kensington underground.* About 5 performances each week during each term at the college or at various churches. Also occasional master-classes.

ROYAL FESTIVAL HALL, *South Bank Centre,* SE1 *(0171*

928 3002). *Waterloo BR/underground*. A wide range of live music in the foyer every day *12.30–2 pm*, including blues, country, jazz, classical, folk and music from other lands. On *Friday evenings, 5.15–6.45 pm* there's 'Commuter jazz', also in the foyer.

ROYAL NATIONAL THEATRE, *South Bank, SE1 (0171 633 0880). Embankment/Waterloo underground*. Early through to contemporary music from around the world including jazz, classical and folk performed in the foyer usually at *6 pm Mon–Fri* and *1 pm Sat*.

ST JAMES'S PARK, *The Mall, SW1 (0171 298 2100). St James's Park underground*. Bandstand concerts *daily* at *lunch-time* and in the *early evening* from the *end·of June* to the *end of August*.

STATION TAVERN, *41 Bramley Road, W10 (0171 727 4053). Latimer Road underground*. Folk, r&b and acoustic blues every evening at *9 pm* and *Sunday lunch-times*.

TRINITY COLLEGE OF MUSIC, *11 Mandeville Place, W1 (0171 935 5773). Bond Street underground*. In each 12-week term there are generally three or four performances of chamber music and recitals each week at the Barbirolli Lecture Hall or the Hinde Street Methodist church nearby.

TROLLEY STOP, *28 Stamford Road, N1 (0171 241 0581)*.

Dalston Kingsland BR. All kinds of bands at this pub, from pop, rock and blues to jazz, folk and funk.

TUFNELL PARK TAVERN, *162 Tufnell Park Road, N7 (0171 272 2078). Tufnell Park underground.* Modern jazz, vintage jazz, world jazz, jazz/funk and just plain old ordinary jazz plus blues and r&b a couple of evenings a week.

WATERLOW PARK, *Highgate High Street, N6 (0171 911 1648). Archway underground.* Jazz and light music in the *summer.*

WATERMANS ART CENTRE, *40 High Street, Brentford, TW8 (0181 847 5651). Gunnersbury BR/underground. Sunday lunch-time* music *from 12.30 pm* including jazz, funk, blues and rock.

WEST HAM PARK, *Upton Lane, E7 (0181 472 3584). Plaistow underground.* In the *summer* on *Sundays,* bandstand music.

WESTMINSTER ABBEY, *Dean's Yard, Parliament Square, SW1 (0171 222 5152). Westminster underground.* The choir can be appreciated at regular services (about 30 a week), and there's an organ recital at *5.45 pm* on *Sundays.*

WESTMINSTER LIBRARIES have a number of lunchtime and early evening classical music concerts throughout the year at MAIDA VALE LIBRARY, *Sutherland Avenue, W9 (0171 798 3659) Maida Vale underground;* MARYLEBONE LIBRARY, *Marylebone Road, NW1 (0171 798 1037) Baker Street underground;* PADDINGTON LIBRARY, *Porchester Road, W2 (0171 798 3696) Royal Oak underground;* VICTORIA LIBRARY, 160 Buckingham Palace Road, SW1 (0171 798 2187) Victoria BR/underground. Telephone the City of Westminster's Arts Officers on *0171 798 2498* for further details.

WHITE SWAN, *13 Blackheath Road, SE10 (0181 694 1160). New Cross BR/underground.* Free admission to see some *evening* rock bands at this south London pub.

NATIONAL TRUST

Lots of people must feel that the admission charges the public has to pay to enter many National Trust properties (which are there for the enjoyment of the nation anyway) are pretty steep – a family visit can easily reach £15. The result is that much of the population cannot afford to pay a visit.

Despite the entry fees, the National Trust reminds us regularly that often the properties do not earn the money required for their upkeep. At present it says that four out of five of its historic houses run at a loss. This must seem hard to believe by anyone who has visited a property in the summer when at times it can appear that the whole county has hit on the same idea at the same time, where the shop (selling identical merchandise to that sold in every other Trust shop) is overflowing with customers, and where there are long queues for the restaurant.

If you escape without being press-ganged into taking out membership you're lucky. Join in busy August and it doesn't take long to realise that there's little time to enjoy membership privileges until the following spring as a large proportion of the properties are closed in autumn and winter.

Every year the National Trust *(36 Queen Anne's Gate, SW1, 0171 222 9251)* sets aside a day when it allows all visitors free admission to many of its properties. In 1996 the planned free entry day is *11 September* (unconfirmed at time of going to press). Leaflets with more details about the day are available from the Trust from the Spring.

The Trust looks after about 1000 ancient monuments, over 200 historic houses, 160 gardens and 25 industrial monuments (such as mines) throughout England, Wales and Northern Ireland. It also protects over 590,000 acres of countryside and almost 550 miles of coast.

In the London area, the Trust owns a section of CHISLEHURST COMMON, 88 acres of PETTS WOOD and 245 acres of adjoining HAWKSWOOD in the Borough of Bromley, 53 acres of EAST SHEEN COMMON, Richmond-upon-Thames, and a nature reserve at SELS-

DON WOOD, south-east of Croydon. All can be visited throughout the year.

Of its 11 buildings around London, these are free all year:

BLEWCOAT SCHOOL, *23 Caxton Street, SW1 (0171 222 2877). Open Mon–Fri 10 am–5.30 pm, Thur until 7 pm. St James's Park underground*. Entry to the School, built in 1709, is free because this is the National Trust's London information centre and shop.

Likewise, THE GEORGE INN, *77 Borough High Street, SE1 (0171 407 2056), open daily during licensing hours, London Bridge underground*, allows free entry as it is run as a Whitbread pub. Appearing in Dickens' *Little Dorrit*, it is the only remaining galleried coaching inn in London, and was built in 1676.

THE ROMAN BATH, *5 Strand Lane, WC2; Temple/ Embankment underground*. The remains of a bath, restored in the 17th century, and which may be Roman, is visible through a window from the pathway.

Entry is free to the formal Stuart gardens and water meadows of HAM HOUSE, *Ham, Richmond, Surrey (0181 940 1950), open Sat–Thur 10.30 am–6 pm or dusk if earlier, Richmond underground*, and to the landscaped park and pleasure grounds of OSTERLEY PARK,

*Isleworth, Middlesex (0181 560 3918), open daily
9 am–7.30 pm or sunset if earlier. Osterley underground.*

MORDEN HALL PARK, *Morden Hall Road, Morden,
Surrey (0181 648 1845). Morden underground.* Has waterways from the river Wandle, a tree-lined avenue,
wildlife-rich meadowland, marshland and woodland as
well as a riverside walk and an information room with
a permanent display on the history of the estate. Old
estate workshops house local craftspeople carrying out
traditional trades like furniture restoration, wood-turn-
ing and stained glass design and restoration, and their
work is on display. A city farm is adjacent.

NATURE RESERVES AND OPEN SPACES OF PARTICULAR WILDLIFE INTEREST

London is extremely lucky that a number of nature
reserves exist within its boundaries despite all the
damage humans have heaped upon the region. Lucky
for us, but also very fortunate for the surprising variety
of wildlife able to take refuge at these places.

Although London would not seem an obvious choice
for wildlife, it has some advantages over the countryside.
Cities are on the whole warmer than the surrounding
areas, the concentration of people means that there is
more opportunity for wildlife to scavenge food, and
there is far less use of pesticides.

Large numbers of birds visit London's resevoirs and gravel pits, a huge variety of plant species abound, fish are tentatively returning to a purer Thames, and habitually rural animals like foxes are in abundance.

There are a number of wholly artificial nature reserves, such as the William Curtis Ecological Park and Lavender Pond Nature Park. These are an attempt to make up for the open space lost each year to new estates, motorways or roads.

Of course, every open space in London not blessed with the title 'nature reserve' is also home to some wildlife, so a few of the better of these sites are included too.

A word of warning: if the last time you picked up a nature book was as a child, and you can't tell a hedgehog from a wart-hog, it may be a good idea to read up on the subject again before visiting one of the reserves. If you don't know exactly what to look for and the best time of year to do it, some of the reserves – especially the smaller ones – can be disappointing at first glance.

If you want further information about nature reserves, telephone the LONDON WILDLIFE TRUST on 0171 278 6612. They also require volunteers to help with conservation tasks, which could be anything from reed-, tree- and hedge-planting to the creation of wildflower meadows. THE LOWER LEA PROJECT (0181 983 1121), the TOWER HAMLETS ENVIRONMENT TRUST (0171 377 0481) and THE BRITISH TRUST FOR CONSERVATION VOLUNTEERS (0171 278 4293) also need volunteers for conservation work. Refreshments may be provided, and it may be possible for volunteers' expenses to be paid.

ALEXANDRA PARK, *Wood Green, N22. Alexandra Palace BR.* The park has woodland, dense scrub, meadow grassland and a pond sustaining plants, insects and wildfowl. From *Alexandra Palace* to both *Highgate* and *Queen's Woods* at *Cranley Gardens, N10* runs THE PARKLAND WALK, with woodland, grassland and scrub at a disused railway line. There's another section from *Highgate underground station (Holmesdale Road, N6)* to *Finsbury Park, N4.*

BARNES COMMON, *Rocks Lane, Barnes SW13. Barnes BR.* Plants, insects, mammals and birds.

BATTERSEA PARK NATURE RESERVE, *Carriage Drive East, SW11. Battersea Park BR.* Nature trails in 'The Meadow' and 'The Wilderness'. There's a leaflet about a tree trail (available from the Pump House Information Centre or ring *(0181 871 6372)*, introducing some of the park's 3000 trees.

BECKENHAM PLACE PARK, *Beckenham Hill Road, SE6. Beckenham Hill BR.* Sixty acres of ancient woodland, a swamp, river and pond.

BENHILL ROAD NATURE GARDEN, *Camberwell SE5.*

Denmark Hill BR. This former prefab site of grass and trees has wild plants, insects (including moths and butterflies) and pond-life.

BRAMLEY BANK, *entrance off Broadcombe, Croydon. South Croydon BR*. Impressive woodland with a big pond, heath and grassland.

BRENT RESERVOIR, *Welsh Harp, The Hyde, West Hendon, NW9. Hendon BR*. Open water with beds of reed and bulrush.

CAMLEY STREET NATURAL PARK, *12 Camley Street, NW1. King's Cross underground/Camden Road BR. Usually open Sat–Thur, ring 0171 833 2311 for further details*. A former canalside coal depot with a variety of habitats that has been internationally acclaimed. Despite being just a couple of acres, the park has a pond, flower-beds, woodland, meadows, a wildlife garden and marshland. Summer play scheme for children.

CANNON HILL COMMON, *Cannon Hill Lane, SW20. Access restricted, ring 0171 278 6612 for details. South Merton BR*. A section of woodland in the centre of the common that is a haven for woodland birds.

THE CHASE, *Dagenham Road, Dagenham. Dagenham East underground*. Of their many sites, this is the London Wildlife Trust's largest reserve.

COLDFALL WOOD, *Crichton Avenue, N10. East Finchley underground.* Thirty-five acres of ancient woodland.

COOMBE WOOD, *between Robin Hood Way and Henley Drive, SW15. Ring for details of access, 0171 278 6612. Raynes Park BR.* Copious woodland flowers and butterflies.

COVERT WAY FIELD, *Covert Way, Hadley Wood, Barnet. Hadley Wood BR.* Scrub, grassland and coppice.

CRANE PARK ISLAND, *Crane Park, Twickenham, Middlesex. Witton BR.* A 4-acre island reached by bridge with nature trails.

DEVONSHIRE ROAD NATURE RESERVE, *Devonshire Road, SE23. Forest Hill BR. Open Sat 2–4 pm.* Nature trail.

DOT HILL, *Dot Hill Road, Plumstead, SE18. Plumstead BR.* Woodland and meadow.

DULWICH UPPER WOOD NATURE PARK, *Farquar Road, SE19. Crystal Palace BR.*

EAST HAM NATURE RESERVE, *Norman Road, E6 (0181 470 4525). Open Mon–Fri 9 am–5 pm, Sat and Sun 2 pm–5 pm (closes at dusk in winter). Visitor centre Sat and Sun 2 pm–5 pm. East Ham underground.* Ten acres of derelict Norman churchyard provide a home for nearly 50 types of wild birds, a number of plants and animals (including foxes, owls, kestrels and pheasants), and more than 20 butterfly species that can be discovered via several nature trails. The interpretative centre has a small display and staff to answer questions. Occasional workshops, open days and other events.

EPPING FOREST, *Chingford Plain, Rangers Road, Chingford, E4. Chingford BR*. Six thousand acres of ancient wood have 150 ponds and rich grassland, many bird species, a herd of black fallow deer and a 12-mile crescent of trees and grass.

FOX WOOD, *Fox Lane, off Hillcrest Road, W5. Hangar Lane underground*. Woodland and small wild flower meadows by Hangar Hill Park, with trail.

FRYENT COUNTRY PARK, *Fryent Way, Kingsbury, NW9. Wembley Park underground*. Get back to nature by helping the Friends of Fryent Country Park and Barn Hill Conservation Group with a variety of conservation projects. Call *0181 206 0492* for details.

GILLESPIE ROAD OPEN SPACE, *Gillespie Road, Highbury, N5. Arsenal underground*. A nature park on old railway sidings with grassland, scrub and a pond.

GREVILLE PLACE, *Greville Place, NW6. Access by ringing*

0171 278 6612. Kilburn Park underground. A large garden in the 1920s, this woodland is rich in plant life with breeding birds.

GUNNERSBURY TRIANGLE, *Bollo Lane, W3. Open most days, ring 0181 747 3881 for details. Chiswick Park underground.* Wood, pond, marsh and meadow.

HAINAULT FOREST COUNTRY PARK, *Fox Burrows, Romford Road, Chigwell. Chadwell Heath BR.* There's woodland, scrub and grassland within this former royal hunting forest.

HAMSTEAD HEATH, *NW1 and NW3. Hampstead underground.* Around Ken Wood is woodland, a wild flower meadow, grassland and scrub. Areas of Hampstead Heath have been designated Sites of Special Scientific Interest by English Nature because of their outstanding natural history and geological interest.

HANWELL SPRINGS, *Church Road, W7. Access by arrangement, ring 0171 278 6612 for details. Hanwell BR.* Situated near some of the best of Ealing's open spaces, the Springs are home to lots of birds.

HYDE PARK, *W1, W2, SW7. Hyde Park Corner/Marble Arch underground.* Woodland, water-fowl on the Serpentine, and The Meadow, a haven for butterflies, as well as a bird sanctuary.

JOYDEN'S WOOD, *Cocksure Lane, Sidcup. Bexley BR.* The wood has a nature trail.

KNIGHT'S HILL WOOD, *Knight's Hill,* SE27. *Access by arrangement, ring 0171 278 6612 for details. West Norwood BR.* Ancient woodland, the remnant of the Great North Wood.

LAMERTON STREET, *Deptford,* SE8. *Deptford BR.* Shrubs, a butterfly garden and pond.

LAVENDER POND NATURE PARK, *Lavender Road, off Rotherhithe Street,* SE16. *Rotherhithe underground.* The pond is home to various fish, dragon-flies and water birds.

LESNES ABBEY WOOD, *Abbey Road, Belvedere. Abbey Wood BR.* A Victorian pond, fossil pit, and lots of wild flowers, weasels, fungi and birds.

LITTEN NATURE RESERVE, *Oldfield Lane South, Greenford. Greenford BR and underground.* Ponds, woodland, thickets and grassland are home to various plants and animals.

MILL HILL, *Dean's Lane, Edgware. Telephone 0171 278 6612 for access details.* An old railway line that is now a wildlife corridor for woodland birds.

NEW CROSS GATE CUTTINGS, *Vesta Road, New Cross, SE14. Open Sun 2–5 pm.* Good bird-watching on this woodland, grass and scrub.

NUNHEAD CEMETERY, *Linden Grove, Peckham, SE15. Nunhead BR.* There are over 100 plant species amongst the woodland and grassland of this 19th-century cemetery.

OLD FORD ISLAND, *off Wick Lane, E3. Access by arrangement, telephone 0171 278 6612. Hackney Wick BR.* An open grassland reserve surrounded by scrub on the River Lee.

OXLEAS WOODS, *Shooters Hill, SE18. Falconwood BR.* This 8000-year-old woodland is home to voles, shrews, foxes, badgers, over 30 species of breeding bird and of tree and shrub, over 100 species of flowering plant and of butterfly and moth, over 200 species of beetle and wild fungus. The perfect spot to put a motorway, as was recently proposed.

RAILWAY FIELDS NATURE PARK, *opposite Haringey Green Lanes Station, N4 (0181 348 6005 for access details). Manor House underground.* There are meadows, woods, a pond and an environment centre with ecological information.

RICHMOND PARK, *Surrey, TW10. Kingston BR.* The

varied landscape of hills, woodland, and grassland abounds in wildlife, including over 600 red and fallow deer.

SELSDON WOOD, *Court Wood Lane, Selsdon, Croydon. Hayes BR*. Woodland, wetland, grassland pasture and a bird sanctuary.

STAINES RESERVOIR, *Stanwell Moor Road, Staines, Middlesex TW18. Hampton BR. Visitors must keep to the public footpath through the central causeway*. A site of Special Scientific Interest and a must for bird-watchers: a winter count recorded an impressive 4000 tufted duck.

STAVE HILL ECOLOGICAL PARK, *Timber Road, Rotherhithe, SE16. Rotherhithe BR*. A variety of natural environments encourage the rich wildlife.

SYDENHAM HILL WOOD, *entrance on Crescent Wood Road, off Sydenham Hill, SE26. Sydenham Hill BR*. Ancient and recent woodland with rich birdlife, unusual grasses and flowers.

TEN ACRE WOOD, *Charville Lane, North Hayes, UB4. Ruislip Gardens underground*. Oak woodland with flower-rich meadows and scrub.

THAMESIDE, *River Road, Creekmouth, Barking, Upney underground*. A lagoon, dykes and grassland.

TOWER HAMLETS CEMETERY PARK, *Southern Grove, E3. Mile End underground*. An overgrown Victorian cemetery transformed into a nature reserve (complete with tombs). Tree trail.

TRENT COUNTRY PARK, *Cockfosters Road, Barnet, Herts. Cockfosters underground*. This country park has over 400 acres with nature trails and an abundance of small wildlife in the woods. There's also a large farm. At the entrance opposite Cockfosters underground station, there's a ¾-mile woodland trail for blind people with messages in braille. Why can't such ideas be commonplace?

TUMP 53, *Bentham Road, Thamesmead, SE28. Abbey Wood BR*. Water, reed-beds, meadow and scrub.

WALTHAMSTOW MARSHES, *Spring Hill, Clapton, E5. Clapton BR*. The only remaining ancient grassland in the Lea Valley, with nearly 400 plant species recorded.

THE WARREN, *Crockenhill Road, Orpington. St Mary Cray BR*. Woodland, pond and marsh.

WILLIAM CURTIS ECOLOGICAL PARK, *16 Vine Lane, Tooley Street, SE1. London Bridge BR and underground*. A wealth of plants, birds and pond-life.

WIMBLEDON COMMON, *Parkside, Wimbledon, SW19.*

Southfields underground. Animals here include badgers, lizards, grass snakes and butterflies and there's rich birdlife on the ponds.

OPERA

THE BIG SCREEN IN THE COVENT GARDEN PIAZZA, *WC2, (0171 304 4000), Covent Garden underground*, is an occasional event where the Royal Opera House relays a free live performance to up to 6000 people standing outside in the Piazza. Just as well it's free – the price for a box with four seats in the Opera House can top £1000 for some performances.

Opera often features in the BROADGATE ARENA SUMMER ENTERTAINMENTS, *Broadgate Centre, Eldon Street, EC2 (0171 588 6565), Liverpool Street BR/underground, from May to September Mon–Fri 12.30–2 pm.*

The two-week COVENT GARDEN FESTIVAL OF OPERA AND THE MUSICAL ARTS, *(0181 944 9467/0171 240 0560), held in May, Covent Garden underground*, typically has mini-operas and an opera troupe performing in Covent Garden shops and bars.

PAPER

Many printers are often overwhelmed with off-cuts of paper and card they will never use, or which are too small in quantity or size for them to use, and therefore they will often gladly off-load some on to you.

PARKS AND OPEN SPACES

ABNEY PARK CEMETERY, *Stoke Newington High Street, N16 (0171 275 7557/9443). Open daily Apr–Sept 9 am–5.30 pm, Oct–Mar 9 am–3.30 pm. Stoke Newington BR*. A mature wildlife-rich mixed woodland.

ALEXANDRA PALACE AND PARK, *Wood Green, N22 (0181 365 2121). Wood Green underground/Alexandra Palace BR*. Wander around the Victorian 'Ally Pally' and its 200-acre grounds, and there are panoramic views, and a small animal enclosure, children's playground, conservation area and boating lake. There are children's shows and workshops in the summer.

AVERY HILL PARK, *Avery Hill Road, SE9 (0181 850 3217). Falconwood BR*. Though not particularly beautiful, this has a covered Winter Gardens *(open daily 10 am–noon, 1–4 pm)* with many species of tropical and temperate plants, a collection second only to the Royal Botanical Gardens at Kew.

BATTERSEA PARK, *Queenstown Road*, SW8 *(0181 871 7530)*. *Sloane Square underground/Battersea Park BR.* Bordered on one side by the river – and views across the water to Chelsea – there's a lot packed into the 200 acres here, including the Japanese Peace Pagoda, a herb garden, the tranquil Old English Garden, an art gallery, a big adventure playground for 5–16 year olds, a deer enclosure, lakes, tree trails and nature trails. Maps, brochures and other information is available from the Park office to the left of the Albert Bridge entrance, and also the Pump House, which has an interactive video on the park's history.

BISHOP'S PARK AND FULHAM PALACE GROUNDS, *Bishop's Avenue, Fulham Palace Road, SW6. Putney Bridge underground.* This was once the biggest moated site in England, but unfortunately the moat has been filled in. Still, you can stroll around the charming herb garden and its Tudor gateway.

BLACKHEATH, SE3 *(0181 305 1807) Blackheath BR.* The 170 acres are rich in history: the Danes camped here in 1011, and James I introduced golf to England here. Greenwich Park is on one side, unspoilt Blackheath Village on the other. There are two ponds, one used for boating at the weekend. An architectural gem, The Paragon, is off *South Row, SE3*.

BUSHY PARK, *Hampton Court Road, Middlesex, TW12 (0181 979 1586). Hampton Wick BR*. North of Hampton Court Palace, this Royal Park of 1099 acres has deer and a children's playground but is best known for the large Waterhouse Woodland Gardens and grand Chestnut Avenue. A children's play programme is organised in the summer.

CALTHORPE PROJECT COMMUNITY GARDEN, *258–274 Gray's Inn Road, WC1 (0171 837 8019). King's Cross BR/underground*. A relaxing retreat.

CHISWICK HOUSE GARDENS, *Burlington Lane, W4 (0181 995 0508/5390). Turnham Green underground*. Although there is a charge to enter the neo-classical villa, the wooded, 60-acre gardens are free to all. There are statues, temples, a lake and an information centre with details of park trails and a display about the garden's history.

CLAPHAM COMMON, *SW4. Clapham Common underground*. A welcome expanse of green (with ponds and a playground) within a large concentration of residential streets.

CLAYBURY WOODS, *entrance via Claybury Hospital, off*

Manor Road, Woodford Green. Woodford underground.
Lots of ancient woodland with an old orchard.

CORAM'S FIELDS, *93 Guildford Street, WC1 (0171 837
6138). Russell Square underground.* Although only a few
acres, there's a paddling pool, an animal enclosure and
playground equipment. Adults only admitted if accompanied by a child.

CROBHAM HURST, *Upper Selsdon Road, South Croydon.
South Croydon BR.* Unspoilt woodland.

CRYSTAL PALACE PARK, *Sydenham, SE19 (0181 778
7148). Crystal Palace BR.* In the park is a maze, a
children's play area, a tiny museum about the huge
Victorian glasshouse, Crystal Palace, which was installed
here but later destroyed by fire, and even a collection of
full-scale models of dinosaurs, which although hardly
Jurassic Park, is surreal all the same.

DULWICH PARK, *College Road, SE21 (0171 525 1554).
North or West Dulwich BR.* A Victorian park of 75 acres.

EPPING FOREST, *Essex (0181 508 0028) Epping/Lough-
ton underground.* This gigantic, ancient forest (over 6000
acres plus an extra 2000 acres acquired over the years to
protect the forest from development) is never more than
a mile from a road yet it is simple to get lost here.
Genuine countryside, with much of the area designated

a Site of Special Scientific Interest. There are regular organised two-hour walks every four to six weeks. About 500 deer roam in the forest and deer sanctuary and there are over 360 rare plant and animal species present.

FINSBURY PARK, *N4 (0181 808 2625). Finsbury Park underground.* A Victorian park with playgrounds and an adventure playground.

FRYENT COUNTRY PARK, *Fryent Way, Kingsbury, NW9 (0181 900 5659). Wembley Park underground.* The park is 260 acres of unspoilt countryside with nature walks and a wildlife area.

GLADSTONE PARK, *Dollis Hill Lane, NW10 (0181 900 5659). Dollis Hill underground.* This 90-acre park was named after William Gladstone, who regularly visited the park's magnificent Dollis Hill House. There's an arboretum housing hundreds of plants and trees from around the world, an art gallery, a children's playground, a wildlife area and an old walled garden.

GOLDERS HILL PARK, *North End Road, NW11 (0181 455 5183). Golders Green underground.* A beautiful walled garden and pond plus a good selection of animal and bird enclosures. There are children's activities and live music in the summer.

GREEN PARK, *W1/SW1 (0171 930 1793)*. *Green Park underground*. So-called due to the absence of flowers, it also lacks a lake yet its mature trees and grassland are a tranquil retreat from the congested centre of town.

GREENWICH PARK, *SE10 (0181 858 2608)*. *Greenwich/Maze Hill BR*. Situated on a hill between Blackheath at the top and the River Thames at the bottom, this park was enclosed in 1433 by order of Henry VI. Successors Henry VIII and Elizabeth I found it a pleasing party venue. Deer were introduced in 1515 and a herd is still in residence in the 13-acre Wilderness. There's a pond with wildfowl, a children's playground, a flower garden and London's longest herbaceous border. There are excellent views, especially at the top of the hill by the Old Royal Observatory (with the meridian line of zero longitude passing through it) where the magnificent panorama takes in the National Maritime Museum (free admission to locals, as with the Observatory) and the Docklands, and (on a clear day) Tower Bridge and St Paul's Cathedral as well. The Observatory's big red ball drops at *1 pm* daily. The information centre at the St Mary's Gate entrance has displays about the history of the 183-acre park. In the summer there are various events such as band performances in the bandstand, open air theatre, café music, children's entertainment and a family day with various events.

HAMPSTEAD HEATH AND PARLIAMENT HILL, *NW3,*

*NW5 (0181 348 9908/0171 485 4491). Hampstead under-
ground.* Four miles from the centre of London are 791
acres of unspoilt heathland, great for walking, with
glorious views. There is kite flying on Parliament Hill
(with its splendid views of London) at the south end of
the heath, as well as a horse-riding circuit, organised
walks, the art collection at Kenwood, and even some
bathing ponds. There are Sunday afternoon band performances on the bandstands at Parliament Hill and
Golders Hill and evening Scottish Country Dancing
sessions in the summer. For children there are a
playground, an adventure playground, play activities for
under-fives (the One O'Clock Club), dog-free enclosures
with play equipment, and in Golders Hill a deer
enclosure and an animal enclosure with flamingoes and
a variety of birds and animals. In the summer there are
shows with clowns, puppets and magicians.

HAMPTON COURT PARK AND GARDENS, *Hampton
Court Road, East Mosely, Middlesex. (0181 781 9500).
Hampton Court BR.* Although admission to Wolsey's
riverside Hampton Court Palace is not free, it is to the
550 acres of deer-inhabited parkland and the formal
gardens, which are well worth visiting in their own
right. The Great Vine, planted in 1768, is supposed to
be the oldest in the world.

HIGHGATE WOOD, *Muswell Hill Road, N6 (0181 444
6129). Highgate underground.* Seventy acres of ancient

woodland with a good children's playground. On the other side of Muswell Hill Road is QUEEN'S WOOD, a smaller but quieter patch of ancient woodland.

HOLLAND PARK, *Illchester Place, Kensington W8 (0171 602 9483). Holland Park underground.* A peacock lawn, rose gardens, a Japanese water garden, woodland, a wildlife pond, an ecology centre and an excellent adventure playground are all crammed into this pretty little park.

HORNIMAN GARDENS, *100 London Road, Forest Hill, SE23 (0181 699 2339/1872). Forest Hill BR.* Has a small children's zoo and a nature trail. If you like working outdoors, volunteers are needed for two hours on Sundays to help with 'ecological management tasks' (i.e. clearing up and repairing) on the Horniman Railway Trail – phone for details.

HYDE PARK, *W1, W2, SW7 (0171 298 2100). Hyde Park Corner/Marble Arch underground.* Peaceful despite being by some of the world's busiest streets. Although 50,000 people may visit it on a good summer day, there's enough space for everyone in the 350 acres of woods, grassland, river and gardens that originally was a Tudor hunting ground. There is a children's playground and a horse-riding track. Speaker's corner is in the north-east of the park, coming alive on Sunday mornings, when it becomes a venue for free and often barmy speech. There are Sunday afternoon concerts at the bandstand in the summer. Every day at approximately *10.30 am* the very colourful Household Cavalry can be seen riding through the park, going from Hyde Park Barracks to Buckingham Palace.

KENSINGTON GARDENS, *W2, W8 (0171 724 2826)*. *Lancaster Gate/High Street Kensington underground*. A continuation of Hyde Park, yet this park strikes a different mood, and is particularly good for children. It has a flower walk, the Round Pond, kite flying, a children's playground, the Albert Memorial, the Serpentine Gallery and the Peter Pan statue. There are puppet shows in the summer.

KENSINGTON ROOF GARDENS, *99 Kensington High Street, W8 (0171 937 7994). Usually open 9 am–5 pm – ring first to check. Kensington High Street underground*. A hundred feet above the Kensington bustle and at over one and a half acres, these are the largest private roof gardens in Europe. There's an English woodland garden with lawns, trees and a stream flowing into a lake; the Tudor garden has restful courtyards and a fountain; and the formal Spanish garden even has a mock convent, palm trees and colourful tiles! The entrance is in Derry Street – take the lift to the top floor of Barker's department store.

LEE VALLEY PARK, *Marsh Lane, N17. Northumberland*

Park BR. Stretches from the East End of London to Ware in Hertfordshire.

LESNES ABBEY WOODS, *Abbey Road, Belvedere, Kent (0181 312 9717). Abbey Wood BR.* Named after the 12-century abbey whose remains are within this 200-acre wood, there's a wealth of wild flowers, birds and a fossil bed. BOSTALL HEATH and its wood adjoin, adding an extra 150 acres of green space.

OSTERLEY PARK, *Isleworth, Middlesex (0181 560 3918). Osterley underground.* Although there is a charge to enter the manor house, there is extensive landscaped parkland with beautiful lakes and some 16th-century stables.

OXLEAS WOODS, *Shooters Hill, SE18. Falconwood BR.* This 8000-year-old woodland is adjacent to Shepher-dleas, Jack and Castle Woods, Eltham and Woolwich Commons and Eltham and Avery Hill Parks – a massive area of green space.

PEAR WOOD, *Wood Lane, Stanmore. Stanmore underground.* Ancient woodland.

PRIMROSE HILL, *NW3 (0171 486 7905). Chalk Farm/ Camden Town underground.* Separated from Regent's Park by a busy road and London Zoo, this 61-acre grassy hill has a children's playground, an outdoor gymnasium, and at the top of the hill one of London's six protected viewpoints.

QUEEN'S PARK, *Kingswood Avenue,* NW6 *(0181 969 5661) Queen's Park underground.* A small park but welcome in an area somewhat lacking in green space. There is a petanque rink and for children there is a playground, a paddling pool and a pet's corner. The summer holidays bring childrens' entertainers such as clowns and jugglers as well as bouncy castles and play schemes with supervised activities. There are also Sunday bandstand concerts in the late summer.

REGENT'S PARK, *NW1 (0171 486 7905). Regent's Park/ Camden Town underground.* Surrounded on three sides by Nash terraces and by Regent's Canal on the fourth, the 300 acres here include three children's playgrounds, the beautiful Queen Mary's Rose Garden (best in June) and a lake rich in wildfowl. There's summer music in the bandstand and cafeteria, even occasional folk dancing, and children's activities during the summer season. If you're meeting someone here, it's best not to arrange to meet at one of the gates as there are about 40 of them.

RICHMOND PARK, *Holly Lodge, Richmond, Surrey (0181 948 3209). Richmond BR/underground.* The largest Royal park, being over 2500 acres (13 miles round the boundaries), which has hardly changed over the centuries.

Richmond Park is so well preserved, it remains more natural than many areas of countryside in Britain. It is big enough for every one of its two to three million annual visitors to find real peace and quiet. There are hundreds of red and fallow deer, badgers, foxes, lakes, woodland gardens, hills and grasslands, and great views. Despite its size, there's only one children's playground, but then it is not a 'statues and bandstands' kind of park. Still, in the summer light music is performed at Pembroke Lodge and there are children's events such as puppet shows, workshops and story-telling.

ROUNDWOOD PARK, *Harlesden Road, NW10 (0181 900 5659). Willesden Green underground.* An aviary, children's playground, floral displays and a wildlife area.

ST JAMES'S PARK, *The Mall, SW1 (0171 930 1793). St James's Park underground.* In the shadows of Buckingham Palace and other interesting and impressive buildings from the Tudor age to modern times, this beautiful but compact park has five acres of lake and a children's playground. There are bandstand concerts in the summer.

TRINITY SQUARE GARDENS, *Tower Hill, EC3. Tower Hill underground.* A war memorial to many merchant seamen lost serving their country. A little plaque near the main road marks the site of the execution of 125 people including Thomas Cromwell and Sir Thomas More.

VICTORIA PARK, *Old Ford Road, E3. Mile End underground*. A big, formal park with lakes, fountains, two playgrounds, a trim trail, a One O'Clock Club *(weekdays 1–4 pm)* for under–5s and their parents, goats, a herd of deer, and numerous events in the summer.

VICTORIA EMBANKMENT GARDENS, *Victoria Embankment, SW1, WC2. Charing Cross BR/underground*. There are many statues, beautiful flower-beds and a lily pond in these gardens by the Thames.

VICTORIA TOWER GARDENS, *Millbank, SW1. Westminster underground*. A quiet and scenic riverside garden with statues and a children's play area.

WATERLOW PARK, *Highgate High Street, N6 (0171 911 1542). Archway underground*. Expanses of water, rose gardens and a children's area are in this hilly park of 26 acres next to HIGHGATE CEMETERY.

WEST HAM PARK, *Upton Lane, E7 (0181 472 3584). Plaistow underground*. Seventy-seven acres with an adventure playground, children's playground and an impressive botanical collection within the gardens. The summer holidays bring childrens' entertainers such as clowns and jugglers as well as bouncy castles and play schemes with supervised activities. There are also Sunday bandstand concerts in the late summer.

WESTMINSTER ABBEY GARDENS, *Westminster Abbey, SW1*. *Westminster Underground*. This beautiful, restful site of over an acre has been the Abbey garden for 900 years, and has lawns, fine trees, a colourful rose garden and a monastic herb garden. All plants are labelled.

WIMBLEDON COMMON/PUTNEY HEATH, *SW19, SW15 (0181 788 7655)*. *Wimbledon BR/underground*. Massive open heath and woodland, stretching for almost two miles. There's a windmill and also pond areas full of birdlife.

PLAYGROUNDS

Many parks contain children's playgrounds, and a number are mentioned in the section on PARKS AND OPEN SPACES. (See also the section on ADVENTURE PLAYGROUNDS.) But if you wish to construct your own one, PLAYGROUNDS FOR FREE by Paul Hogan *(MIT Press)* is indispensable. Although published in 1974, it is still available from libraries and is a comprehensive guide to obtaining and utilising used and surplus materials in playground construction. It explains how to make playgrounds from cast-offs like bins, boxes, tyres and tubes.

POSTCARDS

LONDON CARDGUIDE LTD *(0171 494 2229)* have attractive postcards – 18 new designs each month – in racks placed at 70 (continually changing) restaurants and bars around London (as well as others in Edinburgh, Glasgow and Manchester) such as *Bar Italia, 22 Frith Street, W1 and Harvey Nichols' food hall, 109 Knightsbridge, SW1*. Advertisers are banned from showing the product or logo on the front of the card (which instantly increases their desirability), and can only use a small section of the back for their message, so there's always space for correspondence.

TIME OUT POSTCARD ADVERTISING *(0171 221 5462)* has racks of postcards at around 100 restaurants and bars in London (and another 130 elsewhere in the UK) but some of their cards, although often strikingly designed, have a relatively large amount of advertising on the reverse side.

PUBLICITY

HOW TO GET PUBLICITY FOR FREE, a book by David Northmore, *(Bloomsbury)* explains how anyone, whether amateur or professional, can get no-cost publicity at any level, from a community group wanting a

small announcement in the local rag through to a
national publicity campaign.

SIGHTSEEING AND PLACES OF
INTEREST

A collection of many of London's buildings and monuments of historical and architectural interest and other
major – or just plain interesting – sights:

ABNEY PARK CEMETERY, *Stoke Newington Church
Street, N16 (0171 275 7557/9443). Open daily Apr–Sept
9 am–5.30 pm; Oct–Mar 9 am–3.30 pm. Stoke Newington
BR.* An eery, peaceful Victorian Gothic cemetery.

AFRICA CENTRE, *38 King Street, WC2 (0171 836 1973).
Open Mon–Fri 9.30 am–5.30 pm; Sat 11 am–4 pm. Covent
Garden underground.* This 18th-century building is
devoted to African culture and politics. It houses a craft
shop, an exhibition space and a resource centre with
newspapers, magazines, journals and other sources of
information about Africa.

ALBERT MEMORIAL, *Kensington Gardens by Kensington
Gore, SW7. Gloucester Road/South Kensington underground.* Designed by Sir George Gilbert Scott and
completed in 1872, this ostentatious memorial to Queen
Victoria's consort is extraordinarily detailed Victoriana

in the Gothic tradition. Of the many carvings there are depictions of agriculture, manufacture, commerce and engineering and carvings representing Europe (a bull), Africa (a camel), America (a bison) and Asia (an elephant). If you also spot a can of Fosters it's not representing Australia but is some litter. During the last war the cross at the top of the memorial was blown off – and clumsily replaced the wrong way round. The memorial has had its fair share of critics: even contemporary Victorians called it an 'overgrown reliquary'. Over the road is the ROYAL ALBERT HALL, *Kensington Gore, sw7*, a magnificent red brick and terracotta auditorium topped by a splendid iron and glass dome.

AVERY HILL WINTER GARDEN, *Avery Hill Park, Avery Hill Road, se9 (0181 316 8991). Open daily 10 am–noon, 1–4 pm. Falconwood BR.* Hundreds of plant species in this domed glasshouse with cold, temperate and tropical greenhouses.

BANKS: London's grand and traditional private banks, conveniently located near each other, provide an interesting insight into London's past. The eldest, CHILD & CO., *1 Fleet Street, EC4 (0171 353 4080) Temple underground*, established in 1559, has a display of banking memorabilia, as does GOSLINGS at number *19 Fleet Street (open Mon–Fri 9.15 am–4.45 pm)*. HOARE'S, *37 Fleet Street (open Mon–Fri 9 am–4 pm)* is a particularly good example of a bank of long ago. Although you can hardly fail to miss the brash, modern façade of COUTTS & CO. *(440 Strand, WC2; 0171 753 1000; Charing Cross BR/underground)* each time you leave Charing Cross station, it too has a rich history going back to 1692, and is most well known for being the purveyor of the Queen's cashpoint card and other banking requirements. Telephone the archivist to arrange a tour of Coutts, covering over 300 years of the bank's history. Although he depricatingly described the historical displays as being 'a poor man's Bank of England Museum', you can get to see the boardroom with its splendid 18th-century hand-painted Chinese wallpaper and a replica 17th-century goldsmith's shop.

BLUE PLAQUES: These have been erected to commemorate the residences of famous people and today there are over 600. They include: ROBERT BADEN-POWELL, founder of the Scouting movement, *9 Hyde Park Gate, SW7;* JOHN LOGIE BAIRD, who demonstrated television in 1926 at *22 Frith Street, W1;* WILLIAM BLIGH, captain of the Bounty, *100 Lambeth Road, SE1;* THOMAS CARLYLE, historian and essayist, *24 Cheyne Row, SW3;* CHARLES DICKENS, novelist, *48 Doughty Street, WC1;* BENJAMIN DISRAELI, statesman born at *22 Theobalds Road, WC1;* SIR EDWARD ELGAR, composer, *51 Avonmore Road, W14;* GEORGE ELIOT, novelist, *4 Cheyne Walk, SW3;* BENJAMIN FRANKLIN, American statesman, *36 Craven Street, WC2;* WILLIAM GLADSTONE, statesman, *11 Carlton House Terrace, SW1;* GEORGE

FREDERIC HANDEL, musician, *25 Brook Street, W1;* DR SAMUEL JOHNSON, writer, *17 Gough Square, EC4;* RUDYARD KIPLING, writer, *43 Villiers Street, WC2;* GUGLIELMO MARCONI, wireless inventor, *71 Hereford Road, W2;* KARL MARX, philosopher, *28 Dean Street, W1;* WOLFGANG AMADEUS MOZART, composer, *180 Ebury Street, SW1;* SIR ISAAC NEWTON, scientist, *87 Jermyn Street, SW1;* FLORENCE NIGHTINGALE, nurse, *10 South Street, W1;* SAMUEL PEPYS, diarist, *12–14 Buckingham Street, WC2;* DANTE ROSETTI, artist and poet, *110 Hallam Street, W1;* CAPTAIN ROBERT SCOTT, Antarctic explorer, *56 Oakley Street, SW3;* BRAM STOKER, novelist, *18 St Leonard's Terrace, SW3;* MARK TWAIN, writer, *23 Tedworth Square, SW3;* RALPH VAUGHAN WILLIAMS, composer, *10 Hanover Terrace, NW1;* JAMES WHISTLER, artist, *96 Cheyne Walk, SW3;* WILLIAM WILBERFORCE, abolisher of slavery, *44 Cadogan Place, SW1;* OSCAR WILDE, dramatist, *34 Tite Street, SW3;* SIR CHRISTOPHER WREN, architect, *49 Bankside, SE1.*

BROMPTON CEMETERY, *Finborough Road, SW10 (0171 352 1201). Open daily 8.30 am–dusk. West Brompton underground.* Catacombs by the main entrance welcome visitors to the final resting place of suffragette Emmeline Pankhurst amongst others.

BUILDING CENTRE, *26 Store Street, WC1 (0171 637 1022). Open Mon–Fri 9.30 am–5.30 pm, Sat 10 am–1 pm. Tottenham Court Road/Goodge Street underground.* Exhibitions and information concerning all aspects of the building industry including architecture, restoration, interior design and construction. It's a good source of inspiration if you need ideas for improving your home. There are examples including kitchens and bathrooms as well as new innovations and materials such as tiles and windows.

CLEOPATRA'S NEEDLE, *Victoria Embankment, WC2. Embankment underground*. Presented to the British in 1819 by the Turkish Viceroy in Egypt, this 3500-year-old obelisk wasn't installed for another 59 years. A twin is in Central Park, New York.

CLOCKS: London sure has some interesting timepieces. Of course there's the elaborate clock tower of the Palace of Westminster (the Houses of Parliament) at *Parliament Square, SW1 (Westminster underground)*, popularly known as BIG BEN. It is particularly impressive at night when the clock-face is lit up. A close-up visit, including a walk behind the huge clock-face, is by application to your MP, although there may be a long wait to get on a tour. Strictly speaking, 'Big Ben' is not the name for the clock but the huge bell that produces that famous ring. But there are also clocks that do more than just tell the time; they put on a show. NEAL'S YARD WHOLEFOOD WAREHOUSE in *Shorts Gardens, WC2 (Covent Garden underground)*, has an inventive clock where the minute hand is a tube gradually filling with water until, on the hour, bells ring and the water tips out from watering cans onto the flowers. Before a redesign, it soaked passers by too. The FORTNUM AND MASON CLOCK, *181 Piccadilly, W1 (Piccadilly Circus underground)* springs into life on the hour when models of Mr Fortnum and Mr Mason meet and bow to each other. The Eton school anthem follows, and then the shopkeepers disappear. SELFRIDGES, *400 Oxford Street, W1 (Bond Street/Marble Arch underground)* has a fine art deco clock at the main entrance, and the SWISS CENTRE CLOCK, *Leicester Square, W1 (Piccadilly Circus/Leicester Square underground)* plays tunes on a glockenspiel to a procession of alpine animals at *noon, 6 pm, 7 pm and 8 pm* and at additional times at weekends. If you're still in need of a fix of timekeeping equipment, you can't do better than a visit to the CLOCKMAKERS' COMPANY MUSEUM, *The Clockroom, Guildhall Library, Aldermanbury, EC2 (0171 606 3030). Open May–Sept daily 10 am–5 pm, Oct–Apr Mon–Sat 10 am–5 pm. Bank/Moorgate underground.* Hundreds of exhibits here illustrate 500 years of timekeeping. Try and visit on the hour, at noon if possible.

COLLEGE OF ARMS, *Queen Victoria Street, EC4 (0171 248 2762). Open Mon–Fri 10 am–4 pm. Bank underground.* This recently restored impressive 17th-century building is HQ of the world of heraldry and has some relevant exhibits.

COVENT GARDEN, *WC2 (0171 836 9136). Covent Garden*

underground. There's always a lot happening around the market-place, with many colourful stalls and shops as well as buskers, street entertainers and street theatre including clowns, acrobats, magicians and fire-eaters around the piazza. They've been auditioned, so the standard is generally very high

CROSBY HALL, *Cheyne Walk, SW3. Sloane Square underground*. Built between 1466 and 1475, this great hall, home of wool merchant Sir John Crosby, was moved from Bishopsgate. Shakespeare, Sir Thomas More and Richard III stayed here. The pannelled hall, with hammer-beam roof, can often be viewed on *Saturday* and *Sunday afternoons*.

CROSSNESS PUMPING STATION, *Belvedere Road, SE2 (01689 832290/0181 303 6723). Tours by arrangement one Sunday and one Tuesday each month at 2 pm. Donation requested. Abbey Wood underground*. The tour is of the old works, which contains four of the largest steam engines in the world.

DAILY EXPRESS BUILDING, *121–128 Fleet Street, EC4. Blackfriars BR/underground*. An excellent example of art deco architecture, completed in 1932.

DOWNING STREET, *W1. Westminster underground*. Number 10 has been the Prime Minister's London residence since 1735, and number 11 is the home of the

Chancellor of the Exchequer. Yet this sight has probably been of more interest to metalwork enthusiasts than those interested in politics ever since huge protective gates closing off the street were installed by Margaret Thatcher in the 1980s.

EAST LONDON MOSQUE, *84–98 Whitechapel Road*, E1 *(0171 247 1357). Open daily 9 am–9 pm. Whitechapel underground.* A huge red-brick building blending modern design with traditional Middle Eastern themes. At *1.25 pm* on Fridays the Jumma ceremony is attended by about 3000 local Bangladeshi.

ECOLOGY CENTRE, *45 Shelton Street*, WC2 *(0171 379 4324). Open Mon–Sat 10 am–6 pm. Covent Garden underground.* Shrine to all things green, there's an exhibition space, library and information centre as well as occasional events.

FLAXMAN GALLERY, *Central Dome, University College, Gower Street*, WC1 *(0171 387 7050 ext 7793). Open during term-times Mon–Fri 9.30 am–6.30 pm, Sat 9.30 am–4.15 pm; in vacation Mon–Fri 9.30 am–5 pm. Identification required. Warren Street/Goodge Street underground.* Plaster casts by neo-classicist John Flaxman (1755–1826) are embedded in the walls of the gallery, which is within the college library. There's also a statue by Flaxman of St Michael.

GOLDERS GREEN CREMATORIUM, *Hoop Lane, NW11* *(0181 455 2374). Open daily summer 9 am–7 pm; winter 9 am–5 pm. Golders Green underground.* Over a quarter of a million people have been cremated here since 1902, including Marc Bolan, Peter Sellers, Alexander Fleming, T. S. Eliot and Kipling – Rudyard, not Mr.. Also in Hoop Lane is a JEWISH CEMETERY *open Sun–Fri 8.30 am–5 pm.*

GRESHAM COLLEGE, *Barnard's Inn Hall, EC1 (0171 831 0575). Open Mon–Fri 9.30 am–5 pm. Chancery Lane underground.* Telephone to arrange an appointment to see the beautiful centuries-old wood-panelled hall with its illuminated windows in this unusual college founded by City merchant Sir Thomas Gresham in 1597 and which to this day puts on interesting lectures for the general public.

GUILDHALL, *Gresham Street, EC2 (0171 332 1460). Open May–Sept daily 10 am–5 pm; Oct–Apr Mon–Sat 10 am–5 pm; guided tours by arrangement with the Keeper's Office. Bank underground.* Originally built 1411 and the centre of the City's local government. Only the walls of the 152 x 40-foot Great Hall, crypt and porch survive from the medieval building which was greatly damaged in the Great Fire and the Blitz. The Lord Mayor and Sheriffs are elected here, the centre of many traditional ceremonies. Visitors can attend the ceremony-clad meetings of the Lord Mayor's Court of Common Council every *third Thursday except in August* (ring for more details).

THE HIVE, *53 Webbs Road, SW11 (0171 924 6233). Open Mon–Sat 10 am–6 pm. Clapham South underground/ Clapham Junction BR*. Solely devoted to bees and honey, this fascinating shop has a glass observation hive built into the wall where you can watch over 20,000 bees at work. The owners would appreciate it if you didn't break the glass. There are various bee artefacts around the shop including a wasp nest and there's a 10-minute taped commentary available to talk you through these. You can also often watch honey and royal-jelly-based cosmetics being prepared and beeswax candles being rolled and dipped. There are leaflets and other information available, as well as honey samples to try.

HOUSE OF ST BARNABAS-IN-SOHO, *1 Greek Street, W1 (0171 437 1894). Open Wed 2.30–4.15 pm; Thur 11.30 am–12.30 pm for short guided tour. Donation appreciated. Tottenham Court Road underground*. This charming Georgian mansion built *c.* 1746 has been home to a charity for homeless women since 1862 and provides an insight into a pre-depraved Soho. The tour covers the work of the charity, but visitors also get to see the record rooms and Council Chamber with all their interior decorations preserved including beautiful rococo plasterwork and chandeliers. The courtyard, where Dickens based Dr Alexander Manette's house in *A Tale of Two Cities*, and a little Byzantine-style chapel are also visited. If you would like to go on a full tour lasting around an hour, write requesting an appointment.

THE INNS OF COURT, *Holborn*. London's barristers work from the four Inns (or medieval colleges): Gray's Inn, Lincoln's Inn, Inner Temple and Middle Temple. All allow public access to parts of their peaceful grounds, the best times usually being *mid-morning* or *mid-afternoon* on *weekdays*. Taking a tranquil walk around the Inns (or Honourable Societies of Barristers) is to take a big step back in history as wig and gown-clad lawyers pass by against a backdrop of beautiful buildings dating back to medieval times. Despite extensive damage during World War II, GRAY'S INN has very restful gardens at *Gray's Inn Road, WC1 (0171 405 8164) Open Mon–Fri 10 am–4 pm. Holborn underground*. LINCOLN'S INN, *Lincoln's Inn Fields, WC2 (0171 405 1393), open Mon–Fri 9 am–6 pm, Holborn underground*, is the most beautiful and least altered of the four. Its well-manicured sweeping lawns were used for executions during the Reformation. Soak up the Oxbridge atmosphere. The best feature of MIDDLE TEMPLE, *Middle Temple Lane, EC4 (0171 353 4355)* is MIDDLE TEMPLE HALL. This is open most of the year *Mon–Fri 10 am–noon, 3–4.30 pm – ring and check Hall is not in use. Guided tours available. Temple underground*.

Completed in 1574, this is a good example of Tudor architecture with an incredible hammer-beam roof looking down on stained glass windows, a 29-foot table made from one oak tree and given by Elizabeth I, and various portraits and rich carvings around it. TEMPLE CHURCH, *King's Bench Walk, Inner Temple, EC4 (0171 353 1736)*. *Temple underground*. Modelled upon the Church of the Holy Sepulchre in Jerusalem, this is the only circular church in the capital and contains admirable stone effigies and a 13th-century penitent's cell.

KENSAL GREEN CEMETERY, *Harrow Road, W10 (0181 969 0152)*. *Open Mon–Sat 8.30 am–5 pm, Sun 10 am–5 pm. Kensal Green underground*. Opened in 1833, this was the first commercial Victorian graveyard. It boasts inhabitants including Trollope, Thackeray and Isambard Kingdom Brunel.

KING'S ROAD ANTIQUES: With ANTIQUARIUS indoor antique market at *135 King's Road, SW3 (Sloane Square underground)*, CHENIL GALLERIES at *181 King's Road* and the CHELSEA ANTIQUES MARKET, *245–253 King's Road*, and over 30 more antique dealers in *SW3* you can browse for hours. Opening times are usually *Mon–Sat 10 am–6 pm*.

LAMBETH PALACE, *Lambeth Palace Road, SE1 (0171 928 8282)*. *Waterloo BR/underground*. The imposing Tudor gateway loudly announces what has been the

London residence of the Archbishop of Canterbury since 1207. The chapel and sections of the Palace survive from that time and there is a Great Hall with a hammer-beam roof and a gloomy crypt. Write to the bookings department to arrange a tour; unfortunately it tends to be booked-up for some months.

LIVERY COMPANIES' HALLS, *around the City*. Livery companies, forerunners of trade unions and set up in medieval times, were guilds of craftsmen and traders (such as goldsmiths, fishmongers, vintners and ironmongers) whose duties now are little more than charitable, social and ceremonial. A limited number of tickets to view some of their grand, historic halls at various open days are available from the *City of London Information Centre, St Paul's Churchyard, EC4 (0171 606 3030)*, usually in *January or early February*.

MANSION HOUSE, *Walbrook Street, EC4 (0171 626 2500) Open Mon–Fri 9 am–5 pm. Mansion House/Bank underground*. The official residence of the Lord Mayor during his term in office, this opulent neo-classical building designed by George Dance in 1739 offers tours lasting just under an hour to groups of 14–40 from *Tues–Thur* at *11 am* and *2 pm* by appointment but unfortunately there is usually a waiting list of about six months. Still, you get to see the impressive Egyptian Hall, State Drawing Rooms and lots of gold plate.

MARBLE ARCH, *W1. Marble Arch underground.* Designed in 1828 by John Nash, Marble Arch was based on Rome's Arch of Constantine as a gateway to Buckingham Palace. It was moved from the Palace in 1851 to become the gateway to Hyde Park.

MARX MEMORIAL LIBRARY, *37–38 Clerkenwell Green, EC1 (0171 253 1485). Open to visitors Mon–Thur 1–6 pm. Farringdon underground.* Opened in 1933 to mark the 50th anniversary of Karl Marx's death, this contains a huge collection of political literature and memorabilia. A visit to this interesting building, built in 1737, should include a look at the room Lenin worked from at the turn of the century.

MERCHANT TAYLORS HALL, *30 Threadneedle Street, EC2 (0171 588 7606). Tours by appointment only: write to the Clerk of Merchant Taylors Hall. Bank/Monument underground.* This livery company has been in existence since 1327 and has remained in this street from 20 years after that. The beautiful rooms, painstakingly restored, include the main hall, the great kitchen and a library.

MICHELIN BUILDING, *Fulham Road, SW3. South Kensington underground.* This brash art deco building was decorated in 1911 with tiles, mosaics, stained glass and motoring murals by French artists.

MONUMENT, *Monument Street, EC2. Monument under-*

ground. At 202-foot high this is the world's highest free-standing stone column, a memorial to the Great Fire of 1666. It's height equals its distance from the baker's shop where the fire started.

MORDEN COLLEGE, *19 St Germans Place, SE3 (0181 858 3365). Open by appointment only. Blackheath/Westcombe Park BR.* Those with a particular interest in architecture or almshouses would appreciate the College, built in its own pleasant grounds in 1695 (possibly to Sir Christopher Wren's design) for 'poor merchants ... and such as have lost their estates by accidents, dangers and Perills of the Seas'. Nearby is an excellent crescent of Georgian mansions linked by Doric colonnades, THE PARAGON, overlooking Blackheath.

PICCADILLY CIRCUS, *SW1. Piccadilly Circus underground.* Alfred Gilbert's fountain statue, EROS, the first to be made from aluminium, is dwarfed by the array of gigantic neon advertisements.

QUEEN'S HOUSE, *Romney Road, SE10 (0181 858 4422). Open Mar–Oct: Mon–Sat noon–6 pm, Sun 2–6 pm; Nov–Feb: Mon–Sat 10 am–5 pm, Sun 2–5 pm. Greenwich/Maze Hill BR. Free admission to residents of Greenwich and Lewisham boroughs: either Greenwich's Greenwich Card or Lewisham's Vantage Card (available from local libraries) is required as proof.* Although located in the grounds of the NATIONAL MARITIME MUSEUM *(also free admission to local residents)* and linked to it by beautiful colonnades, many people overlook this, the first example of Renaissance architecture in Britain, an Inigo Jones building begun in 1616. Look out for the Tulip staircase, the country's earliest cantilevered spiral staircase.

ROYAL GEOGRAPHICAL SOCIETY, *Lowther Lane, Kensington Gore, SW7 (0171 589 5466). Open Mon–Fri 10 am–1 pm, 2–5 pm. South Kensington underground.* Only the main hall and map room of this society wholly concerned with exploration are open to the public (the library is too by appointment) but there are over 750,000 maps as well as paintings, expeditions reports and mementoes including those of Livingstone and Stanley.

ROYAL HOSPITAL, *Royal Hospital Road, SW3 (0171 730 5282). Open Mon–Sat 10 am–noon, 2–4 pm; Sun 2–4 pm. Sloane Square underground.* This elegant building with grassy courtyards was built for Charles II by Sir Christopher Wren (who has made more of a mark on London's construction industry than Wimpey and Barratt Homes put together) to house veteran soldiers, and it remains the home of the Chelsea Pensioners who wear distinctive scarlet or navy-blue uniforms. See the hospital chapel off the central courtyard and the grand Great Hall. There's also a small museum and the well kept, pretty grounds, RANELAGH GARDENS. The gardens are closed during the Chelsea Flower Show in *May*.

ROYAL NAVAL COLLEGE PAINTED HALL AND CHAPEL, *King William Walk, Greenwich* SE10 *(0181 858 2154). Open Fri–Wed 2.30–5 pm. Greenwich/Maze Hill BR.* This group of buildings, originally a naval hospital and becoming a college in 1873, were designed by Webb (in the 17th century), Wren (in the 18th century) as well as Hawksmoor, Ripley and Vanbrugh. The Chapel, with its ornate painted ceiling, was rebuilt in the 18th century.

ST KATHERINE'S DOCK, E1 *(0171 488 2400). Tower Hill underground.* Stroll around the yachts, barges and a lighthouse ship at this marina of 19th-century buildings (largely restored) by the Tower of London. There's live music regularly during summer lunch-times.

ST PANCRAS STATION, *Euston Road,* NW1. *King's Cross underground.* Particularly striking on first sight, this is classic Victorian architecture in a Gothic style. The arch, spanning 240 feet, was an astonishing feat in the 1860s.

ST PAUL'S CATHEDRAL, *St Paul's Churchyard, Ludgate Hill,* EC4 *(0171 248 2705). Free admittance Mon–Sat after 4.30 pm but viewing restricted. St Paul's underground.* This masterpiece is rich in decoration inside and out. The largest and most famous City church, it was rebuilt by Wren after the Great Fire. Its outstanding dome towers over the City and would dominate London's skyline if it were not for Canary Wharf. Like Canary Wharf, the cathedral was disliked by many when first built. This is because it had no spire. The tombs of Lord Nelson and the Duke of Wellington are in the crypt.

SHOPS: Although most high streets outside central London are identikit, with the same old chain-store shop-fronts to be seen at whatever town you're in, the centre of the capital has some interesting shops. ALFRED DUNHILL, *30 Duke Street, SW1 (Piccadilly Circus/Green Park underground)* has on display about 200 of the company's collection of about 2500 pipes from around the world including an Eskimo slate pipe, an emu's foot pipe and a Chinese opium pipe. LIBERTY, *210–220 Regent Street, W1 (Piccadilly Circus/Oxford Circus underground)* really stands out, being an eye-catching mock-Tudor department store built in the 1920s from timbers from the Navy's last sailing ships. Nearby is the world's biggest toy shop (full of toys sporting some of the world's biggest price tags), HAMLEY'S at *188 Regent Street, W1.* FOYLES, *113–119 Charing Cross Road, WC2 (Tottenham Court Road underground)* is the biggest bookshop in the UK. There's the extravagance of *Bond Street* and *Old Bond Street, W1 (Bond Street/Green Park underground)* with grand auction houses rubbing shoulders with the likes of CARTIER and VERSACE, and the gold and bejewelled trinkets at ASPREY. SIMP-SON'S the outfitters at *203 Piccadilly, W1 (Piccadilly Circus underground)* has a fine modernist 1930s façade and at number *181* is the Queen's grocers, FORTNUM AND MASON, established in the 18th century. Fronted by magnificent Ionic columns, the huge Edwardian department store, SELFRIDGES, overshadows its location, *Oxford Street, W1 (Marble Arch/Bond Street underground)*. Tea suppliers TWININGS claim that their small shop at *216 Strand, WC2 (Temple underground)* dating from 1710, is the oldest in the capital to be selling the same goods and to be in the hands of the original owners. The history of the tea trade is illustrated. A visit to HARRODS, *Knightsbridge, SW1 (Knightsbridge underground)*, London's biggest and most famous store, is something of an experience, being a gigantic golden consumer palace. Don't miss the Food Halls.

SHOPPING ARCADES: BURLINGTON ARCADE, *off Piccadilly* and *Old Bond Street, W1. Piccadilly Circus/Green Park underground*. Built in 1819, London's longest and most celebrated shopping arcade of mahogany-fronted shops selling luxury goods is complete with two top-hatted, uniformed beadles to discourage anyone from lowering the tone by running, singing, humming or – horror of horrors – opening an umbrella in the Regency arcade. PICCADILLY ARCADE, *off Piccadilly*, is an Edwardian extension to the above and also has suitably grand traditional shops. THE ROYAL ARCADE, which connects *Albermarle Street* with *Old Bond Street*, *WI*, was built in 1879 and has high arched bays topped by a grand glass roof.

SHREE NATHJI SANATAN HINDU TEMPLE, *159 Whipps Cross Road, EII (0181 989 7539). Open daily 9 am–8 pm. Leytonstone underground*. A large temple with shrines to Krishna, Durga, Rama and Shiva.

SOUTHWARK CATHEDRAL, *Montague Close, SEI (0171 407 2939). Open daily 8 am–6 pm. London Bridge BR/ underground*. A fine Gothic building with an interesting mix of architectures, some parts dating from the 13th century. A tranquil retreat.

SPANIARD'S INN, *Spaniards Road, NW3 (0181 455 3276). Open Mon–Sat 11 am–11 pm, Sun noon–3 pm, 7–10.30 pm. Hampstead underground*. This oak-panelled pub built in 1585 has many literary and historic connections, and many interesting exhibits. Keats, Shelley and Byron were regulars and it's in Dickens' *Pickwick Papers*.

SPANISH AND PORTUGUESE SYNAGOGUE, *Heneage Lane, off Bevis Marks, EC3 (0171 626 1274). Open Sun–Wed 11.30 am–2 pm, Fri 11.30 am–12.30 pm. Aldgate/Liverpool Street underground*. Almost everything in this Wren-influenced building is original, including the furniture. Built by Jewish refugees in 1701, this beautifully decorated synagogue is the oldest in Britain. Telephone for a short tour *(donation requested)* which is usually arranged *Sun 11.45 am; Mon, Wed noon; Tues 11.30 am*.

SPEAKER'S CORNER, *north-east corner of Hyde Park, W2. Marble Arch underground*. Soap-box orators have ranted their eccentric or sometimes sensible views at this forum of free speech since 1872 and have included Winston Churchill, Karl Marx and George Bernard Shaw. Popular subjects nowadays are religion, political philosophies, vegetarianism, pacifism and the end of the world. It must be noted that there has been an increase in bigoted speakers or disruptive religious militants of late. It's busiest on *Sunday afternoons*.

STAPLE INN, *Holborn, WC1. Courtyard open Mon–Fri 8 am–8 pm. Chancery Lane underground*. An especially fine half-timbered building with overhanging gables built in 1586 that provides a rare glimpse of London before the Great Fire.

THAMES BARRIER, *Unity Way, Woolwich, SE18 (0181 854 1373). Charlton BR*. Although entry to the visitor centre is not free, you can easily appreciate this feat of engineering, with its 10 huge moveable steel gates, from the riverside. It is the largest barrier of its type in the world and is especially impressive when fully raised during the annual test (usually in early October, ring for the date and times). There's a pleasant riverside walk and a children's play area.

TOWER BRIDGE, *EC3 (0171 407 0922)*. *Tower Hill underground*. Made of steel but clad in stone to not look out of place next to the TOWER OF LONDON (one of London's most historic sites though not free to enter), the bridge is occasionally raised to allow big vessels through – ring to find out when.

TOWER BRIDGE PIAZZA, at *Butlers Wharf, Shad Thames, SE1 (0171 403 6604)*. *London Bridge BR/underground*. Has some interesting shops including 'Oils and Spices' which sells ... well, oils and spices. There are art galleries around the fountain sculpture *Waterfall 1991* and around this exhibit are scattered a walkman, harmonica, books and other items which on closer inspection are sculptured too – a harmless little tease or a pretentious load of old tosh? There's a good view of Tower Bridge off the piazza at the junction with Shad Thames and Horsleydown Lane, next to the Anchor Brewhouse (where John Courage purchased a small brewhouse in 1787) in this area of cobbled streets and wonderful river views. Nearby is HAY'S GALLERIA, *Tooley Street, SE1 (0171 403 4758)*, an elegant arcade of shops with an enormous glass atrium all in a Victorian style, and an interesting fountain sculpture, *The Navigators*.

TRAFALGAR SQUARE, *WC2 (Charing Cross BR/underground)*. The famous traffic island has at its centre possibly London's most well-known landmark, NELSON'S COLUMN. The 170 feet of 1840s Corinthian column and statue dominates the square, host to political demonstrations and New Year celebrations. There are lots of sights on or near Trafalgar Square including Admiralty Arch and The Mall, the National Gallery, St Martin-in-the-Fields and Whitehall, leading to the Palace of Westminster and Westminster Abbey.

TYBURN CONVENT, *8 Hyde Park Place, W2 (0171 723 7262). Guided tours of the shrine daily 10 am, 3.30 pm, 5.30 pm. Marble Arch underground*. The Benedictine nuns here, who may never leave the convent, have a shrine to the Tyburn martyrs, 105 Catholics executed during the Protestant Reformation. The building is near Marble Arch, which was London's principle public execution site from the twelfth to eighteenth centuries when it had a three-legged gibbet known as the Tyburn tree. There are various relics and pictures of the martyrs and a model of the tree in the shrine. There are occasional 'Monastic afternoons' featuring a talk with a slide show, tea, tour and vespers.

UNIVERSITY COLLEGE LONDON, *Gower Street, WC1 (0171 387 7050). Open Mon–Fri 9 am–5 pm. Euston Square/Russell Square/Goodge Street underground*. The Friends' Room can provide a map and leaflet making up a self-guided tour of this impressive neo-classical building, known as the godless college as it was founded for students who couldn't enter Oxford or Cambridge for being non-Anglican. THE COLLEGE EXHIBITION in the North Cloisters tells the story of the founding of the college and features famous staff and students of the past including Sir Stafford Cripps and Marie Stopes. In the South Cloisters of the main building is the skeleton of philosopher JEREMY BENTHAM (whose ideas inspired the founders of the college), displayed in a hermetically sealed mahogany case in his original clothing complete with a wax death mask. University College London also houses the PERCIVAL DAVID FOUNDATION OF CHINESE ART, the PETRIE MUSEUM OF EGYPTIAN ARCHAEOLOGY, the FLAXMAN GALLERY, the STRANG PRINT ROOM, the MUSEUM OF ZOOLOGY and a MAP LIBRARY, all mentioned elsewhere in this book.

WESLEY'S CHAPEL, *49 City Road, EC1 (0171 253 2262). Open daily 10 am–6 pm except during services. Old Street/Moorgate underground.* The chapel and tomb of John Wesley, father of Methodism, are open gratis to the public in 'this acre of Christian heritage', mainly Georgian, that includes seven historic buildings, two chapels, two courtyards, two museums, two pulpits and organs, and a statue of Wesley. Directly opposite is BUNHILL FIELDS, *City Road, EC1 (0181 472 3584)*, once a plague pit and then a burial ground for over 120,000 bodies that include moss-covered headstones of Daniel Defoe, John Bunyan and William Blake. The northern section is a peaceful garden.

WESTMINSTER ABBEY, *Dean's Yard, Parliament Square, SW1 (0171 222 5152). All free Wed 6–7.45 pm; otherwise only nave and cloisters free, open Mon, Tues, Thur–Sat 7.30 am–6 pm, Wed 7.30 am–7.45 pm and between services on Sun. The library is open May–Sept Wed 11 am–3 pm. Also College Garden open Apr–Sept: Tues, Thur 10 am– 6 pm; Oct–Mar: Tues, Thur 10 am–4 pm. Donation suggested. Westminster underground.* Since 1066, the church for British royal weddings, coronations, and burials. The magnificent architecture holds tombs to many kings and queens and memorials to many famous and great people including Chaucer and Dickens. The herb and flower gardens in the 900-year old College Garden, over an acre in size, are a restful retreat from the bustle of central London. Dean's Yard and the tranquil Cloisters are worth visiting as is nearby LITTLE SANCTUARY, *SW1*, a secluded grassed square. It is best to visit the Abbey out of the tourist season or late morning mid-week when it is quieter. There are nearly 30 services a week at the Abbey.

WESTMINSTER CATHEDRAL, *Ashley Place, Victoria Street, SW1 (0171 834 7452). Open daily 7 am–8 pm. Victoria BR/underground.* Head office of the Roman Catholic Church (UK division), this is an imposing building with a vast interior built in 1903 but following an early Christian Byzantine style. It has the widest nave in England at 60 feet. There are Eric Gill sculptures, and columns and mosaics made from many types of marble. Often forgotten, being off the usual tourist route, yet magnificent.

WESTMINSTER HALL, *Parliament Square, SW1 (0171 219 4273). Contact your MP to arrange a tour, which are every morning Parliament sits.* Built in 1099, this is the oldest remaining part of Westminster and has been the scene of many important historical events including the indictment and deposing of Edward II and the sentencing to death of Anne Boleyn. The hall has a 14th-century cantilever roof, the earliest and largest in the world.

WHITEFRIAR'S CRYPT, *Freshfields, 65 Fleet Street, EC4 (0171 936 4000). Open by appointment; contact the premises' manager. Blackfriars underground.* Discovered by building developers in 1987, this is part of a medieval Carmelite monastery. Although you can visit the crypt by arrangement with the law firm resident in the building, it can clearly be seen from the street by looking over the railings into the basement, or walking down the steps on the left.

WHITTINGTON STONE, *Highgate Hill, N19. Archway underground.* It's not worth chartering a plane from

Scotland to see this monument, installed in 1821 to mark the spot where famous, 15th-century mayor Dick Whittington was supposed to have heard the bells summoning him to 'turn again', but it's worth a visit if you're in the area.

SIGHTSEEING AFTER DARK

Many of London's buildings and monuments look even more striking than in the day when lit up at night. A good place to start is the bridge over the lake in *St James's Park*, SW1, which is open until dusk. From here you can see BUCKINGHAM PALACE floodlit over the lake.

THE MALL, SW1, bordering the park, is one of London's finest thoroughfares at night having the Palace at one end and Admiralty Arch at the other, and fine Regency Nash terraces in between. ADMIRALTY ARCH is a huge Edwardian trio of arches dominating the south-west corner of Trafalgar Square.

Passing through the huge arches you come to the illuminated fountains, statues and impressive buildings of TRAFALGAR SQUARE, SW1, including an impressively floodlit ST MARTIN-IN-THE-FIELDS, one of London's grandest churches. WHITEHALL, SW1, on the right, is lined by well lit, generally 18th-century buildings and at the end of this wide, elegant road is PARLIAMENT SQUARE with *the* HOUSES OF PARLIA-MENT and WESTMINSTER ABBEY, *SW1*, the oldest and most eminent of London's great churches. A floodlit BIG BEN towers over WESTMINSTER BRIDGE, *SW1/SE1*, built in 1862 and over 80 foot wide.

A walk along VICTORIA EMBANKMENT, *SW1, WC2 and EC4* takes you from Westminster Bridge to Blackfriars Bridge and passes permanently moored ships and various prominent buildings. On the way HUNGERFORD FOOT BRIDGE, *WC2/SE1*, provides an unforgettable panorama of the river from Cleopatra's Needle to the Festival Hall at the South Bank Centre and slightly further on, WATERLOO BRIDGE, *WC2/SE1*, has particularly good views of the illuminated river, taking in Westminster and the City.

The riverside walk at BANKSIDE, *SE1*, by Southwark Bridge, has good views of the City and St Paul's. Pepys watched the City burn in 1666 from an alehouse here, and the flames must have looked rather pretty, especially when reflected upon the water.

Other bridges worthy of a visit include the triple-arched ALBERT BRIDGE, *SW3/SW11*, whose elaborate Victorian ironwork is enhanced by hundreds of white lights. The nearby CHELSEA BRIDGE, *SW1/SW8*, is also well lit. Opened in 1894, majestic TOWER BRIDGE, *E1/SE1*, was built incorporating Gothic towers so that it harmonizes with the Tower of London nearby; this has led many people to assume it was built in the Middle Ages.

MARBLE ARCH, *W1*, and the huge WELLINGTON ARCH, *Hyde Park Corner, SW1*, are particularly impressive at night. The latter houses a police station.

Both ST PAUL'S CATHEDRAL, *Ludgate Hill, EC4*, considered Christopher Wren's masterpiece desite being widely disliked when it opened for business in 1710, and WESTMINSTER CATHEDRAL, *Ashley Place, SW1*, the imposing Byzantine-style principal Catholic Church, warrant a night-time glimpse.

Even at night you can't escape CANARY WHARF TOWER, *West India Docks, Isle of Dogs, E14*. At two miles high (okay, an exaggeration; to be more accurate you'd need over twelve towers on top of each other to reach two miles), it sometimes seems you can only avoid a view of this, the tallest building in Britain, by entering a windowless room. The TELECOM TOWER, *Cleveland Street, W1*, is a bit more modest.

If you're around the OLD KENT ROAD, *SE1* at *2 am* on a weekend, this is when the pubs close in the area. The resulting chaos is quite a colourful spectacle to observe and invariably includes flashing blue police lights, the projection of vomit of every hue, and messy GBH-style blood sports.

Other areas not to be missed at night include boisterous COVENT GARDEN, *WC2;* the Las-Vegas-style nocturnal version of HARRODS (hope they're on economy-seven), *Knightsbridge, SW7;* the space-station LLOYDS BUILD-ING, *Leadenhall Street, EC3;* wild SOHO, *W1;* the TOWER OF LONDON, *Tower Hill, EC3;* and of course, PICCA-DILLY CIRCUS, *W1.*

SOFTBALL

Softball, a form of baseball that originated in America in the 1930s, remains a popular summer recreation in the capital. London's top players can be seen in action from *mid-May to mid-August every Sunday*, all day from *10 am* at *the University of Westminster Sports Ground, Grove Park, Cavendish Road, W4. Chiswick BR*. Details are available from Bob Fromer of the National Softball Federation on *01886 884204.*

SUN-TANNING

THE TANNING SHOP, with 36 branches around London, offers a trial sun-tanning session for free. Branches: *35 Albermarle Street, W1 (0171 493 1822); The*

Arches, off Villiers Street, WC2 (0171 930 7384); 1 Brampton Park Road, N22 (0171 889 8808); 9 Budge Row, Cannon Street, EC4 (0171 329 8074); 5 Bute Street, SW7 (0171 584 3983); 4 Campden Hill Road, W8 (0171 938 1932); 10 Chichester Rents, Chancery Lane, WC2 (0171 430 1159); 7 Clarence Street, Richmond, Surrey (0181 332 9731); 3b Colonade Walk, SW1 (0171 932 0513); 88 College Road, Harrow, Middlesex (0181 863 2644); 35 Crutched Friars, EC3 (0171 265 0332); 5 Edgewarebury Lane, Edgeware, Middlesex (0181 905 3219); Euston Station, NW1 (0171 383 4260); 482 Fulham Road, SW6 (0171 385 8397); 37 Golden Square, W1 (0171 437 4980); 166 High Street, Barnet (0181 449 8884); 32 High Street, Croydon (0181 688 4171); 254 Lavender Hill, SW11 (0171 228 1382); Liverpool Street Station, EC2 (0171 375 3081); 30 London Road, Twickenham, Middlesex (0181 744 1831); 35 Ludgate Hill, EC4 (0171 236 0013); 27 The Mall, Bromley (0181 466 7996); 40 Mortimer Street, W1 (0171 636 6131); 10 New College Parade, Finchley Road, NW3 (0171 722 1569); 52 New Oxford Street, WC1 (0171 323 0623); 18b Odhams Walk, WC2 (0171 240 5932); 36 Palmer Street, SW1 (0171 976 7292); 151 Praed Street, W2 (0171 402 4856); 8 Putney High Street, SW15 (0181 780 2855); 21 St Thomas Street, SE1 (0171 403 9431); 239 Shepherd's Bush Road, W6 (0181 563 1407); 4 Turnberry Quay, Pepper Street, E14 (0171 418 0008); Waterglade Centre, Ealing Broadway, W5 (0181 840 2294); 110 Wigmore Street, W1 (0171 935 7075); 60 Wimbledon Hill Road, SW19 (0181 944 9724); 15 Windsor Street, Uxbridge,

Middlesex (01895 273622); 52 Wood Street, Kingston, Surrey (0181 546 4070).

SWIMMING

There's no charge to swim in the following open-air ponds, but since they are chlorine-free it is inadvisable to touch the slimy ground. Look out for anglers too. These ponds are deep and for competent swimmers only. Opening times can vary greatly around the year so check first.

HAMPSTEAD MIXED BATHING POND, *off East Heath Road, Hampstead NW3 (0171 485 4491/0171 435 2366). Open summer around 10am–4.30pm.* The pond is hidden by trees.

HIGHGATE MEN'S POND, *off Millfield Lane, Highgate N6 (0181 340 4044). Open summer around 6am–9pm, winter around 7am–3pm.* The summer sees men sunbathing naked by this pond, contravening an old heath regulation. A popular gay meeting place.

KENWOOD LADIES POND, *off Millfield Lane, Highgate, N6 (0181 348 1033/0181 340 5303). Open summer around 7am–9pm, winter around 7am–3pm.* This pond for women only has a changing hut and shower.

PARLIAMENT HILL LIDO, *off Gordon House Road, Kentish Town,* NW5 *(0171 485 3873). Open daily 7 am–9.30 am, doors close 9 am.* Mixed bathing.

TELEPHONE DIRECTORY ENQUIRIES

The standard charge for directory enquiries (dial *192*) and international directory enquiries (dial *153*) is waived for calls made from a public call-box.

TELEVISION AND RADIO SHOWS

Write (enclosing a stamped, addressed envelope) or ring for free tickets as far in advance as possible as some shows have huge waiting lists. You may have to wait for a year or two to see especially popular shows like *Blind Date* and *Noel's House Party*. Even so, you may be able to pick up tickets for some popular shows at very short notice.

Some shows have specific audience requirements, for example visitors to *Paul McKenna's Hypnotic Show* (Carlton) had to sign a form saying they were willing to be hypnotised.

Write for details of forthcoming shows, or state the show you would like to see, to the BBC TV *Ticket Unit, Room 301, Television Centre, Wood Lane, London* W12

7RJ *(0181 743 8000; recorded information and answering machine 0181 576 1227)*.

For LWT, CARLTON and other ITV shows write to *The Ticket Unit, London Television Centre, Upper Ground, London SE1 (0171 261 3971/0171 261 3447)*. The Duty Office at CARLTON TELEVISION (0171 240 4000) or CHANNEL 4 (0171 306 8333) can also give details of shows coming up.

Agents who provide audiences for production companies, like CLAPPERS LTD., *7 Stewards Close, Epping, Essex (0181 505 9596)* and INSPIRED PR *(0121 440 1633)* can put you on their free ticket lists.

Independent production companies like HAT TRICK (*Whose Line Is It Anyway?* etc) and Smith and Jones' TALKBACK place classified advertisements in publications such as *Time Out* and *Private Eye* when tickets are available.

Details of tickets for BBC RADIO SHOWS, to attend anything from music concerts to comedy programmes, are available from the *BBC Radio Ticket Unit, Broadcasting House, London W1A 4WW (0171 765 5243; recorded information and answering machine 0171 765 5858)*. Ask to join the BBC's mailing list to get up-to-date news, and telephone 0171 765 5858 for recorded information on current shows with tickets available.

Also, CAPITAL RADIO, (0171 608 6080) has summer roadshows around London, with live music from top bands and other entertainment.

THEATRE

BATTERSEA ARTS CENTRE (BAC), *Lavender Hill, SW11 (0171 223 2223). Open Mon 10 am–6 pm; Tues–Sat 10 am–10 pm; Sun noon–10 pm. Clapham Junction BR.* BAC continually presents an exciting and diverse range of theatre productions and other events. You can see them for free if you can spare some time in the evenings, joining the friendly Front of House team as a volunteer. Call *0171 223 6557* for details.

BUSHY PARK, *Hampton Court Road, Middlesex, TW12 (0181 979 1586). Hampton Wick BR.* The summer entertainment season often includes open air theatre performances, usually Shakespeare in July. Other open spaces in the Richmond Borough occasionally have summer theatre performances – ring the arts section on *0181 332 0534* for details.

GREENWICH PARK, *SE10 (0181 858 2608) Greenwich/ Maze Hill BR.* The summer entertainment season often includes open air theatre performances (usually Shakespeare in July) and theatre and puppet shows for children – ring for details.

GUILDHALL SCHOOL OF MUSIC AND DRAMA, *Silk Street, Barbican, EC2 (0171 628 2571). Barbican/Moorgate underground.* Matinées in the main house and all plays in the studio are free.

LYRIC THEATRE, *King Street, W6 (0181 741 2311). Open 10 am–7 pm (box office). Hammersmith underground.* The first performance of each of the Lyric's own productions (not staged by other theatre companies) is free to residents of Hammersmith and Fulham borough.

THEATRE MUSEUM, *Russell Street, WC2 (0171 836 2330) Open Tues–Sun 11 am–7 pm. Covent Garden underground.* The museum has play readings, usually of new works by British writers, one or two *Wednesdays* a month at around 5 pm.

TOURIST INFORMATION CENTRES

Most of these offices can provide a free map of central London and public transport plans as well as leaflets and advice. Few telephone numbers are given because the London Tourist Board, which oversees most London tourist information, has all but replaced facilities for personal telephone enquiries with premium rate pre-recorded telephone announcements giving basic general information commonly available elsewhere.

BLOOMSBURY, *35–36 Woburn Place, WC1. Open daily 7.30 am–7.30 pm. Russell Square underground.*

BRITISH TRAVEL CENTRE, *12 Regent Street, W1. Open Mon–Fri 9 am–6.30 pm; Sat, Sun 10 am–4 pm. Piccadilly Circus underground.*

CHELSEA INFORMATION OFFICE, *Old Town Hall, King's Road, SW3 (0171 352 1856). Open Mon–Fri 9 am–1 pm, 2–5 pm. Sloane Square underground.*

CITY OF LONDON INFORMATION CENTRE, *St Paul's Churchyard, EC4 (0171 606 3030). Open daily 9.30 am–5 pm. St Paul's underground.*

GREENWICH, *46 Greenwich Church Street, SE10 (0181 858 6376). Open daily 10.15 am–4.45 pm. Greenwich underground.*

HACKNEY MUSEUM TOURIST INFORMATION CENTRE, *Central Hall, Mare Street, E8 (0181 985 9055). Open Tues–Fri 10 am–12.30 pm, 1.30–5 pm; Sat 1.30–5 pm. Hackney Central BR.*

HARROW TOURIST INFORMATION CENTRE, *Civic Centre, Station Road, Harrow, Middlesex (0181 424 1103). Open Mon–Fri 9 am–5 pm. Harrow and Wealdstone BR.*

HEATHROW TERMINALS 1, 2 AND 3, *Underground Concourse, Heathrow Airport. Open daily 8.30 am–6 pm.*

HILLINGDON TOURIST INFORMATION CENTRE, *Central Library, High Street, Uxbridge, Middlesex (01895 250706). Open Mon, Tues, Thur 9.30 am–8 pm; Wed, Fri 9.30 am–5.30 pm; Sat 9.30 am–4 pm. Uxbridge underground.*

HOUNSLOW TOURIST INFORMATION CENTRE, *24 Treaty Centre, Hounslow, Middlesex (0181 572 8279). Open Mon–Sat 9.30 am–5.30 pm. Hounslow Central underground.*

ISLINGTON VISITOR CENTRE, *44 Duncan Street, N1 (0171 278 8787). Open Mon–Sat 10 am–5 pm. Angel underground.*

LEWISHAM, *199–201 Lewisham High Street, SE13 (0181 297 8317). Open Mon–Fri 10 am–5 pm. Lewisham BR.*

LIVERPOOL STREET, *Underground Station, EC2. Open Mon–Sat 9 am–4.30 pm; Sun 8.30–3.30 pm.*

LONDON DOCKLANDS VISITOR CENTRE, *3 Limeharbour, Isle of Dogs, E14 (0171 512 1111). Open Mon–Fri 9 am–6 pm; Sat 10 am–4.30 pm; Sun 9 am–4.30 pm. Crossharbour DLR.* Free maps and general information about the area as well as an exhibition and an audio-visual presentation.

REDBRIDGE TOURIST INFORMATION CENTRE, *Town Hall, 128–142 High Road, Ilford, IG1 (0181 478 3020). Open–Fri 9 am–5 pm. Ilford BR.*

RICHMOND, *Old Town Hall, Whittaker Avenue, Richmond, Surrey. Open Mon–Fri 10 am–6 pm; Sat 10 am–5 pm; and in the summer Sun 10.30 am–4 pm. Richmond BR/underground.*

SELFRIDGES, *Basement Services Arcade, Oxford Street, W1. Open Mon–Wed 9.30 am–7 pm; Thur, Fri 9.30 am–8pm; Sat 9.30 am–6.30 pm. Bond Street underground.*

TOWER HAMLETS TOURIST INFORMATION, *107a Commercial Street, E1 (0171 375 2549/512 4200) Open Mon–Fri 9.30 am–4.30 pm. Liverpool Street underground.*

TWICKENHAM TOURIST INFORMATION CENTRE, *Civic Centre, York Street, Twickenham, Middlesex (0181 891 7272). Open Mon–Fri 9 am–5 pm. Twickenham BR.*

VICTORIA STATION FORECOURT, *SW1. Open daily 8 am–7 pm.*

VALUATIONS

These auctioneers will value a wide range of antiques and other objects for you if you bring them along:

BONHAMS, *Montpelier Street, SW7 (0171 584 9161). Open Mon–Fri 9 am–4.30 pm. Knightsbridge underground.*

CHRISTIE'S, *8 King Street, SW1 (0171 839 9060). Open Mon 9 am–4.45 pm; Tues 9 am–8 pm; Wed–Fri 9 am–4.45 pm; Sun 2–4.30 pm. Green Park underground.*

PHILLIPS, *101 New Bond Street, W1 (0171 495 0225). Open Mon–Fri 8.30 am–5 pm. Bond Street underground.*

SOTHEBY'S, *34 New Bond Street, W1 (0171 493 8080). Open Mon–Fri 9 am–4.45 pm. Bond Street underground.*

VOLUNTEERING

The NATIONAL VOLUNTEERING HELPLINE on *0345 221133* (calls charged at local rate) can put you in touch with people who can help you become a volunteer.

WALKING IN LONDON

Most Londoners walk regularly – from work to home, from home to the shops – but walking as a pastime in London is so often overlooked. There is so much to see that it is difficult to take it all in. And when you are crammed into a packed commuter train, you just want to get home: a peaceful, leisurely walk is usually the last thing to be considered. A pity, as one of the best ways to get to know the city is on foot.

Of course, location is the important factor when planning a walk, and for that reason most of us would first consider destinations such as the Lake District, the Highlands of Scotland or the moors of Cornwall if we were going to reserve leisure time for walking.

It would seem ill-advised to instead select our polluted, congested and aggressive capital for some free hours to be spent on foot. Walking the Ridgeway in London means nothing more than going from commuter-hell railway station Hayes in the west to a boring Bromley playing field in the east, a somewhat disappointing experience when compared to its 85-mile counterpart situated on the North Wessex Downs, flowing into the Chilterns. Likewise, one can assume that the Pennine Way, off Cotswold Close in Bexleyheath, leaves much to be desired.

Yet even the most cursory glance at the *London A to Z* map shows that the capital can provide a wealth of walks, and even some peace and quiet for the prospective urban explorer. As Disraeli pointed out, London is a nation, not a city.

The areas around Westminster and the City are the original London, but as it grew it swallowed up the villages around it. Until well into the 19th century places like Richmond, Streatham and Islington were able to enjoy a separate existence. Maybe London will eventually become a *notion*, not a city, when it has expanded enough to cover the whole of the south east.

Britain's capital has the advantage of being suitable for walking. Walking is usually the fastest way to travel around the increasingly gridlocked city. From Leicester Square, for example, you can walk to Soho or Trafalgar Square in just a few minutes. Unlike Paris or Rome, cars actually stop for you. Unlike New York, the chances of being attacked are relatively remote in all but the most dubious of areas.

When on foot you notice the smallest architectural detail, a hidden courtyard, a little alley-way. There is probably more culture crammed into London than anywhere else in the world, and there is no better way to take in a bit of culture than by slowly walking around it. And a walk in London, however long, does not require the use of hiking boots, ropes and distress flares.

Even so, tarmac is somewhat harder on the feet than turf and the impure air can exhaust. The incessant noise and bustle in some locations can add to the stress. It's worth bearing in mind that inner-city areas, and especially the City, tend to be quieter at weekends while parks and gardens are emptier on weekdays.

Understanding the intricacies of an Ordnance Survey map is also a skill you will not require. The indexed *London A–Z Street Atlas* (published by Geographers' A–Z Map Co) is quite easy to comprehend – except by a recent minicab driver I used. Less detailed but free London maps are available from underground stations and the London Tourist Board.

There are even walks that are clearly signposted or which have waymarks. There are metal discs set in the pavement along the City of London's HERITAGE WALK. The $12\frac{3}{4}$-mile SILVER JUBILEE WALK is marked by a series of silver crowns in the pavement, and Parliament Square is a good place to start from. Free maps for these two are available from the CITY OF LONDON INFORMATION CENTRE, *St Paul's Churchyard, EC4 (0171 332 1456). Open Apr–Sept daily 9.30 am–5 pm; Oct–Mar Mon–Fri 9.30 am–5 pm, Sat 9.30 am–12.30 pm.*

THE LONDON WALL WALK, follows the course of the old city wall plaques. THE MUSEUM OF LONDON – *150 London Wall, EC2 (0171 600 3699), open 10 am–6 pm Tues–Sat, 2 pm–6 pm Sun* – can provide a map.

If your wish is for open space, Greater London has an enormous amount of it. Every Londoner is in walking distance of it, a unique situation. Not endless fields with nothing but a closed pub at the end of them

– like you'd find in the Lake District – but hundreds and hundreds of parks, public gardens, commons and meadows making up over 60 square miles of the metropolis. There are nearly 400 parks in London of more than 20 acres.

There's Hyde Park, which covers over 350 acres, and there are little patches of green like Embankment Gardens around Charing Cross, as well as many, many municipal open spaces that only the locals know about. Indeed, there are substantial pockets of green on almost every page of a London street atlas.

KENSINGTON GARDENS, HYDE PARK and ST JAMES'S PARK organise occasional guided walks featuring various aspects of their history, wildlife, gardens, plant life and personalities (for details telephone *0171 298 2100*), but attendance hasn't been too good of late, so these events may be curtailed.

The amount of parkland and open space owned by the 32 London boroughs varies enormously. Whilst Hillingdon owns well over 3,000 acres, Islington has about 175. Desperate to imply it is overflowing with lawns and gardens, the borough has the cheek to call a scrap of land off Upper Street 'Islington Green', despite it being barely bigger than a window box.

Henry James wrote over a hundred years ago: 'It takes London to put you in the way of a purely rustic walk from Notting Hill to Whitehall. You may traverse this immense distance – a most comprehensive diagonal – altogether on soft fine turf amid the song of birds, the bleat of lambs, the ripple of ponds and the rustle of innumerable trees'.

It is a miracle that one can still begin a walk from Queensway tube station, go through Kensington Gardens, then across Hyde Park and on to Green Park, and ending up in the south east corner of St James's Park near Parliament Square, with only one or two roads to navigate. Such a stroll must torture property developers as they dream of the marvellously profitable housing estates they could cram into that huge expanse of greenery.

Of course, when the London parks are empty you can find tranquillity but – perhaps this is due to the British reserve – in the height of summer you can sunbathe, lying on your back along with 10,000 others, yet still be quite alone.

The 39-mile signposted GREEN CHAIN WALK in south-east London links the banks of the River Thames with nearly 300 public and private spaces such as woods, parks and gardens. Free explanatory booklets and maps about the Walk are available from the planning departments of the London Boroughs it covers, namely BEXLEY *(0181 303 7777 ext 3210)*; BROMLEY *(0181 464 3333 ext 5743)*; GREENWICH *(0181 853 0077 ext 2259)*; and LEWISHAM *(0181 695 6000 ext 3463)* as well as THE SPORTS COUNCIL *(0181 778 8600)* and public libraries in the area.

You'd think that few people would rush to a sewage treatment works in search of a worthwhile walk. Yet

Thames Water is adamant that the CREEK TRAIL at their works in *Jenkins Lane, Beckton, Barking*, is 'one of the most important ecological locations within the London area'. The wildlife trail has been left in its natural state for 20 years, and has an abundance of reed-beds and grassland, and a variety of birds, plants, insects and other wildlife. Because times available for visiting are subject to tides, ring the works on *0181 507 4721* for further details.

Sewer enthusiasts will also appreciate THE GREEN-WAY at *Wick Lane, Bow, E3*, a four-mile path running on the top of Thames Water's Northern Outfall Sewer embankment, crossing several rivers but also unfortunately the A11, at which point local roads have to be used.

The four-and-a-half mile PARKLAND WALK from *Alexandra Palace* to both *Highgate* and *Queen's Woods* at *Cranley Gardens, N10*, and then *Highgate underground station (Holmesdale Road, N6)* to *Finsbury Park, N4*, is a good country-style walk along a disused railway line. At Croydon, the signposted DOWNLANDS CIRCULAR WALK starts at the main car park on *Ditches Lane*, a mile from Coulsdon South railway station: another easy 'country' walk.

Walking in the countryside proper in Britain often requires generous use of the car beforehand, as one goes in search of signs indicating public footpaths. Even when a footpath is discovered, it may not be suitable. On a recent walk I made outside London, the public footpath ended up in the middle of a golf course in full swing and although the sign indicated that ramblers were entitled to walk over the course, directly across the flight path of balls heading for hole 16, I doubt that many people were courageous or foolish enough to do so.

In London there are no trespassing problems as right of way is explicitly clear. For example, you could explore gigantic Richmond Park (2470 acres) which is next to Wimbledon Common (1140 acres). I mean, how much land do you require for a walk in London?

There are enjoyable waterside walks, the rivers and canals providing some refuge for London's wildlife. The paths are almost continuous, from Docklands in the east to Kingston in the west, on both north and south banks of the Thames. The southern side is generally quieter and less interrupted.

In the centre of town, a walk along the river from Tower Bridge to Parliament Square is to be recommended, as is the river path within Battersea Park. Chelsea Harbour, SW10, is a modern riverside development with a marina, and a agreeable location for a riverside walk. Medieval and modern times merge around the Thames at Wapping and Rotherhithe, whilst a stroll from the path on the southern side of Kew Bridge by Kew Green and ending up at Richmond Bridge is a particularly pretty, peaceful stretch.

An exploration of the area bordered by the Thames from Putney Bridge to Barnes Bridge can take in a couple of cemeteries, Barnes Common and over 80 acres of reservoir where numerous rare birds have been sighted. The Thames tow-path here can in theory be followed as far as Inglesham in Wiltshire, although continuous walking along the river becomes impossible after a few miles, and diversions are necessary.

Although walking the 23-mile tow-path of the River Lee takes you through some Hackney, Tottenham and Enfield industrial estates, there's a variety of country-side, wildlife and historic buildings and you can walk as far as Essex or Hertfordshire. Explore the Bow Back Rivers, starting at picturesque *Three Mills, Three Mills Lane, E3 (0181 983 1121), Bromley-By-Bow underground*, with a myriad of footpaths, tow-paths and river channels.

You could meet up with the Grand Union Canal at, for example, the tow-path underneath Wharf Road in Islington, by The Narrow Boat pub, walking past painted canal boats and not particularly talkative anglers, or alternatively join the canal at Regent's Park or Camden Lock. By following the tow-path from pretty Little Venice to the countryside in miniature that is Kensal Green All Souls' Cemetery, you soon reach the 200-acre Wormwood Scrubs, the largest area of greenery in the district. A leaflet, 'Explore London's Canals', is available from *British Waterways, Toll House, Delamere Terrace, Little Venice, W2 6ND* if you enclose an s.a.e.

Or why not go underwater? An amble past the

space-age architecture of the ludicrous Docklands development contrasts sharply with a stroll the quarter of a
mile through Greenwich Foot Tunnel near Island
Gardens station, a murky old subway built at the turn
of the century for dockers working in the West India
docks. It goes 60 feet down under the Thames, emerging at the other end at Greenwich (see Greenwich
walk that follows). Be sure to take in the magnificent
sight of Greenwich, which Wren believed to be the best
view in Europe, before entering the tunnel on the
eastern side.

London's charm is simpler to understand if the
metropolis is thought of as a cluster of villages. A walk
around districts such as Whitehall, Bloomsbury and
Chelsea or the villages of Hampstead, Wimbledon or
Dulwich reveals different sides of the character of this
great city.

Culture-rich walks abound, from the more grand
such as Mayfair, Old Chelsea, Covent Garden, Monument and Blackfriars, to the less grand but possibly
more lively such as New Cross, Notting Hill and
Stepney. Conveniently, many of London's famous sights
evolved near each other and therefore even the shortest
walk can take many of these in.

There are many organised guided walks on specialist
subjects (such as Dickens' London or Legal London),
typically meeting at an underground station. One firm
offers over 80 walks each week. They typically cost a
few pounds, so the only no-cost option is to walk

alongside the party once it has set off, if you have the nerve.

If you haven't, the RAMBLERS' ASSOCIATION HOT-LINE *(0171 370 6180)* gives information on their guided walks for the week. Or ask for a leaflet detailing the years' guided walks programme around the Epping Forest area organised by EPPING FOREST COUNTRY-CARE, on *01992 788203*. The COUNTRYSIDE HOTLINE *(0171 222 8000)* may be able to give advice about places of interest and where to walk. The LONDON WILDLIFE TRUST *(0171 278 6612)* organises guided walks with a wildlife theme. For guided walks along canals and other inland waterways, contact the INLAND WATERWAYS ASSOCIATION *(0171 586 2510)* which has details of two to four walks each month on *Wednesdays* at *6.30 pm and Sundays* at *2.30 pm*.

Hampstead Heath and the Old Hampstead Society organise walks (centring upon fungus, flora, butterflies, birds and other subjects) on HAMPSTEAD HEATH and the KENWOOD ESTATE on the *first Sunday of each month except January, starting at 10.30 am or 2.30 pm from Burgh House, Well Walk, Hampstead, NW3*. There are also children's walks in the Easter and Summer holidays. A voluntary donation is requested. Ring the organiser of the walks, David Watt *(0181 348 6932)* for further details.

There follow a few walks around London, but for more insight, anecdotes and historical detail visit your library to consult one of a number of books that are available on the subject. These typically feature about thirty different traipses around the same old places – almost always including the likes of Hampstead and 'poor man's Hampstead', i.e. Greenwich and Blackheath, as well as the obvious tourist trail routes, such as Westminster and the City.

Invariably, these books shove into the introduction Dr Samuel Johnson's remark: 'When a man is tired of London he is tired of life; for there is in London all that life can afford'. He's obviously never used the Circle line in the rush hour. Bored of their theme, such books are prone to the inclusion of walks around Windsor, Oxford, Cambridge and Stratford-upon-Avon and then tend to slap £9.99 on the back cover, if you please.

They vary from the lively, briefly informative LONDON WALKS by Tiffany Daneff *(published by Michael Joseph)*; a rather more detailed tome like LONDON WALKS (again) by Anton Powell *(Robson)*; the entertaining, such as A WALK ROUND LONDON'S PARKS by Hunter Davies *(Hamish Hamilton)*; or the rather more pedestrian COUNTRY WALKS AROUND LONDON by Leigh Hatts *(David and Charles)*. WALKING LONDON by Andrew Duncan *(New Holland)* is packed with interest but won't win the Booker Prize with the likes of 'Nearly Connecting Walks' as a subtitle or 'city walking is not like country walking' as an observation.

Other books include SLOW WALKS IN LONDON by Michael Leich *(Hodder and Stoughton)*; 3-D LONDON

(Nicholson); Susan Owen's DISCOVERING COUNTRY
WALKS IN SOUTH LONDON *(Shire)*; WATERSIDE
WALKS IN WEST LONDON by P. and C. Scott *(Spur-books)*; and LONDON WALKS (that bloody title again)
by Guy Williams *(Constable)*.

With such a wealth of walks possible, if you are in
the right frame of mind for it, walking in London can
be as rewarding as any transcontinental explorer's grand
and expensive leisure plans.

A CITY WALK

Leave Monument underground station at the Fish Street
Hill exit and then turn right to observe Wren's 202-foot
high great fluted Doric pillar, the Monument, the City's
memorial to the Great Fire of 1666. The panel at its
base tells its history. To walk its 311 steps up to a great
view of London is not free, costing £1, but it'd almost
certainly give you cardiac complications – which would
be tedious as the emergency phone has been removed.
Those suffering from vertigo would be glad to know
that the viewing platform has been caged in since 1842
as the authorities had to stop people falling off it.

By the Monument, in Monument Street, (and at many
other places around the City), are brown signs pointing
towards places of interest. At this spot alone they indicate routes to the Tower of London, a riverside walk,
Leadenhall Market, London Bridge and one of the City's
38 churches, so there are clearly endless things to do.

To continue the walk, turn left, down Monument Street past a wall plaque on the left explaining how the Great fire was started, and go left again up Botolph Lane. Half-way up the lane on the right is Botolph Alley. Go up this to Wren's St-Mary-at-Hill Church in Lovat Lane. The passage next to the church on the right (which a notice erected by the rector deems to be no right of way although hoards use it shamelessly) leads after another right and left into cobbled St Dunstan's Lane, where there's a Wren church tower and a beautiful public garden. At the other end of the garden turn left, up St Dunstan Hill, cross Great Tower Street and go up Mincing Lane, an historic trading street. On the right is Minster Court, a new development that is impressive if you like overgrown greenhouses, peculiar architecture and overblown statues of horses. At the end of the lane turn left down Fenchurch Street (making a detour on the way to St Margaret Pattens Church in Rood Lane on the left then up Lime Street on the right where you come to Lloyd's of London, the world's leading insurance market. The new Lloyd's tower, with its pipes and protrusions, is clearly a plumber's or air-conditioning duct salesman's ultimate fantasy.

At the end of Lime Street is a possible detour directly over the road, the Church of St Andrew Undershaft. If it's closed, at least you've got a better view of Lloyds. Returning to the end of Lime Street take a left turn into Leadenhall Street and you come to an enclosed market of iron and glass arcades, Leadenhall. Although Victorian, a market has been here since the 1300s. Return to and continue along Leadenhall Street, which becomes Cornhill, home of St Peter upon Cornhill Church. It is not open to the public except by prior arrangement although there is a quiet churchyard dedicated to the art of crazy paving, accessible via St Peter's Alley. At St Michael's Alley, also off Cornhill, is St Michael's Cornhill Church, and further down the alley can be found Jamaica Wine House, an olde worlde characterful pub on the site of London's first coffee house (1692) – jeans not allowed. Returning to Cornhill, go further down until it reveals a perfect spot for statue obsessives – three are on the right at a walkway known as Royal Exchange Buildings, and more around the magnificent pillared Royal Exchange building itself at the end of Cornhill. (Here another detour could be made to the Mayors' and City of London Court up Threadneedle Street).

By the Duke of Wellington monument (at the entrance of the Royal Exchange), a metal Silver Jubilee Walkway guidepost explains the view, which includes the Bank of England (windowless for security reasons) and its free museum, and the Mansion House, home of the Lord Mayor of London, built in 1753 – tours by appointment. Here there are markers on the pavement for the City's Heritage Walk.

Go up Princes Street, which is between Threadneedle Street and Poultry, and left into Lothbury and then Gresham Street to see Guildhall and on the right St Lawrence Jewry Church, rebuilt by Wren after the Great Fire of 1666, then gutted in World War II. Opposite the church, across Gresham Street is King Street. Go down it, then down Queen Street where you can detour to St Paul's Cathedral and St Mary Aldermay Church at the junction with Queen Victoria Street, or go left down Cannon Street at the end of Queen Street, where on the left Salters Hall Court houses peaceful St Swithin's Gardens and Abchurch Lane is graced by St Mary Abchurch Church. Continue along Cannon Street and you are back at Monument tube station.

A WESTMINSTER WALK

Starting at Westminster tube station, a walk around adjacent Parliament Square reveals the Houses of Parliament, the stunning Westminster Abbey and splendid St Margaret's Church plus statues including ones of Churchill, Disraeli, Palmerston and Major. Sorry, wrong about the last one.

Leave the square, going down Parliament Street, passing the Cenotaph war memorial in the centre of the road, more statues and Downing Street, which has housed the Prime Minister's London address since 1731. Moving further on, proceed up Whitehall past the Horse Guards (the Changing of the Guard ceremony is at *10 am* and *4 pm* on *Sundays; 11 am* and *4 pm other days*) and go down Horse Guards

Avenue on the right, with its magnificent architecture.

Turn left into part of restful Victoria Embankment Gardens, or left further down the avenue onto Victoria Embankment, to be beside the Thames. Before you reach Hungerford Bridge (which is shared by pedestrians as well as trains if you wish to look up or down river) turn left into Northumberland Avenue and then right into Northumberland Street. The Sherlock Holmes pub, despite a tendency for displaying pavement signs saying the likes of 'Watson the menu', houses author Conan Doyle's memorabilia and on the first floor an interesting recreation of Sherlock Holmes' study. Further on up the street is Trafalgar Square, one of London's most famous landmarks, with its centre-piece, the 170-foot high Nelson's Column (which took three years to build), and the National Gallery. The square was dedicated to Lord Nelson and named after his great victory, the Battle of Trafalgar.

Pass through the three huge arches ahead, Admiralty Arch, to The Mall, both national memorials to Queen Victoria. St James's, one of the most beautiful of the Royal parks, is on your left as you pass Horse Guards Road, opposite the Institute of Contemporary Arts and a statue of the Duke of York, a cut-price Nelson's Column.

Here you could make a detour further down the Mall to St James's Palace, which was the main Royal residence until George III moved to Buckingham

Palace. Next to the Palace is a large house with a
stuccoed façade, Clarence House, Queen Elizabeth II's
sort of granny flat and the home of the Queen Mother.
Beyond this is another impressive building, Lancaster
House, now used for state receptions. At the end of The
Mall, behind the gilded memorial to Queen Victoria in
the centre of the roundabout, is the Queen's London
home, Buckingham Palace, which is far bigger than it
looks, with state rooms stretching far back from the
frontage.

Returning to Horse Guards Road, walk across the
park to the lake in the centre. The park is the most
royal of the Royal parks – demonstrated by the view of
Buckingham Palace from the bridge over the lake.
Walk on through the thin park to the other side and
you will come to Birdcage Walk. Turn left along it.
Birdcage Walk becomes Great George Street, Parliament Square and Bridge Street and you are back at
Westminster underground station.

A WALK AROUND BLACKHEATH AND GREENWICH
Beginning at Blackheath railway station (where regular
trains from Charing Cross stop) turn left as you leave
the station, and go up Tranquil Vale, passing various
interesting shops that help give Blackheath its village
atmosphere – although there seems to be more than a
fair share of delicatessens, cafés, restaurants and estate
agents. When you reach the heath, there is some
beautiful 18th- 19th-century architecture to your left

and the 1857 Gothic All Saints Church to your right. Blackheath stretches out past the church, and Canary Wharf Tower is in the distance.

Walk to the end of Tranquil Vale to the small roundabout, beside the pond just before the Hare and Billet pub. Turn right, going down Duke Humphrey Road, across the heath (which is often busy with fairs, circuses, kite festivals and sports). At the end of this road, where there is a second pond, enter Greenwich Park, the oldest Royal Park, dating from 1433. Through the gates turn right, away from the tree-lined avenue, into the attractive fenced gardens, walking by the duck-stocked lake. At the other end of the lake, when you reach the expanse of lawn dotted with trees and flower-beds, turn left and walk through the gate. Head past the bandstand (in summer, there is music on Sundays) to the cafeteria and turn right to the end of the tree-lined avenue to enjoy a magnificent view by the statue of James Wolfe. To your left is Wren's Old Royal Observatory. Walk down the great slope Wolfe is looking towards (a worthwhile detour is a walk around the complex of majestic buildings just past the park's boundaries that make up the National Maritime Museum, including the central building, Inigo Jones' 1615 Queen's House). At the bottom, walk left and you will come to the lower main gates of the park. Leave these, walking straight on, down King William Walk, passing the Royal Naval College on the right and a weekend covered market on your left. You end up at the pier next to the Cutty Sark, the world's only surviving wool and tea clipper, built in 1869. In its shadow is the tiny vessel Francis Chichester achieved the first solo circumnavigation of the world in, the Gipsy Moth IV. Here you can follow a riverside path, or take a Thames boat to Westminster (around £5 for an adult single, although the invariably wildly inaccurate commentary provided by a crew member is free), or you could go to the domed entrance of the atmospheric foot tunnel opened in 1902 and walk under the Thames, emerging at the Isle of Dogs.

WORKING LONDON

AUCTIONS BONHAMS, *Montpelier Street, SW7 (0171 584 9161). Open Mon–Fri 9 am–4.30 pm. Knightsbridge underground;* CHRISTIE'S, *8 King Street, SW1 (0171 839 9060). Open Mon 9 am–4.45 pm, Tues 9 am–8 pm, Wed–Fri 9 am–4.45 pm, Sun 2–4.30 pm. Green Park underground;* PHILLIPS, *101 New Bond Street, W1 (0171 495 0225). Open Mon–Fri 8.30 am–5 pm. Bond Street underground;* SOTHEBY'S, *34 New Bond Street, W1 (0171 493 8080) Open Mon–Fri 9 am–4.30 pm. Bond Street underground.* With thousands of pounds rapidly changing hands during a sale, auction houses can be particularly exciting places. Just don't nod your head at the wrong moment. Sales vary enormously and could be for anything from costumes to clocks, coins to carpets.

CARS FORD MOTOR COMPANY, *Thames Avenue, Dagenham, Essex (0181 526 4570). Tours by appointment only Mon–Fri 9.30 am, 1.15 pm. Dagenham Heathway underground/Dagenham Dock BR.* Ring or write to *Factory Tours, Room 3/001*, at the above address to go on a 150–minute tour of the famous Dagenham works, which is 10 per cent larger than the City's square mile and is Europe's biggest engine plant. Prospective visitors are warned that there is a long waiting list to go on the tours (which over 40,000 people take each year) and that three and a half miles of walking is involved – but you do get complimentary refreshments at the end of it. You get to see the manufacturing process of a car including body stamping, robots welding, the paint process and fixing on axles, doors and seats. A museum containing vehicles of the past is also seen.

CIVIL LAW ROYAL COURTS OF JUSTICE, *Strand, WC2 (0171 936 6000). Open Mon–Fri 10 am–4 pm, under-16s not admitted. Temple underground.* Also known as 'the law courts', or the 'High Court', this massive neo-Gothic building holds the country's principal civil cases. Visit one of the 60 court rooms, during a fraud trial perhaps, or instead the small legal museum and the small exhibition of judges' robes. The main hall is worth a visit in its own right, with its huge mosaic floor.

CRIMINAL LAW OLD BAILEY (THE CENTRAL

CRIMINAL COURT), *Newgate Street,* EC4 *(0171 248 3277). Open Mon–Fri 10.30 am–1 pm, 2–4 pm. St Paul's underground.* There are 19 courts here where the country's main criminal cases are tried and it can be fascinating to watch an interesting trial from one of the public galleries although, if you're unlucky, you may find you've looked in on a dull one. The most gripping section of the trial is usually when a witness is being cross-examined by the opposing side's counsel. The oldest courts, numbers one, two and three, usually hold the best trials. When I visited, the murder case in court number one was conducted by two witty barristers convinced they were treading the boards of the Aldwych, an under-intelligent self-incriminating defendant who'd been caught red-handed when attempting to get a 32-inch safe through a 30-inch door frame, and a judge who fell asleep through it all. Who knows, if you get summoned to do jury service here, you can visit and get paid for it too. Under-14s not admitted, along with cameras, radios, food, drink, large bags, mobile phones and Uzi 9mm's.

FINANCIAL FUTURES LONDON INTER-NATIONAL FINANCIAL FUTURES AND OPTIONS EXCHANGE (LIFFE), *25 Dowgate Hill,* EC4 *(0171 623 0444/0171 379 2628). Tours (minimum 10 people) by appointment only. Cannon Street BR/underground.* A chaotic, loud money market with up to 1000 people trading on the exchange floor that's a real spectacle to watch. Traders wear an array of colours indicating the company they work for, using mystifying voice and hand signals, known as 'open outcry' trading.

FISH BILLINGSGATE MARKET, *87 West India Dock Road, Isle of Dogs, E14 (0171 987 1118). Open Tues–Sat 5–9 am. West India Quay DLR*. A huge wholesale fish market with plenty of activity, a large variety of fish, and water spilling everywhere.

FLOWERS NEW COVENT GARDEN MARKET, *Nine Elms Lane, SW8. Open Mon–Fri 3.30–10 am. Vauxhall underground*. Although there is a fruit and vegetable market here, casual visitors aren't encouraged and it's not incredibly interesting anyway. On the other hand, a visit to the wide-awake wholesale flower and plant market in the middle of the night on the way back from a night-club or after a dose of insomnia can be quite surreal. The scents of the thousands of flowers can combine to make a potent perfume.

FRUIT AND VEGETABLES BOROUGH MARKET, *Borough High Street and Stoney Street, SE1. Open Mon–Fri 5.30–10 am. London Bridge BR/underground*. A wholesale market with great atmosphere. From the 13th century the market was held on London Bridge, moving to this site in 1756.

GOVERNMENT THE HOUSES OF PARLIAMENT,

Parliament Square, SW1 (Commons: 0171 219 4272, Lords: 0171 219 3107). Open when the Houses are in session. A taster of our government's bureaucracy follows: *To watch a* DEBATE *in either the Commons or Lords Strangers' (Visitors') Galleries, or in a select committee, either join the queue at the St Stephen's entrance from approximately 2.30 to 10.30 pm or later from Mon–Thur, and approximately 9.30 am–3 pm on Fri for the House of Commons; or from about 2.30 pm Mon–Wed, from 3 pm Thur and from 11 am Fri until debating ends for the House of Lords. Alternatively apply in advance for a ticket via your MP for the House of Commons or a Peer for the House of Lords, or if not a UK citizen, apply to your embassy or High Commission. Obtaining a seat at* QUESTION TIME *(2.30 pm Mon–Thur) is also by prior arrangement with your MP, embassy or High Commission.* TOURS *of Parliament (Mon–Thur) must be applied for in advance from your MP if a UK citizen, and for citizens of other countries by writing to The Public Information Office of the House of Commons. A visit to* BIG BEN *is by application to your MP, although there may be a long wait to get on a tour. Westminster underground.* There has been a royal palace here since the 11th century but after an extensive fire in 1834 this famous sight, the Palace of Westminster, home of our ancient democratic process, was rebuilt in the mid-19th century in a neo-Gothic style and has about 1000 rooms linked by two miles of corridors. The two chambers, the Commons and Lords, are either side of a central hall and corridor. The 314-foot high

Westminster Clocktower on the north west corner of the Palace of Westminster contains Big Ben, the 13-ton bell with a diameter of 9 feet. If you are lucky enough to visit the clocktower you are able to walk behind the illuminated clock-faces and watch the clock ticking and the bells being struck. If you are taking children on a visit to Parliament, there are booklets and education sheets available by sending a postcard to *The Parliamentary Education Unit, Room L210, 1 Derby Gate, SW1A 2DG*, stating what you want. For 8–12 year-olds there are 'The Palace of Westminster' and 'The Work of an MP' and for over-12s there are education sheets on Parliament and a booklet, 'The Glorious Revolution 1688–89'.

GLASS LONDON GLASS-BLOWING WORKSHOP, *7 Leather Market, Weston Street, SE1 (0171 403 2800). Open Mon–Fri 10 am–1 pm, 2–5 pm. London Bridge BR/underground*. Visitors get to see molten glass being blown and moulded into colourful creations.

THE GLASSHOUSE, *21 St Albans Place, N1 (0171 359 8162). Open Tues–Fri 10 am–6 pm. Angel underground*. The public are welcome to see all sorts of blown glass being made in the workshop and on display in the gallery.

MEAT SMITHFIELD MARKET, *London Central Markets, West Smithfield, EC1. Open Mon–Fri 5–10.30 am. Farringdon underground*. With carcasses and bins everywhere full of livers and hearts, and porters wearing blood-stained white overalls, this wholesale meat market is not a place for the squeamish.

METAL LONDON METAL EXCHANGE, *56 Leadenhall Street, EC3 (0171 264 5555). Monument underground.* Telephone the marketing department to arrange a visit to the exchange *(Mon–Fri noon–1.30 pm)* to see this unusual City market at work. The traders sit in a circle quietly to start with but a few minutes later the pace accelerates into frenzied shouting and gesticulating, only to cease at the sound of a bell. Then the process is repeated with a different metal being traded on the floor. There's also a 17-minute video presentation providing background information.

PEWTER ENGLEFIELDS PEWTER WORKSHOPS, *Reflection House, Cheshire Street, E2 (0171 739 3616). Tours by appointment Mon–Fri 10.30 am, 2.30 pm. Bethnal Green underground.* Watch pewter being made the traditional way in the workshops of this firm founded in 1700.

POSTAGE MOUNT PLEASANT POST OFFICE, *Farringdon Road, EC1 (0171 239 2191). Tours lasting an hour are Mon–Fri (except the Christmas period) 10 am, 10.30 am, 2 pm, 2.30 pm and 6 pm. No children under 10. Prior arrangement required, and bookings must be confirmed in writing at least 10 days before visit. Farringdon*

BR/underground. Follow the journey of a letter in Europe's biggest sorting office, including (except for the tours at *10 am* and *10.30 am*) a look at the underground Mail Rail installed in 1927 which carries 10 million sacks of mail around London on automatic trains.

The Mail Rail can also be seen at KING EDWARD STREET CHIEF POST OFFICE, *King Edward Building, King Edward Street,* EC1 (0171 239 5255). *St Paul's underground.* Write to *KEB Visits, Room SG07* at the above address for details of their occasional tours which also includes a visit to the huge sorting office and a buried section of the original City Wall, complete with Saxon bastion.

SILVER LONDON SILVER VAULTS, *Chancery House, 53–64 Chancery Lane,* WC2 (0171 242 3844). *Open Mon–Fri 9 am–5.30 pm; Sat 9 am–12.30 pm. Guided tours by arrangement. Chancery Lane underground.* Thirty-five vaults below ground level display the biggest collection of silver in the world, antique and modern. The traders are happy to talk about their wares, hallmarks and history. It's surprising how much money a tiny, unexciting-looking item can command.

WATER THAMES WATER UTILITIES Telephone customer services *(0345 200800)* to arrange a tour of one of their London water or sewage treatment works to see the processes involved in treating water to make it drinkable. According to Thames Water, visitors are

usually taken aback at the vast scale of the operation,
the immense amount of work and engineering required
to do this. Water treatment works include Ashford and
Hampton (serving south and west London); Copper
Mills (north London); and New Riverhead, a recently
installed ringmain site for the London Ringmain, a
water pipeline around London so large you could fit a
London cab in it. Sewage treatment works include
Abbey Mills (serving north and east London); Beckton
(north east London); Beddington (south London and
Croydon); Crossness (south east London); Esher (Surrey
and south west London); Mogdon and Hogs Mill (south
west London); and Riverside and Nags Head both
serving Essex.

WORKSHOPS AND DEMONSTRATIONS

ALEXANDRA PALACE AND PARK, *Wood Green, N22
(0181 365 2121). Wood Green underground/Alexandra
Palace BR*. Children's workshops during the summer at
the Grove Community Centre.

THE ARTHOUSE, *140 Lewisham Way, SE14 (0181 694
9011) Open Wed–Sun 11 am–6 pm, New Cross BR/under-
ground*. Art workshops for adults and children, such as
life drawings and collage.

BETHNAL GREEN MUSEUM OF CHILDHOOD, *Cam-*

bridge Heath Road, E2 (0181 980 2415). Open Mon–Thur, Sat 10 am–5.30 pm; Sun 2–6 pm. Bethnal Green underground. Children's workshops on *Saturdays 11 am* and *2 pm*.

BRIXTON ARTISTS' COLLECTIVE, *35 Brixton Station Road, SW9 (0171 733 6957). Open Mon–Sat 10 am–6 pm. Brixton underground*. Creative writing workshops on *Thursdays 7–9 pm*.

BUSHY PARK, *Hampton Court Road, Middlesex, TW12 (0181 979 1586). Hampton Wick BR*. Children's workshops and other entertainments during the summer holidays.

COCKPIT WORKSHOPS, *Cockpit Yard, Northington Street, WC1 (0171 831 6761). Open Mon–Wed, Fri 10 am–6 pm. Holborn underground*. Make an appointment to see one of about 80 craftspeople working here. A huge choice including ceramics, glass, woodwork, metalwork, jewellery and textiles.

EAST HAM NATURE RESERVE, *Norman Road, E6 (0181 470 4525). Open Mon–Fri 9 am–5 pm; Sat and Sun 2 pm–5 pm (closes at dusk in winter). Visitor centre Sat and Sun 2 pm–5 pm. East Ham underground*. Occasional children's workshops and other events.

ECOLOGY CENTRE, *45 Shelton Street, WC2 (0171 379*

4324). Open Mon–Fri 10 am–6 pm. Covent Garden under-ground. Occasional green workshops.

401, *401 Wandsworth Road, sw8 (0171 622 6761). Open Mon–Fri 10 am–7 pm by appointment. Stockwell under-ground.* Arrange to see about 30 craftspeople work with metal, textiles, glass and other media, or come to an open day, usually on the *last weekend in November*.

GABRIEL'S WHARF, *56 Upper Ground, se1 (0171 620 0544). Open Tues–Sun 11 am–6 pm. Waterloo/Charing Cross BR/underground.* About 20 craft and designer artists can be watched here making ceramics, sculptures, jewellery, fashion, etc., in their workshops, and there are market stalls.

GEFFRYE MUSEUM, *Kingsland Road, e2 (0171 739 9893). Open Tues–Sat 10 am–5 pm; Sun 2–5 pm. Old Street underground.* Children's workshops at weekends and during school holidays exploring such things as painting techniques, printing, mirror making and dyeing.

GREENWICH BOROUGH MUSEUM, *232 Plumstead High Street, se18 (0181 855 3240). Open Mon 2–7 pm; Thur–Sat 10 am–1 pm, 2–5 pm. Plumstead BR.* Children's work-shops held in the school holidays as well as an activities club each Saturday.

GREENWICH PARK, *se10 (0181 858 2608). Greenwich/*

Maze Hill BR. There are creative workshops and story-telling for children during the summer.

HACKNEY MUSEUM, *Central Hall, Mare Street, E8 (0181 986 6914). Open Tues–Fri 10 am–12.30 pm, 1.30–5 pm, Sat 1.30–5 pm. Bethnal Green underground/Hackney Central BR.* Children's workshops throughout the year.

HAMPSTEAD HEATH, *NW3 (0181 348 9930/9945). Hampstead underground.* From around *May* to *September* horticultural clinics are held in the Flower Garden in Golders Hill Park on some weekend afternoons, and advice can be obtained on gardening topics.

HORNIMAN GARDENS, *100 London Road, Forest Hill, SE23 (0181 699 2339). Open 8 am–dusk. Forest Hill BR.* Horticultural demonstrations are held about once a month on Wednesday afternoons from March to September and occasionally on Sunday afternoons too.

HORNIMAN MUSEUM, *100 London Road, Forest Hill, SE23 (0181 699 2339). Open Mon–Sat 10.30 am–5.30 pm; Sun 2–5.30 pm. Donation requested. Forest Hill BR.* Regular art and craft workshops for three- to seven-year-olds with an adult, and for children aged eight and over. 'Hands on' workshops exploring musical instruments, toys, animals and other subjects.

KENSINGTON GARDENS, *W2, W8 (0171 298 2100).*

Lancaster Gate/High Street Kensington underground. Workshops and other children's entertainment during the summer holidays.

LAUDERDALE HOUSE COMMUNITY ARTS CENTRE, *Waterlow Park, Highgate Hill, N6 (0181 348 8716). Open Tues–Fri 11 am–4 pm. Archway underground.* Occasional children's workshops.

LONDON WILDLIFE GARDEN CENTRE, *28 Marsden Road, SE15 (0171 252 9186). Open Tues, Wed, Thurs, Sun 11 am–4 pm. East Dulwich BR.* Various workshops and training programmes.

MALL GALLERIES, *The Mall, SW1 (0171 930 6844). Open daily 10 am–5 pm. Charing Cross BR/underground.* Various art techniques are demonstrated from time to time.

MUSEUM OF LONDON, *150 London Wall, EC2 (0171 600 3699). St Paul's underground.* Regular workshops on a variety of topics.

MUSEUM OF MANKIND, *6 Burlington Gardens, W1 (0171 323 8043). Open Mon–Sat 10 am–5 pm; Sun 2.30–6 pm. Touch sessions for the blind by arrangement. Donations welcome. Piccadilly Circus underground.* Occasional workshops.

REGENT'S PARK, *NW1 (0171 486 7905). Regent's Park/*

Camden Town underground. Summer children's workshops and other activities.

RICHMOND PARK, *Holly Lodge, Richmond, Surrey (0181 948 3209). Richmond BR/underground.* Summer children's workshops and other activities.

RUDOLPH STEINER HOUSE, *35 Park Road, NW1 (0171 723 4400). Open Mon–Fri 10 am–5 pm. Donation requested. Baker Street underground.* Occasional workshops, meetings, study days and an open day in *June* concerning the works and influence of Austrian philosopher Steiner and his spiritual and mystic teaching.

TOM ALLEN ARTS CENTRE, *Grove Crescent Road, Stratford, E15 (0181 519 6818). Open Mon–Sat 10 am–6 pm. Donations welcomed. Stratford underground.* Regular free workshops for the disabled and for Asian people with learning difficulties as well as an actors' workshop showcase.

VICTORIA & ALBERT MUSEUM, *Cromwell Road, SW7 (0171 938 8638). Open Mon noon–5.50 pm; Tue–Sun 10 am–5.50 pm. Donation requested. South Kensington underground.* Occasional workshops and events which have featured anything from teaching the lion dance of the Chinese New Year, to hair and make-up sessions.

WATERMANS ARTS CENTRE, *40 High Street, Brentford,*
TW8 (0181 847 5651). Open Tues–Sat 10.30 am–11 pm,
Sun 10.30 am–10.30 pm. Gunnersbury BR/underground.
Occasional workshops.